# WORM WORK

# WORM WORK
## RECASTING ROMANTICISM

Janelle A. Schwartz

UNIVERSITY OF MINNESOTA PRESS
Minneapolis
London

Published by the University of Minnesota Press
111 Third Avenue South, Suite 290
Minneapolis, MN 55401-2520
http://www.upress.umn.edu

Library of Congress Cataloging-in-Publication Data

Schwartz, Janelle A.
Worm work : recasting Romanticism / Janelle A. Schwartz.
Includes bibliographical references and index.
ISBN 978-0-8166-7320-9 (hc : acid-free paper)
ISBN 978-0-8166-7321-6 (pb : acid-free paper)
1. Romanticism—Europe. 2. Nature in literature. 3. Literature and
science—Europe—History—18th century. 4. Literature and science—
Europe—History—19th century. I. Title.
pn603.S27 2012
809'.9145—dc23
2012008137

Printed in the United States of America on acid-free paper

The University of Minnesota is an equal-
opportunity educator and employer.

19  18  17  16  15  14  13  12        10  9  8  7  6  5  4  3  2  1

To Mom and Dad, for letting me play
with worms at the dinner table

IT IS NOT SO PERTINENT to man to know all the individuals of the animal kingdom, as it is to know whence and whereto is this tyrannizing unity in his constitution, which evermore separates and classifies things, endeavoring to reduce the most diverse to one form.

—Ralph Waldo Emerson, *Nature*

# Contents

# Acknowledgments

IN 1911, Ambrose Bierce defined the word *edible* in his *Devil's Dictionary* as being "good to eat and wholesome to digest, as a worm to a toad, a toad to a snake, a snake to a pig, a pig to a man, and a man to a worm." I can only hope to be as "edible," to give back as much or more intellectual and emotional nourishment as the following people have given to me: Joelle Underwood, whose scientist's ear and artist's mind helped me execute a successful experiment; Jo Ann Moran Cruz and Melanie McKay, who believed in this project's scholarly import and provided the funds to prove it; Mary McCay, for her inimitable mentorship and dedication to teaching—I count you among my role models; Lynda Favret, whose unflagging southern hospitality should be an inspiration to us all; Loyola University New Orleans and its Department of English, which awarded me a timely research fellowship, precious course releases, and priceless encouragement from colleagues; Hamilton College, which granted me the funds to commission the valuable index of this book; and my mentor–colleagues Peter and Nancy Rabinowitz, Carol Rupprecht, and Vicki Vernon, who taught me how to teach others. Hillary Ecklund, Christopher Schaberg, Katherine Fidler, and Artemis Preeschl offered careful critiques of and challenging insights into my work. You've helped to make this a better book. Holly Combs and Keaton Postler are "pleased as Punch" that they found a worm I hadn't. Zach, whose last name I don't know, reminded me of a little worm who said 'ello. My wonderful readers, Ashton Nichols and Charlotte Sleigh, were both incredibly generous with their encouragement, open to the diplopic vision of so unexpected a subject as worms, and duly penetrating in their assessment of the shortfalls in my argument. Whatever has remained unsaid or unstudied is on me. To all other friends, colleagues, students, and random persons in a crowd who keep piling my desk with wormy circumstance, thank you.

The incredible staff at the University of Minnesota Press deserves more gratitude than I can express. From Doug Armato's immediate warmth and follow-up tweets toward a strange scholar's first-book pitch to Danielle Kasprzak's meticulous editorial guidance and infinite patience to my reunion with an old friend, Dan Ochsner, whose matchless talents I am honored to have had produce my book, I couldn't have asked for a better arrival. I am indebted to the archivists and permissions gurus at Memorial Library, University of Wisconsin; Boxwood Press; the Morgan Library and Museum in New York; Houghton Library at Harvard University; the Tate in London; the Yale Center for British Art; and the Punch Cartoon Library. You helped give this project its "legs."

Special thanks must go to Howard Lenhoff, whose healthy obsession with all things polyp provided my vermicular thoughts with a crucial foundation. Our conversations were as enlightening as they were entertaining; they bespoke of an envious tenacity and munificence of character. I'm only sorry I never made it out to Mississippi. To Virginia Dawson, thank you for your gracious critique and support of the significantly minute details of my analyses. To Michael Bernard-Donals, in case you didn't read it the first time, your sympathetic ear, admirable professionalism, and effortless humility all remain a boon to my psyche. To Nhora Lucía Serrano, my partner in crime, you are more of a muse than you know. To Jonathan Schwartz, whose witty retorts and i-n-d-e-f-a-t-i-g-a-b-l-e support pushed me to push myself further. Finally, to Timber and Roslyn, for taking me on long walks in the park.

Most of all, I am grateful for Joa, who kept me fed, watered, and showered in turnips. *Sans vous je ne suis qu'un ver de terre.*

# Introduction

## VermiCulture

"HUMAN-LIKE BRAIN FOUND IN WORM." This was the headline run online by DiscoveryNews on September 2, 2010, preceding a subtitle that read, "For the first time, a structure comparable to our cerebral cortex has been found in an invertebrate—a humble marine ragworm."[1] By placing a complex vertebrate in direct relation to a simple invertebrate, title and subtitle alike threaten a continued dismantling of the great distance heretofore separating high from low organisms on the chain of being. The suggested proximity of "human" and "worm" provokes in turn a largely pejorative reaction from writer and reader alike. As if the inserted adjective "humble" and the descriptive prefix "rag" were not enough to promote a sense of belittlement toward a worm conceivably six hundred million years our ancestor (and yet still our contemporary) and now understood to share brain structures that anticipate our own, the discussion thread appended to the main article offered up colorful reader responses that range from contempt to ridicule to indifference:

> If you prefer to believe your brain is related to a worm, then so be it. Others have a higher regard for human life.

> Are you saying that we are worm-brain creatures?

> NOOOO! That headline is guaranteed to be cited by some religious nut as proof that evolution is a lie. I can hear it now: "How does EEEEEVVVVILLLLLLUSHUN explain a HUMAN brain in a WORM?!?! Scientisticals done wrote it themselves in that there scientistical

magazine Discovery. Here look at it yourselves: Human-like brain found in a worm. My case is restful-like. God done created it all, periods!"

And to think they are just worms . . .

And the worm turns . . .[2]

Human supremacy appears here to be as carefully guarded (if not as justly organized) as the pecking order of a henhouse. Through nothing more than the rhetoric that frames the summary of and reaction to a scientific study, this article displays an almost unconscious, seemingly inherited repulsion away from the worm. The worm emerges as a creature just shy of a menacing presence; it challenges the supreme position of the human and so deserves our derision and scorn. In short, the worm is reviled not simply for what it is but for what it suggests about the nature of man.

## Worm Work

We wear our hubris well. Or is it that our hubris wears us? This is not a glib question. As the preceding vignette quickly shows, we, as humans, have adopted for centuries the essentially misguided (misappropriated?) idea that *we* are somehow better, more valuable, than *them*. This instance of redressing ourselves—because, to be clear, worms are not the intended audience—for even thinking (much less proving) that in such a low creature we might find progenitive reflections of us is an affront often accompanied by rhetorical acrobatics meant to fortify the lines of separation, however specious.

This is nothing new. One can read of the discomfort provoked by the presence of worms on or near the bodies of humans in the works of Homer and Aristotle just as readily as in the writings of naturalists and scientists from the inception of the microscope through to today.[3] I am also not claiming that this discomfort, or what I understand to be a kind of misaligned allegiance, is unique to the analogy of man : worm. This hubris resonates, for example, in discourses surrounding more complex organisms, such as dolphins and primates,[4] and is perhaps the most visible in the ethnic, gender, and racial divisions that plague our own species. Nevertheless, I am especially fascinated by the entangled relationship of man and worm, particularly regarding the specific threshold of scale these forms exhibit together. I see in it a way to rethink our approaches to organic matter in both our classificatory and narrative practices. And by looking at how man organizes and represents his encounters with the worm, we will see how necessary it is to recalibrate the definitions and aesthetic valuations we assign not only to this lowly being but to ourselves.[5]

To attempt this thought experiment from the time of Homer to today, however attractive, is out of the question for this book. It is simply too broad and too tightly packed of a terrain to cover responsibly here. Instead, this book focuses on a specific historicocultural moment when worm studies enjoyed a particular emphasis and exponential growth—when such studies, as I will show, elicited a root vocabulary for contemporary considerations of the categorically slippery, which continue to hold traction today. Discourses on or about the worm offer a surprising and fertile demonstration of what I propose was a developing aesthetic imaginary from the mid-eighteenth to nineteenth centuries, rooted not in the abstractions of beauty or sublimity but in the very material processes of decay and generation. From the time of Erasmus Darwin to that of Charles Darwin, worms were recognized as much for their literal ability to break down and cast up organic structures as for their figurative utility in the disruption of man-made systems like the classification of organisms and conventional aesthetic judgments. Worms were a taxonomic terror. Their appearance in both natural history treatises and works of poetry and prose often presaged some form of collapse, be it literal or figurative, and hence the need to rebuild meaning. But they also signaled great order in nature as well as a way to express and even preserve such order.

This book traces how worms helped shape, and were shaped by, Romantic culture—how these lower organisms became an instrumental paradox for the Romantics' viable representations of the natural world. I argue that the worm, as an archetypal figure of such processes, recasts the evolution of a literary order alongside questions of taxonomy in the period between 1740 and 1820 (and extended briefly to the 1880s)—making Romanticism a rich humus of natural historical investigation and literary creation.

*VermiCulture* admits, as the medial capitalization in the title to this Introduction insists, a direct relationship between human studies of the worm and this organism's ability to cultivate such study. As I will illustrate throughout this project, both natural historical and Romantic writings share an oftentimes disregarded slippage between an articulation of the material world as inscribed by the figurative and the metaphorical as it is informed by matter itself. This curious yet routine looping exposes two registers of definition that I believe coalesce most readily at worm citings throughout the period: the organic and the aesthetic. It opens up an area of inquiry for thinking aesthetically, on one hand, and in narrative terms, on the other, about organic processes in natural history. These processes in turn affect Romantic literature in a way distinct from the aesthetic categories of the beautiful and the sublime.

This departure from the more conventional pairing of natural aesthetics involves looking at the worm as something *vile,* something that is defined not by any aesthetic qualities it lacks but by a positive understanding of its very substantiveness or materiality. From the Latin *vilem* or *vilis,* meaning "of low value or price, cheap, common, mean, base," the adjective *vile* lends itself to confronting as well as imagining a wholly integrated yet nonetheless disparaged object. It injects a productive and parallel sense of the abject into the actualized lower organisms on which I center this project, allowing for worms to undergird the materiality of a vile nature just as they undermine the values of a culture attempting to assimilate them at the same time it rejects them. In this way can the worm then be realized as that which under-*writes* a Romantic conception of the human and its artistic productions.

At issue in this project are three methodological concerns: to foreground the difficulties and complexities of taxonomic inquiry in eighteenth-century natural history; to reveal the self-conscious aestheticization that develops from the empirical research of natural history to its imagistic and imaginary reconstructions in Romanticism;

and to identify the role of aesthetic sensibility in making natural history as a subject of discourse. Much as Thomas Kuhn, in *The Structure of Scientific Revolutions,* describes scientific revolution as that which disturbs or reshapes scientific consensus, the worm dismantles eighteenth-century efforts to classify it just as it activates and enlivens taxonomic debates about the natural world and the promise of classificatory structures. Such taxonomic irregularity encourages in turn category construction and textual creation at the same time that it unsettles yet continues to induce human agency.

Throughout this project, I offer readings that build on a deconstructive approach with which to realize the figural implications collecting around the worm in Romantic literature. I look for patterns of diplopia, or seeing double, that suggest organic wholeness, such as decay and (re)generation, decomposition and (re)composition, in an effort to indicate a more complex structuring of experience. My approach positions decay or division as positive processes compounded by generation or renewal, thereby making an understanding of organicism contingent on the simultaneity intrinsic to diplopic vision.

With this in mind, it is important to articulate here what I mean by my use of the term *worm*—an articulation that will be developed in detail both in the following discussion and throughout this book. Many of the references to follow will traipse across several of the worm's varied or variable forms: from earthworm, maggot, and caterpillar to two-winged insects like the ubiquitous fly or butterfly to insects in general. Clearly the label "worm" involves much more than what today many of us encounter in our garden (the composting worm, or "red wriggler"), skewered on our fishing hooks (the bait worm, or "night crawler"), or even poking out of a tasty Pippin apple (the codling moth, or "apple worm"). A quick glance at the *Oxford English Dictionary*'s entries for *worm* likewise registers their manifold nature. From *worm* to *wormy,* there are more than thirty entries, which include nouns, verbs, adverbs, past participles, adjectives, and so on. Its figurative uses vie in equal variety with its literal appearances. *Worm,* for example, can be understood as the archaic *wyrm,* for "serpent, snake, dragon" (in the way Milton refers to Satan, or temptation, as a "false Worm" in *Paradise Lost*[6]), or as the broader definition of "any animal that creeps and crawls; a reptile; an insect," or as "applied (like *vermin*) to four-footed animals considered as noxious or objectionable," or in its most common form of "a slender, creeping, naked, limbless animal, usually brown or reddish, with a soft body divided into a series of segments; an earthworm." It is even used today as a computing term for any "self-duplicating program which can operate without becoming incorporated into another program." The terminology employed throughout this book is used to discuss a multitude of specifically *vermiform invertebrate animals,* discovered and/or classified in the eighteenth and early nineteenth centuries, whose shapes resemble (more or less) the shape of a common tubular worm and whose activities display most, if not all, of the wormlike characteristics listed previously. As we will see, it is fitting that such invertebrate animals inspired their technological namesakes because actual worms are as prolific and replicable as their computer counterparts, yet also just as often unincorporable into system building.

The largely unbounded and discomforting worm is of further interest to me given that still today, the scientific study of worms falls under that branch of zoology founded in the late eighteenth century and dedicated to the study of insects: entomology. Its name coined from the Greek *entomon* (insect), entomology identifies the study of insects according to what Aristotle had referred to as *entomos,* or "having a notch or cut (at the waist)." This definition was meant to reflect the visibly segmented division of insect bodies, more overt in those insects with wings than in those without. The general conflation and seeming transposability of *worm* and *insect* are therefore endemic to the communication of naturalist and scientific studies of such organisms—and I will often likewise use the terms interchangeably. Nonetheless, such conflation has seemingly allowed for an omission of the vermicular from any serious critical inquiry into the insect metaphor in literature. For example, neither Hollingsworth's *Poetics of the Hive* nor Brown's *Insect Poetics* makes any mention of actual worms, with the exception of the latter, in which the lore of the mescal worm in a bottle of tequila is taken up briefly alongside novelty candies like the gummy worm (both within the context of entomophagy).[7]

Although ubiquitous, vermicular invertebrates present an immediate discomfort to the observer, often invoking in her that unconscious distancing illustrated at the beginning of this Introduction, so that there is always already something offensive, muddled, or dirty, as well as unknown or elided, when talking about worms. Entomological study is therefore approached in this book in accordance with the way insects and worms often dismantled the very boundaries their eighteenth-century observers set out to reify and how these organisms exposed the crucial paradox of construction and deconstruction that formulated man's approach to both understanding and representing the natural world.

To extend what Giorgio Agamben proposed in *The Open* as the concept of *Homo sapiens*—that is, "neither a clearly defined species nor a substance" but rather an anthropogenic, optical machine "constructed of a series of mirrors in which man, looking at himself, sees his own image always already deformed in the features of an ape"[8]—I choose to look beyond what man viewed as his anthropomorphous equivalent ("an ape"). I look at what resembled him the *least*: the worm. Because man historically recognizes himself in the "non-man in order to be human,"[9] it is not surprising to find that man looks as well to the radically distinct vermiforms in an effort to see continuity where he would see only disruption and division. The causative value of worms in European Romantic thought therefore reveals the nonhuman to be that which restricts the human to, just as it emancipates the human from, the animal that it is.[10]

## A Culture of Worms

Similar in aim to the collection *Romanticism and the Sciences,* my project is concerned with "Romantic modes of understanding Nature, both as they figured in the various natural sciences and as they were manifested in the literature of the period."[11] Specifically, I propose an aesthetics of *worm work* as yet unacknowledged in Romantic scholarship to elucidate the relationship between eighteenth-century natural history and what we classify—not without exception—as Romantic literature.[12]

Navigating what Barbara Stafford identifies as the attempts by naturalists and Romantics alike to make the invisible world visible, to express the inexpressible, and to image the unimaginable,[13] this project realizes the necessity of aesthetic sensibility to bring matter to mind. It labors to do for a teeming portion of invertebrate zoology what Noah Heringman has done for geology and Theresa Kelley is doing for botany[14] so that VermiCulture theorizes an intersection between the materiality of nature's motile minutiae and their aesthetic reformulations. It registers yet another instance of what Kelley describes as "Romanticism's preoccupation with representation and representability—with the problem of relating parts to wholes or even finding wholes for those parts."[15] Even more, it recognizes for Romanticism's experiment in representation what Timothy Morton attributes to fractal geometry: "it's all parts, all the way up and all the way down," until there is "no whole separate from the parts."[16] As such, this project extends efforts to recuperate Romanticism through its natural historical and conceptual contexts, like those found in the work of Ashton Nichols,[17] by concentrating on a particularly slippery, loathsome, and thus often overlooked group of organisms. Just as Heringman mines the intrusively inanimate objects of the natural world ("romantic rocks"), I dissect the agonizingly animate.

As the only extant study devoted specifically to the figure of the worm in late-eighteenth-century literature, Clara McLean's "Lewis's *The Monk* and the Matter of Reading"[18] marks off a significant boundary in the scholarship to which my project responds. McLean's investigation into worm imagery deals in the economies of sex in gothic fiction such as pornography, gender theory, and Freudian aesthetics; she focuses her discussion on figurations of the "phallic worm" and their corruptive, penetrative, digestive, (re)generative, discursive, and narrative implications for reading literature. Although my project thinks through similar metaphoric capacities, it does not revisit the intricacies of the worm's iconographic connection to the serpent and the phallus, nor does it reproduce a full inventory of biblical considerations of the worm. In fact, I have consciously omitted the myriad instantiations of serpents and dragons from my discussion as well as the serpentine and the reptilian. Serpents et al. do warrant a similarly close study to the one I offer here, but the distinctly mystical connotations connected to such creatures would steer my project away from its foundation in empiricism and organic matter. Furthermore, serpents and reptiles are vertebrates and thus more complex organisms (higher on the chain of being) than those on which my study focuses. By contrast, I concentrate on a comparative rendering of nature's lower organisms to the magnitude of man's natural vision—and its resultant textual creations. This book emphasizes a pattern of cultural production by tracing an investigation of the worm through natural historical study and by transferring these findings into a theoretical framework for understanding the Romantic sensibility as it confronts and assimilates such a strangely animate nature.

I show how eighteenth-century natural history studies of the worm provided late-eighteenth-century and Romantic writers with a vocabulary for recognizing the instabilities of classification and for constructing an aesthetic imaginary that could take up those instabilities as its central logic. I do for largely eighteenth-century investigations into the lower animals what Gillian Beer, David Perkins, and Harriet Ritvo have demonstrated as the late-eighteenth and nineteenth centuries' preoccupation with animals higher up on the chain of being.[19] In particular, I examine what Ritvo relates as man's efforts to impose order on nature, even when faced with its apparent outliers.[20] Furthermore, I present the worm as a collection point for what I understand to be patterns of diplopic vision emerging during this period, which in turn recasts Romantic conceptions of the organic and the processual through the development of the largely hidden aesthetic sensibility of the vile.

The first chapter, "Transitional Tropes: The Nature of Life in European Romantic Thought," acts principally to ground the analyses in this book on the objects of natural history, their representative studies and figurative effects. It rehearses eighteenth-century natural history studies of the worm as they manifest at once the exhilaration and the anxiety of discovery, particularly as such discoveries produce the inescapable man : worm analogy. By demonstrating the frequency and deliberation with which the worm (in its multitudinous forms) was being examined, I am able to discuss this organism as an agent of change integral to and transformative of both matter and mind. Because this segment of natural history sees the introduction of modern taxonomic methodologies, I also present here a brief history of taxonomy through the lens of the lower organisms to illustrate classification as a tenuous, if not impracticable, practice. Furthermore, I look at a few literary examples that either immediately predate or coincide with those I will take up later in greater detail to illustrate the worm's metonymic capacity to identify what I have come to recognize as VermiCulture: a culture of thought that secures the substantiveness of the vermicular (developed through the work of both natural philosophers and natural historians) within a vile aesthetic—an aesthetic that gained its fullest expression in writings of the Romantic era.

Chapter 2, "'Unchanging but in Form': The Aesthetic Epistēmē of Erasmus Darwin," presents an extended reading of Darwin's final long poem, *The Temple of Nature; or, The Origin of Society* (1803). A remarkable work constructed of verse and note, *The Temple of Nature* discloses Darwin's vision of organic wholeness in the natural world as an essentially vermicular activity. As I demonstrate, this poem reveals how empirical pursuit gives way to an aesthetic consciousness reliant on figures of twoness to represent a material oneness. Drawing out these figures, which include the linked processes of decay and generation, the relation of man to worm, and the use of empirical narrative inside a mythic frame, my discussion of Darwin's poem registers his attempt to model totality through a simultaneity of extended forms. Moreover, this poem realizes the entangled act of poetic composition as one that relies on decompositional processes. With what I will define as *diplopic,* or double-visioned, paradox, the nature of nature is disclosed rather than disguised by literary enterprise. I thus begin my close readings here because *The Temple of Nature* is itself an exemplary composition dependent on the doubleness I track in subsequent chapters.

Chapter 3, "'Not without Some Repugnancy, and a Fluctuating Mind': Trembley's Polyp and the Practice of Eighteenth-Century Taxonomy," returns to natural history writing to illustrate a kind of lyricism and aesthetic revaluation built into the articulation of empirical study. In doing so, this chapter focuses on a singular vermiform creature, the freshwater hydra or polyp. Discovered in 1740 by Abraham Trembley, this organism displayed (and helped to define) an astonishing variety of wormy behaviors, including the capacity to regenerate from cuttings as if it were a plant. Consequently, previous studies of Trembley's investigations into the polyp emphasize this naturalist's relative obscurity in the history of science against the polyp itself being a celebrated discovery, one that "affect[ed] the orientation of zoological science"[21] in the eighteenth century and helped make the practice of taxonomy into a vital problematic. Although I explore the polyp as the taxonomic anomaly that unsettled previously set ideas on the distinction between plant and animal and the generative or multiplicative behaviors of animate life, I also concentrate on the language used by Trembley and his contemporaries to confront this so-called anomaly. My discussion here submits that Trembley's account of his investigations into the structure and behavior of this creature urges a way of aestheticizing the vermicular that fruitfully combines the more classic repulsion with an inventive appeal to mutability, indeterminacy, and the irrepressibility of the organic, and it is this pattern that gains more prominence in the work of later writers such as that already discussed by Erasmus Darwin as well as that by William Blake, Mary Shelley, John Keats, and Charles Darwin, work that I explore later in this study.

To demonstrate how the polyp, in particular, and vermiform creatures, in general, acted as a figural site for literary reimaginings of life and the place of humans within it, I close chapter 3 with a brief but suggestive examination of Diderot's *La Rêve de d'Alembert* (1769/1830). Retaining its natural–historical characteristics, the polyp is recast in this text from Trembley's actual discovery into what can be read as speculative fiction: the placing of human polyps on Saturn. Both the polyp and insects at large become archetypal figures of taxonomic challenge in a text arranged according to overlapping dialogues between four historical persons: French mathematician Jean le Rond d'Alembert, French philosopher and cofounder of the *Encyclopédie* Denis Diderot, French salon owner Jeanne Julie Éléonore de l'Espinasse, and French physician Théophile de Bordeu. Their conversations reveal mutability to be the property with which to think through the limitations and potentialities of living matter.

Although William Blake should not be thought of as being at the front line of natural historical research per se, I do propose in chapter 4, "'Art Thou but a Worm?' Blake and the Question Concerning Taxonomy," that several of his illuminated manuscripts traverse biblical references, symbolic valuations, and even materialist manifestations of the worm to arrive squarely in an enunciation of this organism's problematic yet productive existence in the natural world—as understood through both text and image. Analyzing the worm as an aesthetic figure made to represent the material consequences of existing in nature, this chapter demonstrates how and why the presentation of worms in Blake's poetry gives way to a positive aesthetic of decay. The worm sutures the phases of decay and generation in such a way as to call attention to perpetual process as a defining, even if vile, characteristic of life. Simultaneously seductive and horrifying, helpless and shrewd, the worm irrevocably demonstrates the slippage of true forms so that its putrid figure is transformed into a constructive agent of cultural representation.

Chapter 5, "A Diet of Worms; or, *Frankenstein* and the Matter of a Vile Romanticism," offers a new natural–historical reading of the relationship between Victor Frankenstein and his creature in Mary Shelley's *Frankenstein; or the Modern Prometheus* (1818). This reading, I argue, supplies a much-needed perspective on Shelley's work, which has been heretofore obscured by a scholarly interest in the novel's thematic implementation of electrochemistry. It foregrounds a material explanation for the creature's existence and its suggestive implications for the creation of narrative. Like those in Blake's poetry, worms in *Frankenstein* appear in part in their capacity to decompose dead matter and so continue to represent the cycle of decay and generation intrinsic to imagining nature as an organic whole. In Shelley's novel, however, worms also expose the potential for creating or actualizing—as opposed to merely discovering—anomaly in nature. In this chapter, I show how Victor ultimately severs figurations of the worm from their natural–historical precedent, suspending process to transpose vermicular trappings into an exaggerated artifice of the vile: the creature. I trace how *Frankenstein* once again reimagines the relationship between the organic and the aesthetic, as outlined in previous chapters, in an effort to present materiality as that which *is* the aesthetic imaginary itself.

The Conclusion, "'Wherefore All This Wormy Circumstance?,'" offers a provocatively brief examination of Keats's *Isabella; or, the Pot of Basil* (1818/1820) and Charles Darwin's *The Formation of Vegetable Mould, through the Action of Worms, with Observations on Their Habits* (1881). My discussion of Keats's poem illustrates how Romantic poetry and prose transform the irresolvable matter of natural history into a powerful and factitious representation of the natural world. This, in turn, allows me to transgress the boundary of my own periodization and discuss how such transformative work can be seen to culminate in the writings of a later age. I suppose that by the time Darwin produces his earthworm treatise, a culture of worms has been definitively cast. Worms therefore inject (revolutionary) movement into Romantic texts without suffering from categorical limitations; they take on the guise of a constant symbol of change.

Whereas the lower organisms disturbed epistemological concerns of eighteenth-century natural history, the vermiforms' ability to cross and elide boundaries provides an extended metaphor of mutability on which to build Romantic literary discourse. Each of the readings presented in this book establishes the terms for understanding how the worm was deployed as a figure to complicate, disrupt, and reimagine ideas of totality. This issue of totality is thus altered from an empirical notion into an aesthetic imaginary by a Romantic interest in organicism, which itself invites a more self-conscious formulation than early taxonomies and aesthetics had imagined.

# 1

# Transitional Tropes: The Nature of Life in European Romantic Thought

BEFORE LAYING OUT a representative catalog of insect study in the eighteenth century, its objects, practices, and rhetoric, I want to discuss two recent theoretical texts: Jane Bennett's *Vibrant Matter* and Timothy Morton's *The Ecological Thought.* Together, these texts present a complementary philosophical treatment of ecology that lends itself to a prescriptive de-centering of the human. In doing so, both texts tread on a meme of worm work today that saw what, I will demonstrate, was its emergent expression in the eighteenth century. This chapter therefore responds in part to an implicit urgency to draw out the founding properties of worm work against its modern and postmodern applications.

That Bennett's and Morton's books appear *now,* released the same year I prepared this manuscript for publication (2010), underscores the timely concurrence of ideas regarding cognitive patterns of (dis)association and classification. Apparently intractable life-forms have increasingly become an idée fixe for cultural geographies seeking to unseat human agency from its self-appointed singularity and supremacy, and so I am especially interested in the way these texts employ organisms ostensibly low and apparently high, as if both questionably other, to articulate ecologies that positively blow your mind.[1]

In *Vibrant Matter,* Bennett plays with the human, nonhuman, and not-quite-human "body of evidence" that reveals what she calls "the vitality of matter."[2] In her convincing effort to expose the philosophical and political implications of rethinking matter as dynamic and active, rather than inanimate and inert, Bennett asks us to ascribe a vital agency to material *things* just as we would to particular *beings,* namely, ourselves. *Vibrant Matter* asks us to realize certain tensions or what Bennett recognizes as assemblages or vectors of causality that inextricably affect our ecological constructions. She "equate[s] affect with materiality"[3] to consider precisely questions of agency and ecology, and she identifies one of the most provocative and promising articulations for remedying the rhetorical, social, and practical problems of confronting matter—of any type: vital materialism or *thing-power.* This system of thought acknowledges the value of any thing that appears to reject categorical assimilation as if something othered,[4] something "out-side," as Bennet writes it, that "refuses to dissolve completely into the milieu of human knowledge."[5] The very insistence of such matter *not* "to dissolve completely" makes the realization and hence revaluation of *thing-power* an exigent call.

Significantly, Bennett chooses to tell "a couple of worm stories"[6] to help sound this call. She considers, for example, Charles Darwin's 1881 treatise *The Formation of Vegetable Mould, through the Actions of Worms, with Observations on Their Habits,* which she reads not as a biological or agronomical text but as an historical one, that is, worms *make* history. Here earthworms act as the exemplum for Bennett's theory of vital materialism because, "when in the right confederation with other physical and physiological bodies, [worms] can make big things happen."[7] Their composting actions can bury small objects and sink great stones so that, as Darwin himself declared, "archaeologists ought to be grateful to worms, as they protect and preserve for an indefinitely long period every object, not liable to decay, which is dropped on the surface of the land, by burying it beneath their castings."[8] Likewise, worms are the *ur*-plough, consistently preparing the land for all types of growth:

> When we behold a wide, turf-covered expanse, we should remember that its smoothness, on which so much of its beauty depends, is mainly due to all the inequalities having been slowly levelled by worms. It is a marvellous reflection that the whole of the superficial mould over any such expanse has passed, and will again pass, every few years through the bodies of worms.[9]

Undoubtedly, worms play an important role in the natural world. But their proposed roles in the developing nature of man and his works still demand further investigation.

As Bennett's worm story continued, it struck me that the way she repurposes, or better, recasts, Darwin's narrative is very wormy behavior indeed. Like Darwin's understanding of the work of the worm, "to sift the finer from the coarser particles, to mingle the whole with vegetable debris, and to saturate it with their intestinal secretions,"[10] Bennett's own analytical work filters the grand theories and subtle insights of her predecessors through those of her own (exchanging, of course, any "intestinal secretions" for intellectual emanations). Bennett not only riffs on Darwin's earthworm studies but does so by passing Darwin's worm story through Michel Serres's *The Birth of Physics,* which is in turn passed through Lucretius's *De Rerum Natura.* Such strategic reformulating suggests a spiraling motion not unlike that of the material decay and (re)generation—not to mention preservation—made possible through the agency of worms, until Bennett's worm story appears finally as an altogether new form. She draws our attention again to *thing-power,* to the "not-quite-human force that addle[s] and alter[s] human and other bodies,"[11] by offering up her own monumental casting of agentic action typified by worm work.

Consequently, Bennett (through Lucretius through Serres through Darwin) and now I (through Lucretius through Serres through Darwin through Bennett) call attention to textual creation and analysis as overtly vermicular activities. Not only do worms recall a kind of Kantian purposivelessness in which worms exist merely to "compete with other (biological, bacterial, chemical, human) agents" yet nonetheless effect significant contributions to human history and culture;[12] they provide an intriguing behavioral model for our critical labors, past, present, and future. "But to truly take worms seriously," contends Bennett at the close of her worm story, "we would not only have to revise our assessment of their activities but also need to question our larger faith in the uniqueness of humans to reinvent concepts now attached to that faith."[13]

This chapter introduces just such a dual reassessment. It positions worms as the very matter with which to rethink the relationship between a material world in constant flux and the human mind working to represent it. By extension, this chapter catalogs examples of what I understand to be instantiations of Morton's "strange stranger," or "other beings, neither me nor not-me,"[14] which inhabit the mesh of life-forms and help initiate the ecological thought. One poignant example, as Morton recalls it, is the theoretical notion that "a worm could become a Buddha, *as a worm.* The ecological thought should not set consciousness up as yet another defining trait of superiority over non-humans."[15] Like Bennett, Morton calls on the worm as an easily cognized figure of low aesthetic value that nevertheless quickly adjusts to high moral worth. Both worm stories therefore signal the trenchant mutability of an organism apparently universal in its coded baseness.

According to Morton, "the ecological thought realizes that all beings are interconnected. This is the mesh. The ecological thought realizes that the boundaries between, and the identities of, beings are affected by this interconnection. This is the strange stranger."[16] Together with Bennett's notion of *thing-power,* this chapter examines a(n) (im)precise segment of the mesh by tracking a particularly slippery strange stranger, which together I have identified as the eighteenth century's culture of worms that informed the Romantic period's consideration of man as both a part of and apart from the natural world. In this way can the mesh be realized through an historical period, with the strange stranger recognized first as the worm and then as the human—thereby making the intersections of man and worm paramount.

Furthermore, if we agree with Morton that the strange stranger "is involved in a shifting zone of aesthetic seeming and illusion," where "camouflage, deception and pure appearance are the stock in trade of life forms,"[17] then empirical studies of the worm can illustrate how the figural frames the literal: as I briefly illustrated in the introduction to this book, actual worms carry with them a confrontation with impressions of the low, the loathsome, and hence the vile. This allows for human aesthetic perception to configure a materiality for these natural *things,* which has itself largely accrued as a result of our own attitude problem: we assume a "loftiness" against the "lowliness" of worms; we have yet to "transcend our impulses" toward making palatable the nonhuman or not-quite-human even as they appear to require a form of tacit rejection.[18]

Consequently, insect studies of the eighteenth century in general and worm studies in particular can be seen to coerce classificatory practices just as they deny taxonomic stability, leaving discovery itself to be revealed as an intrinsically disorienting experience. Such studies at once undermine and reinforce "the unitary, virile ideas of Nature and the Natural that still prevail."[19] Research into the anatomies and behaviors of vermiforms reveals not only the need to revisit and then reassess "lowliness" as a key concept of thought but also suggests that "what makes humans human is not some Natural or essential component of being but a relationship that can never be fulfilled."[20] Worminess, with its paradoxical intimation of a kind of hollow crammed with the organisms responsible for its (negative) construction, can then come to be read as a kind of praxis, simultaneously coding for and creating our attitude(s) of engagement.

## Vermicular Activity

Morton's idea of "a relationship that can never be fulfilled" resonates well with the task set by and to eighteenth-century naturalists: to build a *complete* catalog of the natural world. This was the impossible ideal that fueled not only insect studies but all studies of all forms in the natural world. It promoted the very idea of a whole and unitary (read ordered and hierarchialized) Nature by putting on display a seeming infinitude of individual, organic parts. Although the illusory Catalogue of Nature was, of course, never completed, its attempted achievement remains a significant construction. It betrays that fundamental hubris with which man tackled (and continues to tackle) natural historical study. It displays an insurmountable anthropocentrism in the period, a locus of the human that pits *us* against *them,* by disclosing the irony of holistic formulations.

However, in an effort also to display a correspondingly inescapable biocentrism, or deep ecological current, running beneath the ostensibly anthropocentric natural historical studies of the eighteenth and early nineteenth centuries, I present in what follows an extended snapshot of contemporary research into these organisms set alongside a few vignettes on the vermiforms' traditional literary usages in the period. Similarly *thing*-centric, as Bennett might describe it, and "object-oriented," as Morton might express it, the study of actual worms, as well as the worms' customary metaphorical fashioning, constructs a relay of signification as unpleasant as it is apposite. Such kinetic signification creates in turn the platform from which my discussion of a Romantic culture of the worm will spring in subsequent chapters.

In 1715, hymnodist Isaac Watts delivered his *Divine and Moral Songs for Children, "Against Pride in Clothes,"* within which he wrote "in easy language" what I have positioned as the relatively complicated relationship between man and worm:

> The tulip and the butterfly
> Appear in gayer coats than I:
> Let me be dressed as fine as I will,
> Flies, worms, and flowers, exceed me still.[21]

Read as an interpretive echo of the biblical verse "For the moth shall eate them vp like a garment, and the worme shal eate them like wooll: but my righteousnes shalbe for euer; and my saluation from generation to generation,"[22] the preceding lines employ the nonhuman as a gauge for the virtue of human meekness. By genuflecting to the generative power and artistic beauty of the natural world, the human speaker of Watt's verse draws a practical juxtaposition between himself (dressed in finery) and the vibrant, complex coloring of butterflies and caterpillars, which are themselves arranged with the equally attractive flowers they frequent. "Flies" and "worms" are therefore aligned with a magnificence greater than man, just as their diminutive forms call attention to how little it takes to "exceed [him]."

Whereas the content of the lines themselves concentrates more fully on the first half of Isaiah 51:8 (i.e., on physical disintegration), the form and dissemination of Watts's verse imply the articulated "righteousness" of the biblical verse's second half. Utilizing lyric to defer to the richness of the natural world suggests that the preservation and communication of this virtue are achieved primarily through man's artful rendering. Through Watts's song, the invisible processes of decomposition and absorption, as well as generation, are illustrated. The vermiculated garments of the speaker, and by extension his body, indicate the natural processes that will consume the speaker as so much organic matter. Likewise, such inevitable decay provides the necessary compost in which other life in due course flourishes (e.g., "Flies, worms, and flowers"). There is thus a palpable separateness revealed in these lines, just as there remains an indubitable continuity of forms. With what amounts to a slip in the meaning of *exceed* from moral virtue to physical inevitability, Watts endorses an interconnectivity intrinsic to the natural world that leads inexorably to a representation of the cycle of life.[23] He finally exposes that man, even in his most elegant garb, cannot elude his mortal fate. He cannot escape becoming the food of worms, either euphemistically or literally.

Other eighteenth-century preachers, such as Jonathan Edwards, pursued allied themes and further disrobed man of his pride of place. Edwards takes up the worm, in particular, as a negative image for sinful man in *The Justice of God in the Damnation of Sinners* (1734): "A little, wretched, despicable creature; a worm, a mere nothing, and less than nothing; a vile insect that has risen up in contempt against the majesty of Heaven and earth."[24] In this especially acerbic sermon, Edwards rehearses the sense of Psalm 22:6, "But I am a worme, and no man; a reproach of men, and despised of the people,"[25] by intensifying its figurative use of the worm from a metaphor for the mere lowliness or weakness of man to that of his ungodly and wicked character. Following in like fashion, Edmund Burke hurls the worm as a strong epithet in his 1774 speech "On American Taxation":

> Thus are blown away the insect race of courtly falsehoods! Thus perish the miserable inventions of the wretched runners for a wretched cause, which they have fly-blown into every weak and rotten part of the country, in vain hopes that when their maggots had taken wing, their importunate buzzing might sound something like the public voice![26]

With this, both Edwards and Burke display the common, even classical prejudice against the worm in literature (and in today's popular culture): it is a figure coded for moral and political as much as physical corruption.

The metaphorized worm would only increase in sense, value, and frequency as the scrutiny of the origins and development of the insect world raised to a fever pitch throughout the eighteenth century. As a result of intense study, a zoology of lower organisms emerged in this century to destabilize then-current conceptions of life. Publications from both the Paris Academy of Sciences and the Royal Society of London, for example, provide keen insights into the type and tone of worm studies circulating throughout Europe in the mid- to late-eighteenth century. With a high concentration of submissions between 1731 and 1800, the *Philosophical Transactions of the Royal Society of London* collected numerous treatises about the generation, structure, and behavior of insects from around the Western world. Several of these treatises took the form of letters describing specified worms, such as woodworms or caterpillars, and/or the devastation of their behavior on the land they inhabited. Others focused largely on the discovery of the freshwater polyp, or hydra, the vermiform creature named for its resemblance to the Lernaean Hydra of Greek mythology.[27] Still others were predictably concerned with improving the accuracy of observation and experiment in the work of peers.

In a letter from 1732, Polish physician and Friend of the Royal Society J. P. Breynius (or Johann Phillipp Breyne) provided "some corrections and emendations concerning the Generation of the Insect called by him *Coccus Radicum*." His letter outlined a shift from what he initially found to be this worm's hermaphrodism to what he later determined was a division of male and female metamorphoses. The seeming gender trouble of the worms with which Breynius was confronted revealed a more calculated behavior of generation than he had previously thought. Rather than contain two sexes in one organism, the *Coccus radicum* displayed a more determinate pattern of sexed orientation dependent on need. "Having repeated [his] Observations with the greatest of Exactness, and examined [the worms] in the strictest of Manner," Breynius not only corrected his previous assertion but "freely own[ed]" that the objects of his study were confronted "not without some Repugnancy, and a fluctuating Mind."[28] With this declaration, Breynius exposed how worms promoted an undeniable noxiousness, or "Repugnancy," to accompany the rapidly developing and "fluctuating" field of insect studies.

Dutch physician and naturalist Job Baster submitted "A Dissertation on the Worms Which Destroy the Piles on the Coasts of Holland and Zealand" to the Royal Society in 1739. These worms, having eaten through piles of oak wood "defending the Coasts of the *Netherlands* against the Sea," "threatened very great Damage to the Inhabitants of these Countries." As a result, the "superstitious Populace immediately persuaded themselves, that this new Genus of Animals was created by the divine Wrath for punishing the Sins of Mankind."[29] Immediately, this offending worm is analogized to whatever insult man was supposed to have committed against God. Eventually, Baster identifies the "new" animal as "Xylophagus Worm," which he describes as a type of microscopic water insect that feeds on wood, and he goes on to give "a more accurate Description" of this worm by dividing "the Animal into Head, Body and Tail." He even provides illustrations, "as well as [he] could have them drawn."[30] Such embedded approximate claims like "a more accurate Description" and "as well as [he] could have them drawn" undermines any appearance of specificity and heralds instead the tenuous tone that threads its way through the remainder of the transaction. With such phrasing as "'tis probable," "perhaps," "there can be no certainty," "it seems to be," and "it is probable enough," Baster underscores the inability to understand completely the parts and whole of the organism he so assiduously studied. Moreover, Baster's uncertain diction perfectly reflects the instability of the Dutch littoral, which, even by this time, was a centuries-old problem. In this way can the worm be said to preside over a fragile boundary between land and sea that has everything to do with sovereignty, resources, and so on.[31] Given to deal in probabilities, Baster ultimately leaves his readers with a worm as enigmatic, threatening, and seemingly sovereign as the "divine Wrath" thought to have sent it. He therefore highlights uncertainty and its discomfort as tools for the study of worms in the eighteenth century. His rhetoric reveals the role of probability to be that which produces worm work—rather than that which merely reflects it.

In 1742, Charles Bonnet, Swiss naturalist, philosopher, and member of the Royal Society of London, wrote "An Abstract of Some New Observations upon Insects," which began by using caterpillars both to amend and extend the comprehension of insects' migratory habits, tastes, industries, structures, and sizes, before moving on to a discussion of worm propagation in general and worm regeneration in particular. In this same letter, Bonnet shifts from empirical description to philosophical speculation when he explicitly asks, "Where then does the Principle of Life reside in such Worms, as, after having their Heads cut off, still show not only the same Motions, but even the same inclinations?"[32] Although Bonnet recognized that his observations of the worms "must appear extremely imperfect,"[33] which is to say that he knew what he had to offer were only preliminary findings, his work led him finally to the following questions:

> This wonderful Reproduction of Parts, is it only a natural Consequence of the Laws of Motion? Or does it rather depend on a Chain of minute Buds or Shoots, a sort of little Embryos, already formed, and lodged where the Reproductions are to begin? Are these Worms only mere Machines, or are they like more perfect Animals, a sort of Compound, the Springs of whose Motions are actuated by a kind of Soul? And, if they have within themselves such a Principle, how can this Principle afterwards appear in every distinct Piece?[34]

Appearing to wrestle with certain tensions focused around an understanding of the property of life, Bonnet concludes this portion of the letter by writing, "After all, we must content ourselves with admiring the astonishing Works of the Great Creator, and sit down in Silence."[35] To be a machine possessing a soul conflicted with his belief in Cartesian mechanistic principles and so called into view what the work of La Mettrie and d'Holbach would later construct as deterministic materialism.[36] At the same time, Bonnet relegates any actual answer to his questions to Divine Authority. Significantly, however, this marks only the middle of his letter. Neither "the Great Creator" nor the "Appearances of small living Worms; which makes

[him] still uncertain of the Truth . . . and unable to determine what [he] ought to think"[37] prevent his investigation or silence his inquiries. Both, in fact, urge him—and his peers—to continue.

Another submission to the *Philosophical Transactions* in 1746 reproduces, with added notes, "A Letter from Mr. Henry Baker to the President [of the Royal Society], Concerning the Grubbs Destroying the Grass in Norfolk." Baker, an English naturalist and friend to then-president of the Royal Society Martin Folkes, submits that what the people of Norfolk and Suffolk were calling "grubs" or "maggots" were indeed neither of these. He provides instead alternative and overlapping names for these worms culled from the English, the Dutch, and the French, until the problem of naming gives way to one of identification: having "immediately imagined that they must be the *Aureliæ* or *Chrysalides* of some Species of Beetle,"[38] Baker ultimately concedes that "this, Sir, is all I shall trouble you with at present concerning the Grubs mentioned . . . without distinguishing of what Kind they are."[39] Again, vagaries in worm studies abound, cloaked in an ambiguity drawn out by the empirical labors of the natural historian.

These representative samples of insect study undertaken during the eighteenth century reveal the worm to be a multifarious organism found in a seemingly infinite number of geographical (not to mention anatomical) locations. The preceding transactions identify the vermiform as everything from an earthworm to a larva to a maggot, a flying insect, and the unknown. As a result of its diversity and pervasiveness, *worm* quickly and unremarkably became a general term with which to localize the observation and debate of such varied organisms. Moreover, it became a figure through which to consider the origin and progress of life during a period when each new discovery dislodged previously set categories and frustrated attempts to comprehend a totalized Life through its unbounded parts.

## Life under Scrutiny

At the turn of the twentieth century, a *New York Times* article exclaimed that "the process of regeneration is one of the fundamental attributes of living things. An explanation of which could finally solve the central problem of biology—the problem of life itself."[40] Solutions to this problem are still being pursued today by geneticists and science fiction writers alike;[41] in the eighteenth century, the question underlying this problem—for example, "where, then, does the Principle of Life reside?"—was pondered by philosophers and naturalists, both God fearing and atheist, and it formed the nexus for competing theories of and beliefs in the generation of organisms.

With the invention of the microscope at the close of the sixteenth century, man's gaze turned emphatically toward the minutiae of nature to solve the so-called problem of life (which the discovery of insect regeneration had yet to complicate). With Dutch microscopist Antony van Leeuwenhoek's late-seventeenth-century improvements to this instrument, such minutiae came into focus as a rich and deceptively accessible source of study.[42] In contrast to the vast land and sea explorations of eighteenth-century imperial practices, reaching between what we identify today as Antarctica and Alaska, microscopic study was a more localized process. It lent itself to the detection and presentation of discoveries within one's native land and literal field of vision—and it made insects one of the most significant subjects pursued. This is not to say that investigations of insects were not a part of imperial exploration. As many natural history treatises from the period attest, insects from foreign lands were studied and collected at home with a fervor equal to that of the plants crowding, for example, the public and private gardens of England and France.[43] They similarly crowded the cabinets of curiosity found throughout all Europe.[44] Nevertheless, the ease with which insects in general could be gathered and studied in one's immediate environs allowed for even the most amateur of naturalists to effect in-depth investigations into the generation and classification of life.

The approach to and understanding of insect life did not change significantly from classical antiquity to the start of the eighteenth century.[45] Belief in spontaneous generation, one of the earliest theories of production and reproduction in animals, generally began with an observation of insect behavior. This theory of generation dated back to Aristotle and his claim that worms, or *vermes,* were brought forth by the putrefaction of soil and organic matter under the influence of rain. By the seventeenth century, Descartes replaced the influence of rain with that of heat; thus, as John Farley relates in *The Spontaneous Generation Controversy from Descartes to Oparin,* "for spontaneous generation to occur it was merely necessary for heat, acting on putrefying matter, to agitate the subtle and more dense particles to form an organic being."[46] In this way were maggots believed to emerge from rotting flesh, for example. While the manner and modes of spontaneous generation were argued for centuries, the crux of the debate for the late seventeenth and eighteenth centuries rested not only on how such generation occurred but on the implications suggested by its occurring at all.

In 1688, Italian naturalist Francesco Redi entered the debate with his *Experiments on the Generation of Insects,* which claimed that "all dead flesh, fish, plants and fruits form [but] a good breeding place for [the eggs of] flies and other winged animals."[47] Through his experiments on frog flesh, Redi cast spontaneous generation as an illusion, a false front to what he conjectured were the hidden processes of nature's reproduction via sexual means. To illustrate his hypothesis, he placed both raw and cooked meat in tightly sealed flasks; these produced no maggots. Those flasks he left unsealed, however, revealed a different scene:

> I had placed in a glass dish some skinned frogs, and having left the dish open, I found the next day, on examination, that some small worms were occupied in devouring them, while some others swam about, at the bottom of the dish, in a watery matter that had run out of the frogs. The next day the worms had all increased in size and many others had appeared that also swam below and on top of the water, where they devoured the floating fragments of flesh; and after two days, having consumed all that was left of the frogs, they swam and sported about in the fetid liquid, now creeping up, all soft and slimy, on the side of the glass, now wriggling back to the water until at last on the following day, without my knowledge, they all disappeared, having reached the top of the dish.[48]

Regardless of Redi's failure to recognize the metamorphosis of his maggots ("small worms") into flies, these types of experiments helped distill the empirical direction that eighteenth-century studies of insect life finally took—and quite possibly inspired such iconic fetid scenes as the one related in Matthew Lewis's gothic romance *The Monk* (1796):[49]

> All present then uttered a terrified shout;
> All turned with disgust from the scene.
> The worms, They crept in, and the worms, They crept out,
> And sported his eyes and his temples about,
> While the Spectre addressed Imogine.[50]

While Lewis's worms are credited with having been the germ of the common rhyme "the worms crawl in, the worms crawl out, and the flies play pinochle on your snout" (which has since loaned a kind of levity to the image of putrefying flesh, death, and pulsating decay imaged in the novel proper), their presence in his original text fueled an abject sense of the worm that gruesomely described experiments like Redi's helped engender. Lewis presents the worm as the agent of terror and disgust in the face of (actualized) death, which is further emphasized by the fact that the preceding scene is presented in one of the novel's interior tales, "Alonzo the Brave, and Fair Imogine." The tale, as well as the worms and other unsavory objects contained within it, are at once intimately involved in the text and cordoned off from a more diffuse narrative effect. The tale's title itself serves to underscore the powerful yet isolated combination of strength and beauty, just as the phrase "the worms, They crept in, and the worms, They crept out" functions to mark off the material boundary from which the Spectre (for Alonzo) can speak to Imogine. Once again, worms here recall their biblical counterparts, this time from Job 7:5: "My flesh is cloathed with wormes and clods of dust, my skinne is broken, and become loathsome."[51] Unlike Watts, whose worms could ultimately signal beauty and renewal, Lewis's own apparent biblical adaptation truncates any suggestion of an inviting aesthetic or acceptable natural cycle; instead, he favors suspending the reader at the site of foul decay. Reaching from this episodic tale into the novel as a whole, man is revealed as both the food of choice for actual worms and the "vile insect" referred to in Edwards's biting sermon. Spiritual and physical breakdown can thus be said to collide in *The Monk* at the figure of the worm.

And so Redi's rancid experiments laid out in the seventeenth century what would continue to plague the eighteenth: worms threatened not simply organic collapse; their study also endangered the natural theological belief that experimentation and investigation held the proof of God's existence. In this did Redi's science remain in conflict with his theology so that unless he meant to undermine the omnipotence of God, he could never completely renounce the mechanism of spontaneous generation. Chance production was for him one of myriad ways in which the Divine Creator fashioned being. Even after the experiment detailed earlier, he continued to believe in "the occurrence of animals generated spontaneously from living flesh," which he reasoned to exist from the common presence of tapeworms and other parasites found within animal bodies.[52]

In this regard, Redi serves as an exemplary figure through which to understand the two equally competitive theories of generation that engaged eighteenth-century naturalists in debate.[53] On one hand, Redi believed in preformation, which theorized that organic development is a result of "the mere mechanical growth of a miniature preformed within the parent organism."[54] He therefore supported the idea behind the preexistence of germs, or *emboîtement,* which "teaches that the germ of preformed parts is not produced by the parent, rather it is created by God at the beginning and is conserved in that state until the moment of its development."[55] On the other hand, Redi's successful refutation of spontaneous generation suggested what would come to be called *epigenesis,* or the theory that a more gradual, embryonic development occurred in undifferentiated matter. This self-generation allowed for seemingly new parts to emerge through the growth process rather than appearing only as an enlargement of a preformed entity. Taking both theories into account, Redi's study of insect generation anticipates the divisive beliefs in species variation and the principle of plenitude that would emerge in the eighteenth century. Whereas the latter evinces God's initial foresight in creating all organic forms in an uninterrupted chain of being, the former gives to nature an independent, productive, and creative force. Together, these theories accentuate the rise of Deism throughout the age of Enlightenment. Redi's findings about maggot reproduction were first independently confirmed by Leeuwenhoek. Then other seventeenth-century naturalists, such as the Dutchman Jan Swammerdam and the Italians Antonio Vallisneri and Marcello Malpighi, gathered further evidence to dispel belief in spontaneous generation altogether[56]—even if only temporarily. Such evidence did not dissuade, for example, eighteenth-century naturalists John Turberville Needham and Georges-Louis Leclerc, Comte de Buffon, from believing in spontaneous generation. They continued to understand the vitality of animate beings to be "composed of multitudinous moving molecules," which could "reproduce merely by joining into an autonomous assemblage."[57] Consequently, these seventeenth-century natural philosophers seem to linger in the early modern ability to accommodate opposing ideologies (e.g., Copernican and Ptolemaic; Protestant and Catholic) so that the generation debates can be understood as the very definition of a wormy performative: ideas on the nature and process of life accrue and adjust as a result of their being filtered through the theories of competing naturalists.

Accordingly, soon after Redi's historic experiments, Swammerdam and French entomologist René Antoine Ferchault de Réaumur elucidated a distinction between pupa and egg to reveal the pupa as a stage in, rather than an origin of, the life cycle of a lower organism. In other words, all three men, working simultaneously in different countries, revealed changes in the form and structure of an insect that rejected the idea of its suddenly appearing as or transforming into a distinct organism. Together with the refutation of spontaneous generation, this explanation of metamorphosis went a long way to show that insects, like their more complicated counterparts higher up on the chain of being, conformed to a general pattern of reproduction—even if the theory behind this pattern continued to spark debate.[58]

Crowded with physical as well as metaphysical implications, investigations into the structure and behavior of insects complicated then-circulating theories of generation at the same time as they disrupted fledging taxonomic practices striving to decipher the whole of the natural world. Apparently indicative of a chaos of life, insects encapsulated something much larger and virtually uncontained in the eighteenth century than they do today. They remained a kind of default name for all invertebrates incompletely understood or posing classificatory hurdles until John-Baptiste Lamarck, in 1809, definitively separated invertebrates into the genera with which we are familiar today and finalized, in the early nineteenth century, a categorical separation of worms from insects that Linnaeus had only begun in the eighteenth.[59] The very idea of insects (and worms), therefore, betrayed an inherent leakiness, a net of definition oozing with variables and irreconcilable differences. Réaumur, for example, did not hesitate to place "anything that was not a quadruped, a bird, or a fish" into the class of insects. "Slugs, starfish, snakes, or lizards were all insects. A crocodile was a 'furious insect,' but an insect all the same."[60]

Further exposing the discomfort that accompanied this period's worm work, Bonnet wrote in 1766, "I have given the name *insectology* to that part of natural history which has insects for its objects: that of *entomology* would undoubtedly have been more suitable but its barbarous sound terryfy'd me."[61] Entomology's so-called barbarous sound reflects what was indeed unrefined in the study of insects: taxonomic fixity. Even the formal title for the field that covers the study of insects went from natural philosophy to natural theology, through the short-lived insectotheology, until finally emerging as entomology (as understood today), which opened a space in which man could submit his own designs for ordering and accounting for the natural world. So the displeasure that Bonnet felt toward "entomology," over and above its being the more "suitable"—because more classical, perhaps—name for the field he himself helped shape, stemmed in part from a fear of severing the theological from the natural. Having made this perhaps trite statement some twenty years *after* the discovery of parthenogenesis and regeneration in lower organisms, Bonnet's insistent, though informal, labeling of a "part of natural history" focused on insects also paradoxically encouraged man-made systems over seemingly natural–theological ones.

What to do with all the wormy insects, then, was a necessary question. The problem of accommodating multiple discrepancies and infinite variety within one bloated category helped make the study of natural history almost synonymous with the developing practice of taxonomy. As if the sheer number of vermicular organisms was not enough to dissuade attempts to comprehend the vastness of nature, an awareness of so-called anomalous organisms within this vastness further challenged efforts at classification. Worms would figuratively crawl through the very boundaries meant to reify them so that any attempt to construct categories was quickly elided by the very organism also functioning to define them. Naturalists therefore fixated on the unprecedented fluidity of these creatures' taxonomic means: their mutable, even capricious, properties.

Early taxonomists of insects, from Aristotle through the fifteenth century, relied on structure and utility to construct a cognitive framework for placing worms into specified categories. On one hand, these organisms were identified by their visible structures such as the "notch or cut (at the waist)" of the *entomon* or an insect's wing type. On the other hand, these organisms were categorized according to how they were used in relation to man. For example, maggots, leeches, and other parasitic worms were commonly employed to dispose of the placenta after childbirth or in the practice of bloodletting, and so such worms were grouped together. With use value being the dominant organizing factor in Aristotle's inchoate system of classification, animals hunted for food, for sport, or out of fear were likewise each given their own category. Plants, too, were divided in terms of utility, most often according to their medicinal values, so that every physician by virtue of the profession was also an herbalist and a botanist, even an invertebrate zoologist. In this, we encounter an early example of the ambivalence of categories in taxonomy: as the example of the physician-cum-botanist–zoologist informally illustrates, a living form has the potential to exhibit more than one categorical attribute.

At the start of the sixteenth century, anatomical and morphological criteria now took precedence over any utilitarian relationship between classified and classifier, or what Scott Atran identifies as the "existence-determining physical properties" immediately visible to the observer.[62] This revision ushered in a debate over so-called natural and artificial systems of classification prevalent from the sixteenth to the eighteenth century. The debate revolved around the question of whether such systems were reflective of real affinities in nature or were merely products of human contrivance and convention. Were classifications made according to a Platonic ideal of organic form, or did they emerge from the nominalist philosophy which theorized, first, that the real essence of things was hidden irretrievably from human knowledge and, second, that the metaphysical conception of natural forms presented a continuous series or chain of being?[63]

With the rise of empirical influence over theological perspective in the late seventeenth and eighteenth centuries, such inquiries gave way to a recognition of what seemed to be intermediary figures. These were neither ideal forms nor discrete links in the chain but rather transitional organisms that suggested both infinite variety in nature and an intrinsic order. The *Mimosa pudica,* or sensitive plant, for example, had already been discovered as one such organism in the seventeenth century. Familiar to eighteenth-century naturalists, the sensitive plant was introduced in 1637 by Tradescant the Younger after his return to England from a trip to Virginia. Robert Hooke, author of *Micrographia* (1665), is credited as one of the first to investigate the movements of this plant: in response to external stimuli, such as the touch of a breeze, the alighting of an insect, a drop of rain, or the absence of light, the sensitive plant contracts its reticulated leaves and its leaf stalk droops. After some time has passed, the leaves expand and the stalk returns to its original position.[64] As a result of its seeming irritability, the sensitive plant was also called the "sensible" or "humble" plant, anthropomorphizing it further not only to mimic man's physical attributes, and his emotional and intellectual capacities, but also to underscore such mimicry as a distancing technique. The sensitive plant was both like and wholly unlike the human form. Although its movements suggested an animate nature, its literal rootedness set it within the inanimate. Its existence therefore raised questions about animation, about living and nonliving, and about plant and animal—that is, about category (de)construction—that would reappear in the eighteenth century with the discovery of the *Chlorohydra verdissima,* a particularly "attractive" freshwater polyp, given its greenish coloring.

This latter, almost microscopic vermiform heralds a heavy traffic in natural historical writings of similarly anomalous organisms, helping to make aberration or monstrosity appear normative. The freshwater polyp was for the eighteenth century what the platypus and the kangaroo were for the nineteenth: "representative rather than idiosyncratic anomalies." "What guaranteed the continuing appeal of these animals was the fact that the oddity was not confined to the merely physical but extended to the level of theory or system."[65] With its mostly tubular body, wormy behavior, and extraordinary ability to regenerate, the polyp became quickly imbued with a significance beyond its physical existence. The traditional symbolic value of worms as harbingers or producers of death and decay was further complicated by the opposite value of regeneration and renewal being now not just allusion but material reality. This in turn allowed vermiforms to serve as ready figures of an instrumental paradox with which to envision nature as process and to problematize and even reconfigure material and aesthetic categories.

Consequently, a conflict between particulars and preestablished general laws arose in eighteenth-century taxonomic practices. Throughout the century, empirical attempts were made to organize nature into a system discernible, definable, comprehensible, and ultimately controllable by man, and it was this need for or assumption of control that at once opposed and promoted the establishment of general rules for categorization. Naturalists like Linnaeus approached taxonomy as if it were a finite task. He indeed looked at nature like a catalog, one that would account for and classify all organic forms. But as the impossible ideal that held throughout the eighteenth and nineteenth centuries (and into today), the attempt to complete a catalog of nature ignored, for the most part, that to which Réaumur attested early on: that human knowledge "did not reach beyond the first crust of several of the small particles of the universe."[66]

With a privileging of the visible reinforced (and amplified) by the popular use of the microscope, eighteenth-century naturalists believed themselves capable of finally discovering and cataloging all nature's secrets. Tiny landscape scenes, mixed from the weird fauna and flora found in dirty ponds and ditches, for example, contained accessible metaphors of a larger, ineffable creation; they intimated what Susan Stewart expressed as the manner in which "all the material world shelters a microcosm."[67] Through their drive to watch these micro-cosmic scenes under an enlarging lens, naturalists disclosed a tacit desire to control and direct them.[68] Microscopy, as Barbara Stafford elucidates, "foster[ed] a sense that small, foul, yet self-sufficient and self-generating elements crowded out and obliterated any encompassing *corpus*."[69] "Under the remorseless lens," Stafford continues, "a well-behaved anthropomorphic unity was pulverized into tiny and teeming minima. Not only were individuals overwhelmed by their corpuscles, but animals seemed to dissolve into the strangeness and indescrib-ability of irregular polyps and multitentacled hydras."[70] In effect, the minute exhibition did not simply promise to order, via analogy, the chaos of life. It also disclosed insects as exactly those "small par-ticles of the universe" capable of challenging the construction and control of an encompassing system of classification—adherence to general laws or specific analogical affinities notwithstanding. While "common sense," declares Atran, "is an indubitable source of truth for knowledge of the readily experienced local world," it is "fallible as a means of insight into the scientific universe."[71]

As the founder of modern taxonomic practices, Linnaeus believed in the proclivity of man to classify those objects placed within his field of vision. In his *Systema Naturae* (1735), Linnaeus states that "natural objects belong more to the field of the senses than all the others and are obvious to our senses anywhere."[72] He also defines a naturalist as one "who well distinguishes the parts of natural bodies *by sight* and describes and names all these rightly in agreement with the threefold division" of animal, vegetable, or mineral.[73] Natural history is therefore "that classification and that name-giving of the natural bodies judiciously instituted by such a naturalist,"[74] leaving natural history and taxonomic practices to intersect at the point of the visible. Not surprisingly, Linnaeus utilized the visible structural similarity of natural objects to create what he felt was an intuitive binomial classificatory system, *Genus species*.[75] Yet he recognized the visible as a body of evidence subject to misinterpretation: "very few people are lightly to be trusted, as far as observations go."[76] With this remark, Linnaeus draws out an emergent distinction between the amateur naturalist and the specialist as well as highlighting the limited vision of any system-making endeavor—including his own. Such limits of Linnaeus's systematized vision of nature are perhaps most obvious with regard to his definition and treatment of the insect world. In his *Systema Naturae,* he devoted a mere one-third of one page each to insects and worms, respectively, offering to expand on what Lamarck and others had proposed as a separation between the two forms. Within these groupings, however, he also included reptiles and the questionable zoophytes thought to bridge the plant and animal kingdoms. During this same period, Réaumur was at work on his six-volume treatise on the history of insects, *Mémoires pour servir à l'histoire des insectes* (1737–48), in which he supposed that these organisms greatly outnumbered "the twelve or thirteen thousand plants already named."[77] Because he hypothesized insects to be of a largely unknown quantity, Réaumur approached his study of them without the use of preset laws.

Regardless of one's approach to classification, a certain plasticity and rational simplicity had to be maintained. For example, by dividing insects according to their wing number—four wings, two wings, or no wings—Linnaeus consistently had to rearrange his taxonomies to reflect what he thought of as nature's own concern for affinities and transitions. "Probably the nicest illustration of [this] concern," remarks Mary Winsor, is Linnaeus's "shuffling the fish around until the last one, just preceding the first insect, was the flying fish. After some rearrangement, the beetles began with typical genera and faded out with some insects which, beetle-like in some ways, have softer or smaller wing-covers."[78] In effect, although Linnaeus studied the natural world according to general laws, he presented his system of classification as if tracing or tracking an inherent natural order in much the same way that Réaumur and other naturalists working against general laws also strove to represent nature's totality in its sectioned components. In both approaches, insects consistently frustrated attempts to contain them within—and so uphold—an organized accounting of nature's myriad objects.

According to Alain Corcos, "the outstanding feature of life is the continuous creation of an extremely high degree of orderliness."[79] In this view, classificatory practices can be thought of as a reflection of this order. However, the privileging of the visible that motivated such practices, coupled with the notion of life itself as "continuous creation," also disclosed the seeming infinity of natural objects, in form and function. Like Baster's rhetoric of probability, the methodology of classification complicates the reflection of order with its ability to produce it—however frustrating such production might be. As embodiments of this impossible ideal, insects therefore became as repugnant in their categorical waywardness as they were attractive.

### "Whence This Contrivance and Design"

"But the worm is only a worm," declared Mademoiselle de l'Espinasse in Denis Diderot's *La Rêve de d'Alembert*; "that is, its smallness, by concealing its organization from you, takes away the element of wonder."[80] Rather than dismiss any further discussion of this lowly creature, l'Espinasse's comment serves to beg the question of what the worm conceals—or what it can reveal, even organize—beyond the visible barrier put up by its minute form. As both the literary vignettes and natural historical treatises discussed throughout this chapter have illustrated, the worm is indeed something more than the sum of its segments. Its appearance in literature alone has made it at once a moral teacher and a corrupt adversary, a symbol of death and decay and a signal of renewal. It carries an intractable aesthetic burden, and as l'Espinasse attests to, it projects an overwhelming materiality in an outwardly unimposing form. So when William Paley, in *Natural Theology: or, Evidences of the Existence and Attributes of the Deity, Collected from the Appearances of Nature* (1802), finally took up the subject of insects at the turn of the nineteenth century, not surprisingly, he began with the now prosaic admission that these small creatures were poorly understood compared to their larger counterparts:

> The structure, and the use of the parts, of insects, are less understood than that of quadrupeds and birds, not only by reason of their minuteness, or the minuteness of their parts, (for that minuteness we can, in some measure, follow with glasses) but also, by reason of the remoteness of their manners and modes of life from those of larger animals.[81]

Insects, owing to their diminutive size, their more or less hidden structures, and their puzzling behaviors, continued to represent a kind of visibly invisible organism that threatened the accepted purposiveness with which natural theology credited the Creator. According to Paley, "there cannot be a design without a designer; contrivance without a contriver; order without choice."[82] But when confronted with insects, "the question, which irresistibly presses upon our thoughts, is, whence this contrivance and design."[83] Unlike the dismissive yet altogether alluring tone of l'Espinasse's assertion, Paley's rhetoric reveals a more clinical interest in the minuteness of the insect form to secure his belief in natural theological design or the idea that every system in nature, each part of every system, and all functions within these systems reveal the existence and attributes of God (as the extended subtitle to Paley's text claims). This same rhetoric, however, also constructs an essential (if subtle) "remoteness" of the vile insect *from us* by "reason of" its distinction from "larger animals."

Like the more secular naturalists, whose formal approach to nature was plagued with classificatory inconsistencies, Paley struggles with categories in his own natural–theological project. For instance, he places mollusks and crustaceans—those animals, "whether belonging to land or water, which are covered by a *shell*"—in his chapter on insects "for want of a better place."[84] According to Jacques Roger, insect studies at this time "threw scholars out of their ruts, refused to be placed in traditional frames of reference, ruined the most solid analogies and the most accepted laws."[85] They not only demonstrated nature's insatiable appetite for variety in organized life[86] but also revealed active metamorphoses as natural processes and the mutability of form as an innate characteristic.

Founded on the premise that all creation came from God, natural theology designated a course in natural history that contained a priori the moral of the good, the positive, and hence the judgment of the beautiful in God's work. Such aesthetic coding provided natural history with the right (read virtuous) motivation: it signaled an endeavor to understand divine creation and to acknowledge God's creative presence as an engendering force. However, it also assumed a certain aestheticism for natural history that the study of insects often undermined. Paley, for example, closes his chapter on insects with a pithy justification of insect existence: "what one nature rejects, another delights in. Maggots revel in putrefaction."[87] As the final words on the subject, disgust and corruption represent the matter in and out of which insect life appears to thrive, leaving the sacred to provide completely for the profane through the idea of a wholly incorporated body of living matter.

Juxtaposing delight and disgust, Paley also brought life and death into close relation. Being and not being formed a common system in which the matter of decay gave rise to further abundance. This view of organicism further confused the boundaries of the sacred with the profane and left the vermicular world to infest more than the bodies that fell victim to decay. Worms permeated the work of naturalists and philosophers, who strove to uncover the wide-ranging anatomies, principles, and behaviors of these organisms, just as preachers, poets, and novelists endeavored to understand the design and function of their own living bodies against such intimately animate things. "In some times and places," writes Bennett, "the 'small agency' of the lowly worm makes more of a difference than the grand agency of humans."[88] *Now* in the ecology of things, as *then* in the theorizing of organicism, are two such times and places.

# 2

# "Unchanging but in Form": The Aesthetic Epistēmē of Erasmus Darwin

ERASMUS DARWIN WAS THE DEFINITION in the eighteenth century of what today we would peg as an interdisciplinarian: his interests, always forward thinking, crossed through a mixture of fields and their methodologies. He was a physician and an inventor, a natural philosopher and a poet. But he never devoted intense time to scientific research, nor was he ever a worshipped poet.[1] Darwin was simply industrious, balancing the breadth of his scientific insights with the richness of his literary output. Combine this with the varied forms in which he presented his ideas, from natural historical treatise and engineering schematic to casual missive and formal poem, and Darwin fell easily between categorical distinctions. The convoluted labels of "scientist–poet" and "poet–naturalist" with which he has been tagged over the centuries affirm the slippery taxonomy within which Darwin resides and the suggested holism his myriad projects strove to present.

Born at Elston Hall, Nottinghamshire, England, in 1731, the "friendly, sociable and full of teasing humour"[2] Darwin matured into a rotund pioneer of evolutionary theory before dying of a respiratory tract infection in 1802.[3] With his encyclopedic interests rivaled only by the multitudinous forms found in the natural world, he came well suited to the art and rigor of eighteenth-century natural history study. The great collecting fervor from the previous century had continued to flood Darwin's time, helping to make such study the fastest growing branch of science during the eighteenth century.[4] Combined with the rapid technological advances of this century's industry, the collecting enterprise outgrew cabinets of curiosity, expanding from mantelpieces, gardens, and private salons to include the whole of the natural world. Regarding nature was that exercise wherein phenomena were observed and studied to reveal larger systems of functionality—"as if knowledge were conveyed directly, visibly, tangibly" by its comprehensive objects.[5] Having lived when the newly born wonder, "infant science,"[6] transformed naval exploration into scientific expedition, Darwin saw thousands of new species—of plants, birds, insects and reptiles, fish, and mammals—not only discovered but sketched and collected at every exotic landfall, to be then sent back to England.[7] On English soil, therefore, a plenitude existed (or soon arrived) to keep a mind like Darwin's running on full steam.

In this chapter, I look long at Darwin's final and most obscured work, *The Temple of Nature; or, The Origin of Society* (1803), as a poem that fruitfully mounts an accumulated empirical vision onto an expansive aesthetic form. By filtering the elements of natural history through the body of poetry, *Temple* transforms unfathomable nature into a sound cultural artifact. This fundamentally vermicular activity projects in turn the challenge and necessity of representing the natural world as an aesthetic work, that is, within the space of literature. It relies paradoxically on decompositional processes, on the productive dismantling of an apparent organicism, to compose an aesthetic epistēmē wherein figures of twoness represent a material oneness.

Exemplifying Darwin's interdisciplinary practices in their most mature shape, *Temple* invites a strategy of scopic reading that successfully extrudes a totalized image of the natural world through an effected double vision, or diplopia. As a visual disorder not diagnosed as such until 1811, diplopia is a useful term with which to mediate the likewise anachronistic appearance of Darwin's posthumously published poem. Just as diplopia relied on such a designation to bring it firmly into the cultural consciousness (while no doubt the condition itself predated its formal classification), so must *Temple* be acknowledged at once separate from and dependent on its creator for its comprehensive philosophical achievement that to imagine nature is in fact to create it.

Defined by the *Oxford English Dictionary* rather simply as "an affection of the eyes, in which objects are seen double," diplopia manifests a cognitive inconsistency between what is perceived and what is actually present. One tree in reality is, for instance, figured as two identical trees in the mind's eye so that seeing the tree means perceiving two images superimposed, overlapped, or side by side. In *Temple,* however, this diplopia is slightly modified not to present identical objects per se but to communicate a simultaneity of forms requisite to understanding these objects in the totality of the natural world. For example, Darwin decisively submits that ants and worms must be seen, or realized, as man's coarticulating actors; he projects both man and insect as a twofold feature of nature, drawing out their material affinity with lyrical resonance:

> —Stoop, selfish Pride! survey thy kindred forms,
> Thy brother Emmets, and thy sister Worms![8]

Playing in part on the discomforting yet pervasive aligning of high and low organisms found across genres in the eighteenth century, Darwin's final poem explores a flattening out of such deceptive, if attractive, hierarchical constructions on an epic scale. At the same time, the poem itself performs the interaction between poetry and natural history, making matter and aesthetics mutually constitutive. Thus, to understand the full impact of the man : worm analogy in particular, and vermicular analysis in general, we must recognize diplopia less as an impairment of the eye and more as a kind of coding of vision that allows for the necessary de-centering of the human—and, by extension, the irony of singularity to be that which is neither differentiable nor single valued—in favor of a more holistic rendering of the aesthetic imaginary.

Whereas common diplopia produces an illusion of doubleness, thereby creating a false impression of a single object, what I call diplopic paradox compounds this process so that such illusive doubling discloses rather than disguises the nature of nature. In an effort to demonstrate that a physics of nature and a metaphysics of nature are dual aspects of a project for which no objective "nature" preexists its construction, *Temple* resolutely displays *di-vision,* in which there was only ever unity. It promotes the cooperation of organic forms as they work toward the highest attainable standard of development as well as the collaboration of textual forms as they are able to capture this movement. With what I will discuss at length as its conceptual juxtaposition of a mythic Nature to the empirical developments of natural matter, as well as its formal deployment of lyrical verse along-side philosophical note, *Temple* produces not just a narrative on the origin and progress of life in the universe but an argument for man's ability to define and experience it through art.

"Might not," Darwin asks, "such a dignified pantomime be con-trived, even in this age, as might strike the spectators with awe, and at the same time explain many philosophical truths by adapted imagery, and thus both amuse and instruct?"[9] This machination of a "dignified pantomime" is precisely what I claim *Temple* does/is; the poem is ex-ecuted by a single voice, that of the Poet's (and, ultimately, Darwin's), able to inhabit and express all voices across space and time, animate and inanimate natures. The poem reads as a proper gesture of assent to "both amuse and instruct" its audience. Moreover, the poem itself is the answer *within which* the preceding question appears—thereby convoluting the order of inquiry so that the root query performs as little more than a rhetorical signpost to guide the reader toward the poem's imposing response. The didactic aim of the poem is thus compounded by its aesthetic charge, leaving the poem itself to be read as a series of double visions and redoubled images. Darwin's hypothesis of an effectively "contrived" representation of the natural world is consequently embedded within the rehearsal of its answer.

Because the previously quoted contrivance of the dignified pan-tomime appears in one of the notes that extends from a line of verse in Canto I of *Temple,* its presence evokes what Dahlia Porter has rec-ognized as the "paratextual" relationship between "primary text and dependent supplement."[10] In *Temple,* however, positioning the verse as primary to its notes, or even turning such an "explanatory trajectory of note to verse" on its head,[11] would elide the functioning diplopia of the dignified pantomime to simultaneously propose and explain Darwin's creative—and nonetheless empirical—efforts. So rather than assume any actualized hierarchical valuation, the relationship between

*Temple's* two formal elements must remain richly indeterminate. Thus does the introduction of diplopic paradox invite a critical leveling of the elements of Darwin's final poem and elide recourse to any one point from which or on which the poem might unfold. It recasts our reading of *Temple* as a constant negotiation of content, style, and form; as the poem sifts through the objects and actions of natural history, it produces a lasting monument to organic impermanence.

## The Scientist Poet

Darwin shied away for much of his life from positioning himself as a skilled poet. As a successful physician,[12] as well as an elected member of the Royal Society of London and a regular correspondent to its *Philosophical Transactions,* he instead published extensively on his experiments and inventions as well as on his medical investigations. Darwin's first paper, on the "Ascent of Vapor," appeared in the *Philosophical Transactions* when he was twenty-six, followed by treatises on "An Artificial Spring of Water" (1785) and the "Mechanical Expansion of Air" (1788). Although he wrote his first poem, "The Death of Prince Frederick [of Wales]" (1751), at the age of twenty, while a student at St. John's College, Cambridge,[13] and worked his poet's quill alongside the surgical tools of his professional trade for the extent of his life, he also recognized what his contemporaneous biographer, Anna Seward, described as the public's prejudices that "so much excellence in an ornamental science was not compatible with intense application to a severer study." Just as "Nature . . . added the seducing, often dangerous gift of a highly poetic imagination" to the "many rich presents" of Darwin's "generosity, wit, and science," Darwin also "remembered how fatal that gift professionally became to the young physicians, [Mark] Akenside and [John] Armstrong."[14]

Favoring with his publication history an "application to a severer study" over the appeal of poetry (that "ornamental science"), Darwin carefully drew up his own book-length treatises on human and plant care, *Zoonomia; or, the Laws of Organic Life* (1794/1796) and *Phytologia; or, the Philosophy of Agriculture and Gardening* (1800), respectively. He ushered in what Seward called "a new era of pathological science,"[15] with *Zoonomia* in particular helping to secure Darwin's honored place as the preeminent physician of the English Midlands for over five decades and serving as a boilerplate for his burgeoning ideas on life's evolutionary development:

> that all warm-blooded animals have arisen from one living fila-ment, which THE GREAT FIRST CAUSE endued with animal-ity, with the power of acquiring new parts, attended with new propensities, directed by irritations, sensations, volitions, and associations; and thus possessing the faculty of continuing to improve by its own inherent activity, and of delivering down those improvements by generation to its posterity, world without end![16]

Begun in 1770 and first published in two volumes in 1794 and 1796, respectively, *Zoonomia* is described proudly by Seward as

> the gathered wisdom of three-and-twenty years embracing, with giant-grasp, almost every branch of philosophic science; discov-ering their bearings upon each other, and those subtle, and, till then, concealed links by which they are united; and with their separate, conjunctive and collective influence upon human orga-nization; their sometimes probable, and at others demonstrative, power, under judicious application, of restoring that regularity to the mechanism of animal life, which is comprehended under the term health.[17]

And while the "doctrines of the *Zoonomia* are not always infallible," continued Seward, "it is a work which must spread the fame of its author over lands and seas, to whatever clime the sun of science has irradiated and warmed . . . throwing novel, useful, and beautiful light on the secrets of physiology, botanical, chemical, and aerological."[18]

Perhaps what provided Darwin the most readily with said "fame," however, as well as what made him his own best example of life's civilizing nature, were the many inventive plans for industrial ma-chinery, such as carriage steering, a steam car, a canal lift, a copying machine, a horizontal windmill, and even a rocket engine, that he devised, circulated, and attempted to implement throughout the late eighteenth century.[19] Likewise, he was well known as the entrepreneur of Wychnor Ironworks in Staffordshire, a founding member of the Lunar Society of Birmingham, and creator of the Lichfield Botanical Society, which he charged with translating the works of Linnaeus from Latin into English.[20] Thus was Darwin effectively known as that man of "severer study," prompting *The Midland Naturalist* (1878), journal of the Associated Natural History, Philosophical, and Archeaological Societies and Field Clubs of the Midland Counties, to declare that "had [Darwin] lived now [in the late nineteenth century] . . . we believe he would have been a bright luminary in biology; that he would have been a popular poet may not be so certain."[21]

Nevertheless, at age fifty-eight, Darwin published the first of three widely circulated didactic poems dedicated to representations of the natural world and human society: *The Loves of the Plants* (1789), which was inspired to completion by his own thorough translation of Linnaeus's *Systema Vegetabilium*.[22] With its goal to "inlist Imagination under the banner of Science,"[23] this parodic poem offered sexualized images of flora after the fashion of the Linnaean classification system in an effort to restore a shared sense of animality between all animate things. He then followed up this poem with *The Economy of Vegetation* (1791), which exchanged representations of the natural world for the technological, celebrating industrial innovation and political progress. Both poems were later collected together into *The Botanic Garden, a Poem in Two Parts* (1799), with the latter *Economy of Vegetation* packaged as its first part—as if to position Enlightenment ideals against and before the emerging character of Romanticism. After the success and scandal of these poems[24] came Darwin's third and final poem, *The Temple of Nature; or, the Origin of Society* (1803). Published a year after Darwin's death, this long poem disclosed in earnest his vision of organic wholeness from "one living filament" to the rise of human industry and society. The release of all the previously mentioned poems are what led to Darwin being acknowledged as a seminal English poet of the nascent Romantic period, even hailed by Coleridge (albeit fleetingly) as the "first *literary* character in Europe, and the most original-minded Man."[25]

Given the versatility and impact of his writings overall,[26] Darwin appears as radical a figure in the eighteenth-century landscape as both the French Revolution he staunchly supported and the Industrial Revolution he helped to ignite. His considerable accomplishments as both naturalist and poet helped to position him as a linchpin of the English Midlands enlightenment and to make him the leading English philosophe of his era.[27] Viewed in this way as an intellectual revolutionary, Darwin easily manifests what Michael Page describes as his "desire to grasp and synthesize a wide range of thought in many diverse areas," which in turn "reveals him to be a figure who deserves further attention as one of the key transitional figures who straddle the Enlightenment/Romantic divide."[28] Through his long poems in particular, Darwin demonstrated at once the cooperative properties of physics, chemistry, and natural history with imagery, analogy, and allusion. He harnessed poetry's strength and grace of metaphor to imagine the generation and progress of life according to the physics of nature.

### The Naturalist's Poem

Originally bearing the unadorned title *Origin of Society,*[29] *The Temple of Nature; or, the Origin of Society* is considered by modern scholars to be Darwin's best poem with regard to its epic and robust treatment of the natural historical record performed over four cantos of verse and pages on pages of notes. Unfolding what Martin Priestman describes as a "total vision of life in a continuous sequence," *Temple* details Darwin's progressivist view of nature as it moves from matter's inception and gradual development in Canto I, to asexual and sexual reproduction in Canto II, then on to the development of the human mind and human society in Canto III, to conclude in Canto IV with "an attempt to outweigh the awareness of life's cruelties with a vision of ever-increasing organic happiness."[30]

Written in the same format as *The Botanic Garden,* which was itself modeled on Alexander Pope's *Dunciad Variorum* (1729), *The Temple of Nature* presents an immediately arresting visual effect. Virtually every page of the poem is divided between verse and note, what

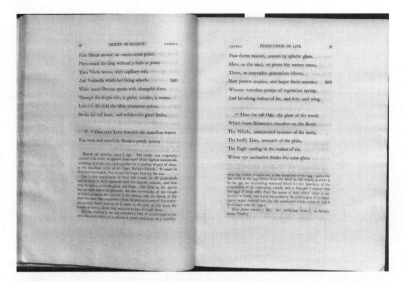

FIGURE 2.1. Erasmus Darwin, *The Temple of Nature; or, the Origin of Society*, Canto 1: 295–302. Courtesy of the Department of Special Collections, Memorial Library, University of Wisconsin–Madison.

Priestman describes as "two types of language,"[31] so that reading is a staccatoed traverse between the top of the page and the bottom and, when necessary, from one page to another and from the front of the text to its back (see Figure 2.1).

Just as a glance at Darwin's poem forces the reader to see double, given its verse–note format, the appearance of the poem's subtitle, "A POEM. WITH PHILOSOPHICAL NOTES," insists further that this double vision is manufactured, that is, constructed on the page with a punctuated break. The poem's visibly split format is thus predisposed to suggest a separation between epistemic modes—between a physics of nature and its metaphysics. It causes the reader not merely to see double but to read doubly, as if to inscribe disorder as the ordering practice for the poetry of nature, for the mutually constitutive "nature writing" and "writing nature." Forced to vibrate visually between verse and note, the reader must construct a category of "nature" at the same time as the natural world is being continuously defined through its interconnected objects. To disclose rather than disguise the nature of nature becomes, then, a kind of *taunt*-ological exercise: a tautology that carries and echoes its own ontological value, thereby creating a personality or character of Nature simultaneous with an acknowledging of nature as a category identified primarily through human experience. The poem literally *taunts* its reader with a theory of being, of animality, of life's emergence; its insistent demand to *re-vise*—to see again and again the interplay of form and content, matter and mind—is what results finally in the diplopic paradox.

As the literal as well as figurative vehicle for Darwin's poetic writings in general, and *Temple* in particular, diplopia more accurately accounts for what modern critics have thus far identified as the effected "marriage"[32] between science and poetry. *Temple*'s employment of the "two types of language" of verse and note creates an illusory (albeit pronounced) separateness, which the figure of marriage largely attempts to organize into a unified arrangement. Beginning in 1941, with Clark Emery's statement that while Darwin "did not wed science and poetry]" in his *Botanic Garden,* "he made a mighty effort,"[33] marriage emerged as the predominant metaphor with which to approach Darwin's work through modern criticism—regardless of whether the so-called marriage was successful. A little over two decades after Emery, Irwin Primer wrote specifically of *Temple* that "as an imaginative book, [it] appeals to us precisely in its attempt to envision the marriage of poetry and science."[34] Desmond King-Hele went further, attesting in 1999 not only to the celebration with which Darwin's poems present the union of science and poetry but also to the "marriage of humans and nature."[35] But the idea of marriage is implicitly hierarchical, carrying with it a traditional sense of yoking and subduing that ostensibly leads to reproduction. While the procreative potential of this metaphor is undoubtedly significant for Darwin's project, perhaps even providing a cheeky reference to Darwin's personal life of two marriages and fourteen children (at least two or three of whom were illegitimate), its allusions to women as property, male dominance, and other such sexist essentialisms[36] are too coincident with features of an eighteenth-century culture that Darwin himself sought tangentially to revise.[37] Consequently, the marriage metaphor ultimately limits our encounter with the poem as a progressive, even modernizing text, distinguished for its capacity to keep science and poetry in balanced tension and thereby projecting division as constitutive of totality.

Perhaps in an effort to recalibrate the burdened implications of such a metaphor, current criticism has moved away from a direct citing of marriage as a defining characteristic of Darwin's poetry and more toward a sense of interconnection or synthesis. Alan Richardson claimed in 2002 that because Darwin wrote "about matters of wide intellectual and popular interest—'earth, air, stars, bodies,'" he "approache[d] these topics with an 'experimentalist' ethos that linked scientific studies to poetic researches." Accordingly, Richardson described Darwin's career as "an example of overlap, if not fusion, between literary and scientific endeavor."[38] This, in turn, resonates with what Priestman and others have lately described as Darwin's writing of the "scientific poem."[39]

Clearly the proliferation of combinative language is striking, whether the word *marriage* actually appears or other words appear with similar, if less culturally weighted, connotations, for example, *link, overlap, fusion*. As recently as 2007, Darwin's poetry is said to be "melding literary and scientific practice," while yet "maintaining the boundary between science and imagination."[40] This juxtaposition of "melding" and "maintaining the boundary" quickly shows diplopia as an inherent, if disregarded, characteristic of how we are coming to understand Darwin's poetic strategy. It also draws out the irony of the marriage metaphor's profusion in Darwinian criticism: joining together, of any kind or bias, carries with it a fortification of prior separateness to recognize convergence as such. Consequently, the marriage figure and its rhetorical analogues are at once too specific and too vague for the mutually constitutive scientific thought and literary enterprise that Darwin used to represent nature as an integrated yet segmented system. Instead, the apparent doubleness of natural history and poetry in *Temple* exhibits what Wordsworth had imagined as "something far more deeply interfused" in the terminal poem of the *Lyrical Ballads* (1798):

> . . . And I have felt
> A presence that disturbs me with the joy
> Of elevated thoughts; a sense sublime

> Of something far more deeply interfused,
> Whose dwelling is the light of setting suns,
> And the round ocean and the living air,
> And the blue sky, and in the mind of man;
> A motion and a spirit, that impels
> All thinking things, all objects of all thought,
> And rolls through all things.[41]

*Temple* demonstrates a fundamental and self-conscious entwining of the unsettled, developing materiality of nature ("all objects of all thought") with a disturbing yet joyful aesthetic sensibility needed to articulate an organic whole (like a "sense sublime" and a "presence" that "rolls through all things"). In contrast to the marriage metaphor, therefore, which privileges at base the idea of bringing two distinct entities together, the paradox of diplopia allows for a neutral consideration—or continuous settling—of the relationship between natural history study and poetic form. Moreover, whereas the marriage metaphor is concerned with product, with the resultant union of the two modes of inquiry under consideration, diplopia manifests the process, however paradoxically, by which totality itself can be comprehended. It seizes on the oscillation of separations and separateness—never clearly maintained as such, yet also never resolved—to realize "nature" as both a categorical and an aesthetic construct. It presents a priori the parts making up the whole, which is to say, it reveals the whole as always already a disassembling of unified parts.

This involution of the visual with the conceptual, of an aesthetic epistēmē that refuses easy distillation into (an) individual aspect(s) in favor of indefinite expression, largely informs what has become the unresolved contest of the poem's generic value. Scientists like Richard Keynes and Desmond King-Hele have effectively presented the evolutionary ideas in *Temple* to modern biologists and historians of science, among other related disciplines. And literary critics like Elizabeth Sewell and Irwin Primer have been fascinated by Darwin's use of the Orphic and Eleusinian mysteries as a framework and generator of evolutionary ideas.[42] As Priestman's advertisement for *Temple* enthusiastically declares, the poem reads as a prolonged act of defiance, for the first time integrating [Darwin's] evolutionary arguments within a single sustained theory of the material basis of the formation of the universe and, finally, of the human psyche and social organization; investing this vision with an imagery far grander than the somewhat ingratiating nymphs and sylphs of his earlier poems, but also—through its battery of sometimes essay-length notes—daring his critics to counter it on its own scientific terms.[43]

Perhaps because of *Temple*'s "battery of . . . notes," which appear alongside and almost exceed in bulk the work's lyrical structure of heroic couplets organized into continuous cantos (which are themselves ornamented with original engravings by Henry Fuseli[44]), modern criticism of the poem remains stubbornly convoluted. Against an extolling of its meticulous representations of the natural world, many of these same scholars remain largely unimpressed "by the performance [of *Temple*] as poetry."[45] They go so far as to cite the work as a failure of poetic form and Darwin himself as an uninspired poet—even as they submit that it is indeed his most scrupulous poem.[46] Touted as an "amazing compendium of scientific theory and lore,"[47] *Temple* seems to suffer from its own categorical waywardness; it appears to ask its readers to read science in the form of poetry. Or is it poetry in the form of science? This interpretive challenge is what at once sustains and undermines the work's aesthetic effectiveness and what allows for it to be critiqued as both Darwin's greatest achievement and a supreme disappointment.

At the time of its publication at the turn of the nineteenth century, *Temple* was met with similarly mixed reviews; however, these earlier reviews were understandably concerned more with its proposed theory of evolution than with its execution of genre. In contemporaneous English publications like the *Monthly Magazine* and *Gentleman's Magazine*, the *British Critic*, *Critical Review*, and the *Anti-Jacobin*, Darwin found his work regarded as both "genius" and "glaringly atheistical" as well as both horrifying and full of splendor.[48] Coleridge spared no asperity in his eventual condemnation of his once-praised predecessor, writing in a letter to Wordsworth in 1815 that the idea of "Man's having progressed from an Ouran Outang state" was "contrary to all History, to all Religion, nay, to all Possibility." And what's more, it was wild speculation, or "Darwinizing with a vengeance."[49] (And this is to say nothing of how, decades later, the author of *On the Origin of Species* would be equally praised and condemned for completing in prose what his grandfather proffered in poetry.[50])

West across the Atlantic, Darwin's work enjoyed no greater critical reception, though the poem was a popular conversation piece. Just as it remained predominately Darwin's "ideas, not the verses" that were "target[ed] for abuse" in England,[51] American readers too had a hard time accepting the premise not only that man progressed from primates but that life itself evolved from microscopic creatures. On one hand, such a premise could lead inevitably into atheism, perhaps first settling on the concept of an unmoved mover, then to elide finally any originary causal function in favor of a kind of parthenogenesis. On the other hand, it suggested that we look for our ancestors toward the lower end of the chain of being, placing humans once again into that loathsome proximity to "sister Worms."

By embracing what was conceivably vile, critics notwithstanding, Darwin was able to promote plasticity as the most attractive aspect not only of man as an evolved species; he designed *Temple* to celebrate the agility of man's emergent intellect as that which can comprehend— better, represent—the magnitude of his developmental process. In what follows, I focus primarily on the first two cantos of *Temple* because their explicit illustrations of the production and reproduction of life make up the "adapted imagery" needed to perform and thus define that dignified pantomime of nature. The third and final cantos certainly continue the discussion outlined earlier, but they are more concerned with the intellectual and moral development of humankind; my interest lies in representations of the material schema of nature. It is thus within Cantos I and II that Darwin exposes the four philosophical truths, or principles, with which *Temple* displays an organized, if frenetic, nature in process: the brevity of life, immutable mutability, a living web, and organic happiness. Much as Aristotle identified the four kinds of causation as material, formal, efficient, and final,[52] so Darwin insists that four interrelated principles govern the natural world. By defining and delineating each principle of change, I am able to sketch the epistemology of nature as Darwin imagined and created it.

To acknowledge a kind of vital materiality[53] in *Temple*'s innately doubled presentation, without falsely dividing and reuniting it into modern generic components or harnessing it to a specious hierarchy of forms, diplopic paradox remains the more precise approach to envisioning *Temple*'s (de)construction of the natural world. Specifically, it keeps visible the setting of Darwin's work of natural history against its frame of the Eleusinian mysteries, leaving a classical mythic structure to transmute "the origin and progress of society": in his preface to the poem, Darwin notes that "in the Eleusinian mysteries the philosophy of the works of Nature, with the origin and progress of society, are believed to have been taught by allegoric scenery explained by the Hierophant to the initiated, which gave rise to the machinery of the following Poem."[54] In short, he employs epic, eternal figures in their transience to convey natural, finite processes as a flexible continuum. Like his poem's format, this artificial doubling of the historic and the mythic is crucial to understanding how and why Darwin constructed his lasting vision of nature *as poem*. Recognizing the marriage of poetry and science thus functions only insofar as it reflects the discursive ambition of Darwin's project. He wishes to demonstrate the logic of nature, and to do so, he must articulate a rapidly alternating current of its imagined and apprehended processes.

## Materialism and Myth

Following in the tradition of empiricist philosophers Francis Bacon, Isaac Newton, and John Locke, Darwin worked to advance his theory of a mechanistic, self-sufficient, and progressive system of nature. He looked to nature as the basis for advancing order and unity in accordance with sensible matter.[55] Just as Lockean methodology dictated the superior importance of visual images in Enlightenment thinking, material idealists sought to reveal what Donald Hassler recognizes as "a comprehensive [matter-based] world view . . . to replace the supernatural world view" of entrenched and immaterial religious beliefs.[56]

"'Clear thinking' is a direct result of reducing complexity to nonmisty outlines that can be 'seen.'"[57] One of the consequences of this materialism was that God was relegated to the "Great First Cause"[58]—not necessarily in denial of God's role as Creator but certainly placing him into the dimly lit corner of what Darwin evasively named the "Ens Entium," or "Parent of Parents" or "Cause of Causes."[59] Such a deistic perspective allowed Darwin to set Nature as the consummate child of God in *Temple* and God as the undetectable, originary act of creation used merely to kindle the poem's own unfolding.

This perspective led to Darwin's eventual condemnation and loss of popularity because neither his scientific insight into biological evolution nor his experimental method(s) of representation could convince the staid, God-fearing public of eighteenth-century England. In this way, *Temple* followed in the same scandalous vein of perceived atheism of which *The Botanic Garden* and *Zoonomia* were accused. Natural history, not theology, was endowed with the task to interpret and even translate *Temple*'s imagistic content of the natural world and the origin of its mysteries. As such, it would be Nature—not God—revealed as the force behind all life. The practically simultaneous publication of Darwin's *Temple of Nature* (1803) and the third edition of his *Zoonomia* (1801) with Paley's *Natural Theology* (1802) emphasized a continued strain between religion and science at the turn of the nineteenth century. As King-Hele notes, Darwin's contemporary readers

> were much happier with Paley's *Natural Theology*, which was seen as the Church's riposte to *Zoonomia*, and refuted Darwin's speculations with the certainties of theo-zoology. Paley had no doubts: "Design must have had a designer. That designer must have been a person. That person is GOD." 'And who was GOD's designer?' Darwin might wickedly have asked if he had not been dead."[60]

As Darwin states in the preface to the third edition of *Zoonomia*, "the great CREATOR of all things has infinitely diversified the works of his hands, but has at the same time stamped a certain similitude on the features of nature, that demonstrates to us, that *the whole is one family of one parent.*"[61] Although Darwin was no atheist, he did relegate God to a suspiciously finite role of original creation. Working outside a natural theology and its popular analogy of clock to clockmaker, Darwin's deism does not mimic the divine; rather, it acknowledges itself as a descendent of, but not dependent on, the Cause of Causes. Nature, assuming her familiar mantle of "mother," demonstrates a remarkable independence in Darwin's poem. His "evolutionary theme," notes King-Hele, "seem[ed] wildly improbable to most readers" of the eighteenth and early nineteenth centuries, given that it flew in the face of "both Christianity and human dignity."[62]

Like his continental counterparts d'Alembert, Diderot, la Mettrie, and d'Holbach, Darwin was a materialist who supposed that all life could be explained mechanistically. This materialism was based on speculative atomism, which held that living beings were organized according to the motion of "permanent, indivisible atoms in empty space."[63] Popularized by Lucretius's *De Rerum Natura,* a significant classical influence on Darwin's systematized thinking, the doctrine of atomism was the foundation for the Enlightenment's diffuse scientific belief that life provided its own evidentiary existence. Moreover, speculations about the future development of life, concerning the progress of nature and all entities contained therein (from plant to human life and on to the patterning of meteorological events and the formation of the universe), grew logically from evidence visible to human perception. As Robert Ross accurately observes, Darwin "enlisted the support of the visual imagination . . . because it was felt that the most potent of senses resides in the eye."[64] This, again, brings diplopia to bear as the visual metaphor capable of supporting the confrontation of matter with the imagination.

Significantly, the speculations or hypotheses concerning the material nature of life carried a certain irony, just as all discussions of materialism necessarily do. When philosophes like d'Holbach, following Locke's cue, began "attributing mental characteristics, such as sympathies and antipathies, to the fundamental material atoms,"[65] they drew attention to the idea that much of scientific knowledge is in fact immaterial—understood more through the mind's eye than the eye itself. Just as the words that make up a specific language are arbitrary, albeit given toward a general system of substantive comprehension, that which actually constructs the physical world at its base is always unseen. Out of the reach of man's phenomenal field, even when aided by increasingly advanced instruments, lie those "permanent, indivisible atoms of empty space" reminiscent of the shadowy bower of First Cause to which God had been consigned. As a result, the material world presented by Enlightenment thinkers could only ever be one of approximation; in turn, this paradox of representation demands that the language of analysis be one of "vivid, visual imagery in which the ideas imaged are never completely seen"[66]—and yet these ideas are nevertheless clearly represented. The imaginative act of Darwin's pantomime therefore renders "the whole world visible"[67] so that Darwin necessarily came to rely on adapted imagery to promote his vision.

Although Darwin held fast to materialist ideals, his varied modes of communicating his natural philosophies strayed from the strict theorizing of his predecessors—perhaps in an effort to reconcile empirical limitations with his aesthetic vision. Ross again observes that Darwin's "poetic problem was, in fact, how to move from the distinctness of phenomena in the eye to the indistinctness of phenomena within the mind."[68] But because he "delighted in the half-knowledge of mystery without relinquishing the world so graphically before his eyes,"[69] Darwin, in the most practical sense, labored to display the mysteries of nature with all the weight visual imagery could bear, paradoxes notwithstanding. His organicism celebrated what Fredrika Teute identifies as "the social affections and sensory pleasures found in nature,"[70] just as much as it venerated the transformations of physical matter itself. So that while Darwin had to contend with "the futility of trying to give mechanical explanations to organic phenomena," he nevertheless strove to provide a "unifying concept for an infinitely complex materialism."[71]

For this reason, Darwin's writings are said to "offer a wide picture of the world that challenges all our deepest notions about how things are and ought to be."[72] This is indeed the challenge of *Temple*, beginning with its preface. Initially, the preface offers a curiously superficial "aim" "simply to amuse," to the humble fault of any "deep researches of reasoning,"[73] as if to suggest discrete, even incompatible roles for the "ornamental science" of poetry and the "severer study" of natural history. However, in what immediately follows this suspect statement of purpose, Darwin effectively revises his goal: he discloses his method of adapting "beautiful and sublime images" to represent "the operations of Nature."[74] Such images are said further to occur "in the order . . . in which the progressive course of time presented them,"[75] resulting in a compound of aesthetic and mechanistic approaches needed to understand a sensible nature. In addition to the material causes operating in the natural world, therefore, Darwin maintains that a prescribed order governs the presentation in its entirety. This order, we come to learn, is understood as the "firm immutable immortal laws" that dictate "how rose from elemental strife / Organic forms, and kindled into life."[76] The rhyme of "strife" with "life" capitalizes on sound to promote process (and tension) over product. It not only designates struggle as a fundamental attribute of being; it also stresses the harmony of such activity through its punctuation of the lines' iambic tetrameter and pentameter, respectively. The overall design of Darwin's poem thus echoes Horatian dictum by adding to its prefaced amusement an unmistakably didactic dimension, which in turn realizes the dual goal of the dignified pantomime—both to amuse and to instruct—and makes the choice to employ a synthetic binary format suitably evident, if visually misleading. Proposing here what looks on the face of it to be that popular figure of marriage between poetry and science, *Temple*'s preface performs instead the very re-vision necessary to decipher the poem's comprehensive diplopia, which in turn is the necessary activity needed to represent "the operations of Nature" that follow in the poem as a whole.

Darwin opens Canto I, "Production of Life," as he does each of his four cantos, with a straightforward table of contents, or general inventory, reminiscent of the form used to introduce topics in his *Zoonomia* or any similar eighteenth-century natural history treatise. By laying to view each segment of the whole—however inseparable instrumentally—such categorical anatomizing guarantees a sense of the empirical, thereby emphasizing the didactic sense of the poem. Each topic is listed according to the order in which it occurs in the canto and is identified by line numbers marking each stanza-like section—as if superimposed on nature's own arrangement:

> I. Subject proposed. Life, Love, and Sympathy 1. Four past Ages, a fifth beginning 9. Invocation to Love 15. II. Bowers of Eden, Adam and Eve 33. Temple of Nature 65. Time chained by Sculpture 75. . . . Shrine of Nature 129. Eleusinian Mysteries 137. . . . IV. Urania 205. GOD the First Cause 223. Life began beneath the Sea 233. Repulsion, Attraction, Contraction, Life 235. Spontaneous Production of Minute Animals 247. . . . V. Vegetables and Animals improve by Reproduction 295. Have all arisen from Microscopic Animalcules 303. . . . Venus rising from the Sea, emblem of Organic Nature 371. All animals are first Aquatic 385. . . . The Hierophant and the Muse 421–450.[77]

From the progenitive roles of Love and Sympathy ("Invocation to Love") to Genesis retold ("Bowers of Eden, Adam and Eve") and an initiation into the "Eleusinian Mysteries," Darwin introduces his "Subject proposed" in mythic terms. Similarly, the presence of a "Temple" and "Shrine of Nature," as well as naming "GOD the First Cause" and recalling the Old Testament, all evoke religious or spiritual tones for the poem. And yet, once inside the "Temple of Nature," we are told how "Life began [spontaneously] beneath the Sea" from "a fifth beginning," thereby suggesting from the beginning that we are already beginning again with the materials of Life. We are also provided here with the contingent properties of Life's generation ("Repulsion, Attraction, Contraction") as well as its ability to "improve by Reproduction." Myth, therefore, is used to communicate natural history, as realized through the divine conversation between "The Hierophant [Urania, Priestess of Nature] and the Muse [of Poetry]."

The Muse, called on by the Poet to "attend [his] song" and "write [his] verse,"[78] acts for the Poet as Virgil did for Dante, guiding a charge to realize an image of existence. And yet, to continue the analogy, just as Beatrice (in place of Virgil) ultimately led Dante to his enlightenment, the Muse defers to the Priestess of Nature, Urania. Hence the Poet is piloted into a classical model of Eleusinian myth as an initiate of Urania, who instructs him in the origin of natural phenomena by amusing and inspiring him with its divine disclosure. As a result of this piloting, the Poet is able to translate the natural world into the aesthetic work of the poem itself. In doing so, he calls on his reader, whose "soft-rolling eyes engage, / And snow-white fingers turn the volant page,"[79] to experience his adapted vision as it performs the interaction between poetry and nature.

In contrast to a mythic Nature, however, with its progenitors Immortal Love and Sympathy, the reader is more closely tied to the ephemera passing in and out of life in a day. Suggestive of sacrifice, this young, virginal reader[80] becomes a conduit from the mythic, abstract frame of the poem to its historic, material depiction of the natural world. Read as an analogue of mortal life, the reader, whose innocence will be forfeit through the act of reading itself, signals the brevity of individual life relative to the total system through which the natural world evolves.

By opening Canto II, for example, with the exclamation, "How short the span of life!"[81] which repeats in turn Canto I's closing testament to the "brevity of life,"[82] Darwin reveals his difficulty of demonstrating the infinite progressions that occur in the natural world.[83] Given that he is as mortal as his reader, he lacks the panoramic vision of time. With the "precision of careful observation and the broadly intellectual powers of myth,"[84] Darwin sets *Temple* the task to overcome this empirical inability to witness how "with finer links the vital chain extends, / And the long line of Being never ends."[85] Thus the challenge of reading Darwin's poem lies in large part in its intrinsic diplopia of mythic and historic perspectives. Because our representations are predisposed to juvenility (ourselves "young," like the reader, in the eyes of Nature), and so lack the long perspective accorded to the grand scale of the natural world, but also grant us the necessary plasticity of mind (with our "soft-rolling eyes engage[d]"), Darwin invents time within the space of his text "by [the] palsied repetition"[86] of individual examples drawn from an observable, recorded nature.

## Toward an Organic Happiness

"Hence without parent by spontaneous birth / Rise the first specks of animated earth."[87] Once Darwin acknowledges life's brief duration, he is free to focus his attention on exemplifying how spontaneously generated life is stimulated into a rich and diverse plenum. In Additional Note I, which directly follows the close of *Temple*'s verse, significant detail is expended to lay out (1) the "prejudices" against the doctrine of spontaneous generation, which in turn serves to preserve Darwin's deism and materialism together; (2) "preliminary observations" to support spontaneous generation; (3) the "experimental facts" ostensibly proving spontaneous generation, which cite contemporary naturalists Buffon, Réaumur, and others; and (4) Darwin's own "theory of spontaneous generation," which builds on both Lucretian and Linnaean theories. Finally, Darwin provides an appendix, beyond the additional note, that lists spontaneously generated organisms, divided into classes and briefly discussed. As a result of this careful progression and itemization of ideas, Darwin contends that

> there is therefore no absurdity in believing that the most simple animals and vegetables may be produced by the congress of the parts of decomposing organic matter, without what can properly be termed generation, as the genus did not previously exist; which accounts for the endless varieties, as well as for the immense numbers of microscopic animals.[88]

He commits to representing nature in its "endless varieties," compounding example onto example to illustrate the progression from simple to complex organism and from asexual to sexual reproduction. In accordance with progressive principles, Darwin displays nature as a changeable and changing continuum so that

> when we reflect on the perpetual destruction of organic life, we should also recollect, that it is perpetually renewed in other forms by the same materials, and thus the sum total of the happiness of the world continues undiminished.[89]

In formal terms, the individual cantos and additional notes of *Temple* offer the dignified pantomime of classical personifications that demonstrate the four principles that are for Darwin mingled in the natural world: again, the brevity of life, a living web, immutable mutability, and organic happiness. By exposing the constructedness of his poem not simply in its verse–note format but through the transparent fiction of a mythic frame needed to communicate the materialist principles of an organized nature, Darwin seeks to preserve nature's characteristic structure—its motile and protean organicism.

In *Temple,* the principle of organic happiness resonates as the ironic final goal or purpose toward which Darwin directs his pantomime of nature. In other words, we are to understand that "when an aged or unhealthy animal dies, the amount of happiness lost is small; while much happiness is gained by the insects (and other creatures or plants) that feed on its remains."[90] "Pleasure in the entire biotic realm," states Nichols, "is increased not only by the prolific reproduction of 'insects' and the microscopic organisms but by the death and organic regeneration of larger creatures."[91] As telos, organic happiness carries with it the three remaining principles of a nature in process. Through it we can recognize the interrelatedness of life in nature (as the living web), the constancy of change (or immutable mutability), and life's brevity. Similar to Aristotelian logic, "all four causes are relevant to" Darwin's schema. Likewise, just as "the formal, efficient, and final causes frequently coincide" in Aristotle's *Physics, Temple* presents the living web, immutable mutability, and organic happiness all of a piece. However, whereas Aristotle's "physical explanation" is dependent on either a "stat[ed] *end* (i.e. the final cause) or the antecedent *necessity* (i.e. the material cause) of a process,"[92] Darwin's poem relies on the simultaneity of final and material causes to activate his progressive, binocular vision of nature.

To understand, for example, why the "reasoning reptile" is "linked" "to mankind,"[93] we must consider how the brevity of life and organic happiness synchronize to reveal the living web of life—the formal cause of Darwin's schema. In recognizing that "our vaunted wisdom is not so different from the instinctive wisdom of the wasp, bee or spider,"[94] or the industrious behavior of the ant or worm, Darwin emphasizes the interconnectedness of all organic life; be it simple or complex, such life shares a transitory existence, a common albeit ineffable origin, and analogous developments (e.g., instinct and reason). By what Stuart Harris depicts as "linking phenomena over vast stretches of space and time," Darwin attempts to relate an "organic unity of life at all levels."[95] But he also works to reveal "a Nature that aims at plenitude and seems remarkably careless of individuals."[96] By progressing his poem from the First Great Cause to the Truth Divine, organic happiness can thus be read as Darwin's own rhetorical call for humility, in which "sister Worms" are indeed those phenomena deserving of our esteem because they inhabit the immediacy of our space and time.

According to A. O. Lovejoy, the "notion of the full and infinitesimally graduated Scale of Being" brought with it several implications that "tended definitely to lower man's estimate of his cosmic importance and uniqueness," one of which intimates that man's place on this scale is "not midway in the series [toward the infinite, or God], but well down toward the lower end of it. [Man] was the 'middle link' in the sense that he was at the point of transition from the merely sentient to the intellectual forms of being."[97] What Darwin did was to reimagine the linearity of this chain as a nonhierarchical mesh, making the capacity to continually evolve contingent on interconnection and cooperation.[98]

On the basis of its representation of the web of life, and its invocation of a progressive chain of being, *Temple* effectively denies the human species its ascendency of reason in favor of associating reason to instinct. Darwin projects, as his grandson Charles would do decades later to more lasting effect,[99] that

> Imperious man, who rules the bestial crowd,
> Of language, reason, and reflection proud,
> With brow erect who scorns this earthy sod,
> And styles himself the image of his God;
> Arose from rudiments of form and sense,
> An embryon point, or microscopic ens![100]

Tying end to end, "man" to "microscopic ens," as two such kindred forms, Darwin shows that indeed, even the most complex of nature's organisms have direct relation in "form and sense" with those more simple beings, the reptile or worm or embryonic entity. According to the poem, and reflective of the natural philosophy and burgeoning geology of the eighteenth century, this evolving relation stems from the generative theory that all "Organic Life began beneath the waves."[101] Presenting water as the source for all life on earth begs the question of a source for earth—and thus also of the natural elements and nature itself—in much the same way that Darwin might be thought to have questioned who designed God. Not only does Darwin equate the chain of being with the web of life; he is careful to trace back the beginnings of an "earthy sod" to "shoreless earth,"[102] and then still back so that "from each sun with quick explosions burst, / . . . second planets issued from the first."[103] This then recalls "the fifth beginning" pronounced in the first canto's table of contents, further helping to cement the image and idea of a web of life over and above that of a chain.

But there is a problem with presenting the origin and development of our known natural world from within the context of a planetary cataclysm: the relative instantaneity of a world thrown into existence is not only inconceivable to man but also immediately unempirical. Unable to witness or experience this birth, itself always a kind of rebirth from preexisting planetary bodies, vapors, or other elements, Darwin is forced to lay claim, through analogy, to an elusive "beginning or birth"—as that which is the source for life on earth. This, in turn, circumvents empiricism's demand for sensible experience simply by eliding origin with its infinite doubling. In doing so, Darwin is free to draw on then-current evidence to speculate backward toward an approximate creative act.

Further complicating this creative act is the personification of Nature. When "Young Nature lisps," for example, this construction is meant to reveal not only that "she is," indeed, "the child of GOD"[104] but also that she is relatively young. She is a system not yet—because not ever—matured. In this way, Nature is figured as both progeny and progenitor. Although Darwin preserves God's role as *the* Creator, at the beginning of time, he repels God's role as *active* Creator throughout time. In doing so, he can maintain Nature as an empirically if metonymically hermetic system indicative of a "globe . . . gradually enlarging":

> The perpetual production and increase of the strata of limestone from the shells of aquatic animals; and of all those incumbent on them from the recrements of vegetables and of terrestrial animals, are now well understood from our improved knowledge of geology; and show, that parts of the globe are gradually enlarging, and consequently that it is young; as the fluid parts are not yet all converted into solid ones. Add to this, that some parts of the earth and its inhabitants appear younger than others; thus the greater height of the mountains of America seems to show that continent to be less ancient than Europe, Asia, and Africa; as their summits have been less washed away, and the wild animals of America, as the tigers and crocodiles, are said to be less perfect in respect to their size and strength; which would show them to be still in a state of infancy, or of progressive improvement. . . . The juvenility of the earth shows, that it has had a beginning or birth.[105]

Darwin insists that the natural record proves his theory of the earth. Detailing "progressive improvement," his "natural argument" relies on an illustration of growth predicated on youth and on a youth predicated on constant rebirth ("*a* beginning or birth" is the quotation, rather than "*the* beginning or birth") to demonstrate how the "living web expands"[106]—be it on a cosmic scale of universal naissance or on the relatively minute scale of individual generation.

The telescopic view with which Darwin presents his theory of the earth, however, would have the same representational problems of origin discussed earlier if he did not then center it on the wholly observable model of minute scale. Darwin cautiously maintains the empirical ground of his poem by inserting other illustrations into the poem that are native to a naturalist's study. "[V]iew'd through crystal spheres in drops saline"[107] suggests, for example, the ubiquitous water droplet. A world of "progressive improvement" cannot only be witnessed in such a space, it can be replicated. With every drop of water comes yet another microcosmic instantiation of nature's "changeful form[s]."[108] From "Mucor-stems" to "animated rings," to "Vibrio waves" and "Vorticella whirls," Nature as a whole is replicated in cross section by the observable movements from "a globe, a cube, a worm," until

> Last o'er the field the Mite enormous swims,
> Swells his red heart, and writhes his giant limbs.[109]

In an effort to cement such "kindred forms" as man and worm, their relative repugnancy notwithstanding, Darwin traverses this particular evolution of form merely through the invocation of scale; all named organisms retain insect characteristics—from the microscopic Vorticella to the giant Mite.[110] Moreover, the size of each organism likewise indicates an increasing complexity: from continuous globe to contiguous cube to segmented worm, each form reflects in contour the structure of its predecessor.

Viewing the living web expanding in this manner once again recalls the so-called origin of life in the natural world, causing Darwin to repeat here, "ORGANIC LIFE beneath the shoreless waves / Was born and nurs'd in Ocean's pearly caves."[111] But rather than reiterating a cataclysmic event, Darwin collapses the telescopic view of the natural world into the microscopic investigations characteristic of an eighteenth-century naturalist. The "First forms minute," said to "Move on the mud, or pierce the watery mass," "establish that the organisms described [prior to these] were not the first."[112] By alluding to organisms spontaneously generated, Darwin continues to elide any presentable origin, this time not from the perspective of the cosmos but from its minutiae. Depicting nature in this way moves arguably closer to that microscopic representability needed to fortify Darwin's empirical materialism.

Just as Darwin's representational strategy of the dignified pantomime is defined in a footnote and presented as a rhetorical question, Darwin inverts the usual trajectory of observation, in which nature's myriad forms lead to their being recorded in the annals of man. Instead, he causes "progressive improvement" to appear as if in repetition of what can be captured in and around a naturalist's study. When "successive generations bloom" outside in nature, they might appear to double the contents of powder jars (precursors to the petri dish) inside a naturalist's study, thereby creating an observable diplopia.[113] Lacking any true experiential base, Darwin effectively manufactures one out of the analogue between a nature enclosed under glass and the one endlessly, though sequentially, bursting forth "in countless swarms."[114]

Akin to the minutiae trapped to view in droplets of water, the observable (and thus recordable) habits of individual organisms also offer solid evidence of a world in constant transformation. Canto II abounds with instances to illustrate this topic, focusing on the transition from asexual to sexual reproduction—from budding trees to hermaphroditic aphids to the trials and conquests of man.[115] By grouping these illustrations in close proximity, Darwin acknowledges both the order of nature, as it moves from simple to complex organism, and the ostensible perfectibility transmitted through such an order. Whereas asexual reproduction suffers at length from mortal decay so that "The feeble births acquired diseases chase, / Till Death extinguish the degenerate race,"[116] sexual reproduction overcomes this difficulty through, for example, natural hybrid variation and thus a greater stride toward organic happiness: "Form'd by new powers progressive parts succeed / Join in one whole," to "[save] the sinking world."[117]

This trajectory from asexual to sexual reproduction, however, only underscores a linear progress needed to secure a flawless nature. The immutable aspect overriding such mutability has yet to be determined. By combining the brevity of life, which requires reproduction, and immutable mutability, which makes constant the flux of life itself, change in nature is revealed to be both fixed and variable simultaneously. This such diplopia allows for cyclic activity to be reconciled to linear progress:

> HENCE when a Monarch or a mushroom dies,
> Awhile extinct the organic matter lies;
> But, as a few short hours or years revolve,

Alchemic powers the changing mass dissolve;
Born to new life unnumber'd insects pant,
New buds surround the microscopic plant;
Whose embryon senses, and unwearied frames,
Feel finer goads, and blush with purer flames;[118]

This passage from the fourth and final canto of *Temple* augments the cyclical illustrations flooding Canto II. It portrays how new life must be understood to grow out of the decay of the old such that the moldering forms of the butterfly ("Monarch") and mushroom, over time and by way of natural chemical laws, nourish "the microscopic plant" that will reengender the life cycle—in an improved state, with "finer goads" and "purer flames." As Priestman rightly submits in his annotation to this passage,

the juxtaposing of monarchs and mushrooms has a nicely republican ring, as well as reaffirming Darwin's constant theme of the unity of all organic life. . . . The idea that the new insects and plants which feed off dead bodies feel "finer goads" and "purer flames" [IV.390] can be related to the argument in [Darwin's] *Phytologia* that new organisms are "more irritable and more sensible" than those they feed on, and hence "more pleasurable sensation exists in the world, as the organized matter is taken from a state of less irritability and less sensibility, and converted into a state of greater."[119]

To superimpose such activity within the filled space of nature, and thus preserve the repeatability of change over time, Darwin not only must follow sexual reproduction to its apex, "And give SOCIETY his golden chain,"[120] he must track its inevitable demise.

The mythic Love said by Darwin to attract one sex to another carries with it an instrumental tool of decomposition: the "Demon, Jealousy" rises and "lights the flames of war,"[121] making the natural world into a savage battleground where decimation and death pave the way for rebirth. Darwin spends over one hundred lines just prior to the close of Canto II illustrating this exchange from incipient love to war to love again, and birth to death to rebirth, by integrating myth with natural forms.[122] He depicts Helen and Philomel alongside "Contending Boars" and "The incumbent Linnet."[123] He shows as well how "Despotic LOVE dissolves the bestial war" and "Pair after pair enamour'd shoot along / And trill in air the gay impassion'd song."[124] Like asexual reproduction, sexual reproduction suffers from prolonged generation, ultimately needing to wipe the proverbial slate clean and begin anew. This repetition of beginning again reveals nature's striving toward perfection as just that: a striving or struggle to complete itself in final form rather than an accomplished or accomplishable act. As Darwin demonstrates, such perfectibility is only ever defined in suspension; as process deferred, the system of nature suggests development in each individual in each generation through time immemorial. But by bracketing examples of periodic transmutations together, Darwin effectively extends his ability to speculate on the principles of a unified system while still remaining safely within empirical confines.

While the preceding discussion encompasses virtually the whole of Canto II, tracing the generation and regeneration of life through the ages and across species, this same canto turns to a succinct example of this recycling system: the butterfly. Cited by Darwin as "the ancient emblem of the soul after death as rising from the tomb of its former state, and becoming a winged inhabitant of air from insect creeping upon earth,"[125] the butterfly functions as a solitary symbol of life's metamorphoses (and its accompanying superstitions). Through each state of its development—from egg to larva or caterpillar, to pupa or chrysalis, to adult or winged insect—this organism immediately represents the birth, death, and rebirth demonstrated broadly earlier. Moreover, this organism allows for an empirical eye to spy the totality of its development—and thus to justify its symbolism.[126] Beginning life in its lowliest form, the butterfly exchanges one form for another in its journey toward "perfection." As if to draw in one stroke the sense of beginning again that he arduously sketches throughout *Temple*, Darwin conspicuously refers to this organism in process, in the stage of its rebirth *from* "insect creeping" *to* "winged inhabitant of air." In doing so, he is able to posit renewal as intrinsic to linear growth and nature's loathsome, unsettling aspect as fundamental to its attractive, moral expression. He fixes process, like a pinned insect, to reveal a plastic nature.

"Unchanging but in form,"[127] each preceding example establishes the immutable mutability needed finally to imagine the organic happiness of an organized nature in "progress to greater perfection"[128]—that is, in ironic teleological motion. If nature is understood by Darwin's empirical eye as a cyclical, yet infinitely linear system, which imposes the confrontation of cycle and progress, then his aesthetic sense attempts to mimic this repetitive and paradoxical system in his final poem. Specifically, by transmitting verse with note, myth with natural history, *Temple* stands as the mature and cohesive product of Darwin's wide-ranging imaginative and empirical vision. It is, ironically, the single vantage point from which to view his holistic representation of the natural world.

By deconstructing the development of life in nature over and again, utilizing his four interdependent principles, Darwin constructs an extended poetic simile of nature's "progressive movement" in revolution. The fact that all life is said to begin "beneath the Sea" is consistently returned to in the first two cantos of *Temple*; it is, however, prevalent in the last two as well. That Darwin does not begin his poem with the origin of life, but always begins *again* this natural process, is established by an historic repetition proving its constant rotation. Proclaiming in an example from man's own history that "the art of painting has appeared in the early state of all societies before the invention of the alphabet," Darwin discusses how Cortez and the Spanish adventurers communicated by drawings correspondent with Egyptian hieroglyphics, thereby linking the figurative fashionings of antiquity to their more modern counterparts.[129] This linking of verse to note, subject to subject, which parallels the associative path from Urania to reader, suggests that Darwin's note, as he himself declares, is meant to "nudge us into relating the Muse's request [to enter the Temple] to the idea that Nature's real processes have long been recorded in Egyptian hieroglyphics and other non-verbal depictions, giving rise to myths of gods, heroes and beauties which now need decoding back to their real scientific meaning."[130] As a result, *beginning again* is both a process and a theme reiterated throughout the poem, suggestive of the cyclical nature of "happy" life that Darwin wishes to establish (or recode) and vital to constructing Darwin's unified theory.

Given that the first two cantos of *Temple* are concerned with the production and reproduction of life, the "origin of society" is effectively reestablished as the titular process manifesting its own variable growth. By extension, then, the *Temple of Nature* is turned into a placeholder (which I will discuss at length in the following section). It must become the stage for that "imaginative act" capable of perceiving the progress of life as it emanates from its fabricated "origin":

> From this first altar fam'd Eleusis stole
> Her secret symbols and her mystic scroll;[131]

Darwin's note to the preceding couplet claims that "the Eleusinian mysteries . . . consisted of scenical representations of the philosophy and religion of [ancient Egypt and then in Greece]."[132] Moreover, Priestman first interprets the "first altar" as Nature, being the logical origin from which "the ancient Greek Eleusinian Mystery rituals" were founded,[133] and then goes on to clarify Darwin's allusion by elucidating several of the historical sources—literary and religious—on which the poem draws. In doing so, Priestman reinforces the clothing of myth in what Darwin himself claimed were the recorded trappings of a lived history. "Repeatedly," states Priestman, "[Darwin] concludes that [myths] are based on real ancient scientific knowledge"; the "Eleusinian Mysteries . . . revealed only to an initiated elite that the 'vulgar' mythology was a misreading of real material truths as the conservation of matter from organism to organism."[134] By consistently grounding myth in historical event—social or natural—Darwin is able to turn from abstraction into experience, to negotiate infinite and finite realms simultaneously, all the while remaining within the demonstrable site of organized nature. This, in turn, returns his poem to the telescopic perspective needed paradoxically to project his microscopic, mortal vision beyond the limitations of its inherited empiricism and into the greater scale of nature's infinitely changing track.

However, Darwin's writing also registers the key events of his time: industrialization (to which his own experimental projects happily responded) and the French Revolution. For example, his note accompanying the preceding couplet suggests that the mythic frame in which nature is set mirrors the historical perspective of his vision.[135] It follows the invention of the Eleusinian mysteries from Egypt to Greece and into Europe as well as these mysteries' representations in the sixth book of Virgil's *Aeneid* and on the Portland Vase.[136] He outlines "Death, and the destruction of all things" as the first stage in the origin of society; "the reproduction of living nature" the next; "the resuscitation of all things" after this; and "lastly, the histories of illustrious persons of the early ages . . . enacted [by hieroglyphics]"[137]— all, incidentally, immediately preceding his noted rhetorical plea for the dignified pantomime.

Such enacted analogies of birth, death, and rebirth crop up almost without break from the preface through to the final "agreeable hope" with which Darwin wraps up his additional notes to *Temple* and thus the work itself:

> I conclude with an agreeable hope, that now war is ceased, the active and ingenious of all nations will attend again to those sciences, which better the condition of human nature; and that the alphabet will undergo a perfect reformation, which may indeed make it more difficult to trace the etymologies of words, but will much facilitate the acquisition of modern languages; which as science improves and becomes more generally diffused, will gradually become more distinct and accurate than ancient ones; as metaphors will cease to be necessary in conversation, and only be used as the ornaments of poetry.[138]

As King-Hele notes, Darwin kept his radical view and enthusiasm for the French Revolution even after the Revolution degenerated into the Terror[139]—even if his open praise of the revolution cautiously dimmed. *Temple* ends, not surprisingly, in the obstinate optimism of (r)evolutionary advancement. But he transfers the burden of change from military hands to systematic minds, charging the intellectual plane, rather than the planed-edge of the guillotine, with "better[ing] the condition of human nature." He all but states that familiar devices such as analogy, metaphor, and allusion are as much at work in science as they are in poetry, perhaps in a move to show that the "ornamental science" of poetry is in fact as effective and necessary in this period's scientizing as others have proclaimed it useless and distracting. And because Charles Darwin could not ultimately avoid (even if obliquely) a sense of indebtedness to his grandfather's theoretical foresight, and maybe even to his grandfather's narrative know-how,[140] Erasmus Darwin's anticipation (and illustration) of the theory of natural selection emerges as a practical example of how one idea is built from/on the decayed remains of another. Revealingly, by foreshadowing the theory on which his grandson would later stake an illustrious history, this elder Darwin could be said to orchestrate in death the rebirth of a (r)evolutionary insight into the origin of species.

Because Darwin draws consistently from communicated history, the "production of life" is already a reproduction of the recorded musings and experiences of civilizations long since dead. It is the literary echo of the transposed record of natural history with which Darwin sees the whole of nature within a single powder jar. From its inception, then, *Temple* juggles the three stages of birth, death, and rebirth in an effort to begin (or, more accurately, begin again) working toward its goal of representing an extant organicism. Like the Catalogue of Nature, *Temple* is its own impossible ideal. With this, literature, like the natural world, appears to "generate itself out of past forms, rejuvenating or demystifying them by exposing the conventions that legitimate them. Literature becomes in this way an ironic history of itself."[141] Birth, death, and rebirth all conspire to form a cycle of empirical detection, with neither beginning nor end, yet nevertheless represented as moving from a (revolving) origin toward a specified (inaccessible) telos. As the recycling system in which Darwin was most interested toward the close of his life, the generation, decay, and reproduction of life in the universe serves as the ancillary model for the subject Darwin claims his poem patternistically represents.

Considering Darwin's noted "interest in visual, non-verbal forms of communication,"[142] out of which he fashioned the mythic frames of his poetry, his final long poem materializes as an intriguing experiment in the dynamism of adapted imagery: the immediate interplay between the mythic and the empirical, between aesthetic objects and material images, results in a wholly novel representation of a nature at once seen and unseen, inert and stirring. In an attempt to make words speak images, Darwin presents what Catherine Packham labels as the "analogies of science . . . to produce poetry's animation."[143] In other words, Darwin is showing the "young" reader how to imagine movement in a petrified text by repetitively including imagery bespeaking the four principles of a recycling nature. Even more, the addition of Fuseli's illustrations cement his participation in a key feature of eighteenth- and nineteenth-century science: the inclusion of visual aids to augment a work's written description.[144] But *Temple*'s internal rhetorics act most effectively as their own visual aid, representatively doubling and redoubling the dynamism of the natural world.

By setting the human imagination to work within nature's myriad forms in *Temple*, Darwin attempts to unravel his Gordian knot of representation. Deceptively simple, Darwin's final poem synchronizes content to form so that the subject and the space of its telling conflate into a frozen image nevertheless suggestive of timeless activity. The paradox of a vision doubled, as it were, thus appears in the lucrative contradiction between material encounter and aesthetic sensibility and in their appearing together as empirically grounded speculation—as the imaginative act that defines an aesthetic imaginary.

## Raising the Temple

Just as Darwin had to invent time in his poem, so, too, did he have to create space. But *The Temple of Nature* as a poem with philosophical notes remains too abstract a form to carry the burden of experience. So Darwin actualized a Temple of Nature[145] within his text to explicate the vision of nature offered by the poem itself. This Temple therefore appears as a casting from which we can witness the construction of *Temple* as poem. Met with the challenge of elucidating change over time from within the confines of his empirically driven belief in a material nature, Darwin had to make his poem capable of representing what is patently beyond the reach of the empirical: the beginnings of "organic life" from "beneath the shoreless waves" to the "first forms minute" and their eventual development into the society of man. Designed as the place in which the space of literature is shaped,[146] defined by its own performativity, the Temple of Nature "goes some way to being the 'dignified pantomime' [of nature] recommended" by Darwin.[147] Furthermore, by doubling the sacred structure—putting a Temple in *Temple*—in an attempt to reveal nature's multifaceted image, Darwin firmly inscribes diplopic paradox as the means to approach a seeming totality of the natural world.

"We might say," explains Ludmilla Jordanova, "that [nature] is simply a word for the physical world which we understand as having an existence separate from and prior to human life . . . [making] nature that which is *un*tainted by human hands."[148] By extension, the Temple of Nature is the charted location within the fold of the actuated text *(Temple)* where uncontaminated nature can be expressed. This sacred yet manufactured space serves to construe linguistically a boundary—however boundless—within which to depict the infinite progression of a changing natural world. Darwin's play here with adapted imagery allows for a perfectly consistent negotiation between the mythic realm in which the story of Nature is told and the empirical world from which nature unfolds. It allows, in short, for metaphor to perform its literal function of transport—to move *The Temple of Nature* inside the Temple of Nature for purposes of representability.

Just as Urania, Priestess of Nature and mythic guide, recalls that "the mute language of the touch is sight"[149] and that "the first LANGUAGE enters at the sight,"[150] Darwin ensures his Temple a paradoxical materiality of imagined form. He provides concrete—albeit intangible— attributes of its physical figuration. Darwin's "usual prioritizing of the visual keeps his poetry firmly to its purpose of clarifying abstruse science through a series of mental pictures" so that his "richest and most seriously meant of all his poetic images: that of his last poem's eponymous Temple of Nature,"[151] becomes the illustrative structure of the poem it inhabits. The Temple acts as the staging platform for *Temple,* and the success of Darwin's dignified pantomime hinges on the readability of the form *within* the space of literature, in which diplopic construction deliberately (re)produces the totality of an idea:

Here, high in air, unconscious of the storm,
Thy temple, NATURE, rears its mystic form;
From earth to heav'n, unwrought by mortal toil,
Towers the vast fabric on the desert soil;
O'er many a league the ponderous domes extend,
And deep in earth the ribbed vaults descend;
A thousand jasper steps with circling sweep
Lead the slow votary up the winding steep;
Ten thousand piers, now join'd and now aloof,
Bear on their branching arms the fretted roof.[152]

According to Priestman, "the Temple's positioning on the 'desert soil' suggests both the post-Eden myth of fallen Nature it is replacing and the lifeless, pre-organic earth on which life has miraculously reared itself."[153] While this observation speaks directly to Darwin's technique of adapted imagery, and to the instantaneous transformation of allegory into philosophy, imagery into scientific analogy,[154] it also maintains the Temple as a positive paradox of construction. "Form," "air," "storm," and "earth" all refer to the natural world. Be it in structure, atmosphere, or substance, Darwin anchors the universal Temple in the imagery of an empirical terrain.[155] By adding the "winding steep" to connect the immeasurable lengths of the Temple's "vast fabric," itself comprising a fabricated "dome," "vaults," and "step," Darwin calcifies the sublime edifice by expressing it through geological descriptions of magnitude—of a land transformed and transforming. At the same time, these very expressions serve to evoke the synthetic fabrications of the society of man, the irony of which cannot go unnoticed. By setting the Temple in ahistorical Time, "Ere Time Began,"[156] yet building it according to the speculations of equally vermicular and human architecture (while still purportedly "unwrought by mortal toil"), and indicative of the natural order it intends to re-present, Darwin effectively circumscribes a theatrical space that is precisely the dignified pantomime he adopts—even as it throws into relief a performance of the same. In short, the Temple becomes visible as archetype and metonymy, idealizing the space in which it figures the traverse of a natural order. The Temple, because construed through the man-made text of *The Temple of Nature,* is only ever a doubled structure of Darwin's design. It is both within and without Time, yet always already spatially cognized.[157]

Mention of the Temple's support structure, defined by its "piers, now join'd and now aloof," further frames this ideal yet staged space with precisely the simultaneity necessary to create diplopic paradox. Because the grand scale of the Temple prohibits any single vision from finally grasping the totality of its form, standing as it does "high in air" *and* "deep in earth," the vertical pillars ("piers") appropriately figure the two opposing but complementary approaches to unveiling its mysteries. Like the aerial prop roots of a banyan tree, the fusing of one or more structural supports together ("join'd"), while leaving others disconnected ("aloof"), augments the overall strength of the building—and, symbolically, points the way toward enlightenment, toward conceiving of the natural world as infinite segments of a set totality.[158]

Accordingly, the Temple remains both imagined and unimaginable, allowing for its construction to warrant disorientation and explanation at the same time. With the Poet (and by extension the reader) up against an altogether befuddling portal to enlightenment, Darwin effectively grants his poem, and especially the voices within it, the translational power necessary to open it. The projection of growth from initiate to initiated, innocence to experience, reveals the thread with which Darwin navigates an ironic exit to his revelatory maze: in the middle stands Urania (speaking for Nature), who schools the Muse; the Muse then inspires the Poet; and the Poet is left to reveal terrestrial mystery to the innocent reader. Under a "fretted roof" of verse and note, a totalized vision of the natural world in process unfolds, reliant on the ricochet of voiced revelation.

To protect this initiate–initiated dynamic, and thus confirm the circumscription of epistemic space, Darwin oftentimes moves the conversation between Urania and the Muse from what reads like an exterior position to the literal Temple into its vast interior, with little indication. When, for example, the Muse is led "with pausing step" to wander down "sun-bright avenue" and "green recess," such nature-strewn paths—themselves prey to Darwin's superimposition of constructedness—yield "trophied walls," "statued galleries," and "pictur'd halls" of a collected History.[159] Precisely because the Temple predates Time, eternal in its vision and infinite in scope, and yet it contains within it the trappings of mortality ironically immortalized, the movement in and out of the Temple suggests the continuous surface on which matter exists, multiplies, and dies. It proposes that nature be read in its ostensible accessibility—a synchronic image of what can only manifest diachronically—rather than in its unapproachable mysteries. Consequently, this access is dependent on the tensive relationship between novice (Poet and reader) and emissary (Urania and Muse).

With its stubborn, if dizzying, manifestation of a solid amorphousness, the witnessed conversation between Urania and the Muse elicits an immeasurable landscape nevertheless circumscribed in its multitiered representations. Darwin intimates an adamantine bond between past and future, progress and communication. He projects a mythohistorical past and inevitable future together, falling backward as he does to the "Four past eventful Ages" of the universe to propel his argument simultaneously forward and "give the fifth, new-born of Time, to light."[160] Once again, we are made aware that to begin is always to begin again: to enter the "fifth Age" already assumes a fourth and a sixth, ad infinitum.

By placing "proud pyramid, and arch sublime" as structures artistically rendered in the Temple's "galleries," Darwin is able to juxtapose the timeless monument to its generated reproductions. Moreover, because such reproductions are depicted on "Earth-canker'd urn" and "medallion green with time,"[161] Darwin exposes timelessness to inevitable decay. In doing so, he makes art a natural preservative and nature an artful image. Aesthetic objects,[162] therefore, act to generate what only ever decays and disclose what always needs recuperating: a totalized image of the natural world. Objects in the Temple, as well as the Temple itself, go a long way toward recognizing the danger of ignoring this paradox of holism. To distinguish the natural world from its individual representations would at last damage the organic vision of life that Darwin's poem works strenuously—repetitively—to promote.

As a requisite performance space for Darwin's schema, the literal Temple is presented architecturally as both a place of worship and the threshold of wisdom. It is a sacred space of nature's mysteries framing the work as a whole, yet all the same remaining captured within it, constructed by it. By simultaneously signifying the space of literature and collapsing this space into the confines of an imaged building, Darwin effectively redoubles the metonymic structure of his poem. The interior form thus contains and is contained, creates and is created by, the totality that is *The Temple of Nature*. To capture the enormity of this transposed vision, the poem must therefore be approached in the simultaneity of one manufactured form being in and around another. With this seemingly incongruous positioning, constant only in its spatial interplay, the poem itself becomes that definitive space in which nature can be read. The literal Temple is now the obvious figure that helps the reader grasp the diplopic paradox of *Temple*'s arcane project.

## What Can and Cannot Be

While I agree with the general premise that Darwin "combine[d] the two sides of his life, poetic feeling and scientific realism,"[163] to produce *The Temple of Nature*, I maintain that this combination needs to be recast to reveal an essential diplopia not previously accounted for. To do this, I have proposed that this poem be read with respect to the whole it proposes to image forth, according to its countless pieces. If Darwin's *Temple* represents that "total vision of life in a continuous sequence," then his work is met with the acute dilemma of having to configure a fluid unity from seeming disparity—a unity that travels necessarily between form and content. Just as *Temple* relies on both verse and note to format the entirety of its subject, comprehending this subject likewise depends on Darwin's ability to fragment the flexible continuum of nature's developmental processes, to lay bare its essential and constitutive components while maintaining it as a progressive, holistic category. For the reader to realize nature, in its magnitude, as just such a process in motion—working toward the ideal of organic perfection (itself unimaginable outside the abstraction of concept)—Darwin must break down and rebuild his vision. He must, in short, fragment totality to imagine it as whole. This is the representative challenge that Darwin's final long poem conquers with its consistent manufacture of diplopic paradox.

As one final instantiation of this representational paradox, Darwin ends his poem with a revelation that both can and cannot be: it is an important omission that Darwin never finally presents the figure of Nature, especially given his perhaps incessant brooding over form throughout the poem. With "Silence hover[ing] on unmoving wings," Darwin draws the verse of *Temple* to a stark but elegant close:

> With trembling awe [Urania] the mystic veil withdraws,
> And, meekly kneeling on the gorgeous shrine,
> Lifts her ecstatic eyes to TRUTH DIVINE![164]

While we are told that the veil has lifted, presumably to reveal arcane Nature beneath, we are carefully not shown what stands there. What the Priestess Urania, and at length the Poet, impart to the reader through pantomime is nothing more than the communicated action of a disclosure. Merely presenced in the poem, *not* presented, Nature, as a singularity, continues to rely on the divine proxy of Urania's storytelling and the placeholder of a "gorgeous shrine." Even the frontispiece to the poem illustrates precisely this moment. When we open the physical work, we see the scene of the veil lifted: Nature is exposed as a triple-breasted female, signifying the fertility and ensuing myriad reproductions of the natural world (and perhaps the resultant fecundity of imagination's coupling with science). But like Darwin's verse, Fuseli's engraving merely symbolizes Nature without presenting her. Moreover, because it serves as a pictorial foreword to the poem, yet depicts the poem's final scene, the placement of this particular engraving intimates the selfsame cyclicality of which the poem as a whole partakes.

Essentially eliding any insinuated image of an actualized Nature, Darwin suggests that to behold Nature is not finally to see her as Being; rather, it is to realize nature as an eternal and infinite collection of beings, a taunting that is always coming to be and passing away. Nature's palpable absence at the close of Canto IV thus recalls us to the process, like a kind of prosopopoeia, with which we came to grasp the totality of nature: our reading of *Temple* is exactly that which formulates (our idea of) the natural world.

With the final lines of his verse, Darwin effectively forces us to begin again our approach to the Temple of Nature. He draws us back into the poem itself, to the imaginative act responsible for recoding a mythic ideal back into its integral natural histories. With the final muting of Urania's "sweet voice" ("silence hovering"), originally responsible for "chain[ing] the Muse's ear with fascinating strains,"[165] the space of literature is clearly revealed as that which yields an evolving nature. *The Temple of Nature* thus manufactures nature's crowded image, while the Temple of Nature serves to signal this image's manifesting. In the closing silence at the Temple proper, the reader is made, like Darwin himself, to recognize the necessity of procession: knowledge arises from the mirroring processes of progressive movement between nature's objects and the reader.

Although Darwin's *Temple* does, as Primer notes, "abound prophetically and forebodingly with the difficulties of reconciling traditional faith in a rational cosmos with the empirical evidence of an expanding and evolving organic Nature,"[166] its ontoepistemological exercise primarily establishes the power of the imagination as that which "improv[es] nature by the exertions of art."[167] On one level, *Temple* is comfortable within the limits of knowledge that often plagued naturalists in the eighteenth century. On another level, the poem validates the strength and necessity of human creativity to supplant the impossible ideal of not only completing a Catalogue of Nature but of comprehending nature to the fullest effect of its organic form.

Darwin's "mighty effort" emerges in his creation of a work accepting of what the human mind uneasily encounters as the enigma of nature and transforming it into an attractive image paradoxically capable of exposing its impenetrable secrets. Initiated by its verse–note format, *Temple* actuated the struggle to maintain an epistemic totality of materialist ideas and aesthetic impulses. Moreover, the poet–naturalist Darwin preserved what Priestman indirectly recognized as the coded vision that the scientific poem of *Temple* emits: "a double image," or "fertile ambiguity which would be destroyed if we could visualize either state completely clearly."[168] Thus did Darwin hold diplopia to be part of, not apart from, this totality. My revisionary reading of *Temple* recognizes the poem's ironic suggestion of separateness as its effort to define and maintain an extant organicism. Darwin, if not able to overcome contradiction, imagined the benefit in it.

## Coda

In October 2006, Martin Priestman produced the first annotated edition of *Temple*. Significantly, this edition of the text has been executed only in a digital format, as part of the *Romantic Circles* online journal.[169] It is a testament to the original work's structural density and intricate subject matter that it took over two hundred years for such an edition to be tackled. As Priestman acknowledges, because "the published [original] *Temple of Nature* is . . . already extremely well supplied with footnotes of its own, as well as [with] fifteen Additional Notes," the annotated poem risks appearing as a dizzying "hall of mirrors," reflecting "notes on notes on notes."[170]

Perhaps it is only now, with the advent and widespread use of tools for digital reading, that this particular work could feasibly be read as an annotated text, "allow[ing] readers to travel at will as far down the annotation trail as they wish,"[171] without the threat of irresolvable disorientation. Priestman's virtual representation and augmentation of *Temple* allow readers to call up at will specific sections or retrace their steps through the textual maze; locate a pattern of particular words and images; or jump instantaneously between verse, note, additional note, and (now) editorial note. The digital searchability performed in this space transforms the materiality of the poem from hard text to hypertext, exchanging as it does the static format of the original for the constantly shifting, more ephemeral "hall of mirrors" of its representation. It echoes what I have demonstrated was the immaterial base on which Darwin and his fellow philosophes built their materialist approximations of a phenomenal nature. In effect, virtual space appears quite possibly the best space in which to present (or contain, or construct) the largely unmanageable yet wholly methodical text of

*Temple.* It confirms the intrinsic diplopia of both form and content by performing the more rhizomatic exercise of reading multiplicity,[172] of endlessly establishing interpretive connections from within a single cultural work, against the vermicular activity of filtering an original poem through its new media iteration.

# 3

# "Not without Some Repugnancy, and a Fluctuating Mind": Trembley's Polyp and the Practice of Eighteenth-Century Taxonomy

DURING SUMMER 1740, Genevan naturalist and soon-to-be Copley Medal recipient Abraham Trembley chanced on what would become one of the most transformative organisms discovered in the first half of the eighteenth century:

> Having noticed various small animals on the plants that I had taken from a ditch, I put some of these plants into a large jar filled with water, placed it on the inside sill of a window, and then set about examining the creatures that it contained. . . . The novel spectacle presented me by these little animals excited my curiosity. As I scanned this jar teeming with creatures, I noticed a polyp fastened to the stem of an aquatic plant. At first I paid little heed, for I was following the livelier little creatures which naturally attracted my attention more than an immobile object.[1]

While employed as a tutor to the sons of Count William Bentinck, himself a curator at the University of Leiden and Friend of the Royal Society of London, Trembley identified the "novel spectacle" of the polyp. The preceding casual slip from "small animals" to "little creatures" to what, eventually and after much debate, Trembley would identify as an "aquatick insect" or "worm," "the Fresh-water *Polypous*" is indicative of an essential ambiguity and sense of wonder with which Trembley confronted this unusual organism. All but subsumed by the myriad "livelier little creatures" that initially "excited" Trembley's "curiosity," the polyp is classified today (not without its own flexibilities) as a freshwater cnidarian or coelenterate or hydra, a marine invertebrate with distinctly vermiform associations. Moreover, what Trembley found, indeed, what he was finally, if not immediately, drawn to, was a specific species of polyp, the *Chlorohydra veridissima*, or green hydra.

Named in part for its ingestion of the algae *Chlorella*, which continues to live inside and produce food for the host organism, thereby imparting to it a greenish hue, *C. veridissima* most likely attracted Trembley in the first place with its promise of a plant's familiar color and seemingly "immobile" structure. Today this particular polyp is recognized as a close relative of the jellyfish, displaying a comparable anatomy as well as corresponding regenerative behaviors. Though more rooted than its buoyant cousin, the polyp sports a distinctly wormlike tubular body capped off by several stinging tentacles, with which it captures prey and protects itself from predators. In an effort to inhabit locations heavy with food traffic, the polyp is usually found in the freshwaters of shallow ditches, ponds, or streams "hanging" upside down or "standing" right side up. When movement is required, it performs a nimble exercise much like that of the common inchworm. In many ways, the freshwater polyp is as ubiquitous a marine vermiform as the earthworm is a subterranean one. And yet our seemingly instinctive understanding of its existence, if not our acute awareness of it, remains more attributable to the Greek myth of the Lernaean Hydra, virulent guardian to the Underworld slain by Heracles, than to the matter of Trembley's decidedly less hazardous (though in my opinion just as impressive) discovery.

Recounted in Hesiod's *Theogony* as a chthonic water beast spawned by Typhaon and Echidna,[2] the Lernaean Hydra outwardly conflates the marine with the subterranean vermiform so that this mythic creature somehow anticipates, in a single colossal form, the varied types and shared behaviors of certain smaller and categorically lower organisms first uncovered in the mid-eighteenth century. Accordingly, the freshwater polyp can be understood, on one hand, as one such mundane projection (in miniature) of its legendary namesake—as if to suggest that what Hesiod imagined in his epic poem bespoke of the as yet unidentified albeit analogous creations existing out in the natural world. On the other hand, the polyp offers up its own exceptional nature, provoking Trembley and others to reimagine life and the consequences of vitality from worm to man.[3]

With what began as an afterthought in his research into the plants and insects inhabiting freshwaters ("at first I paid little heed"), Trembley would help to revolutionize eighteenth-century ideas on taxonomy and generation. His empirical observations and meticulous experiments regarding one tiny aquatic creature would inaugurate a paradigm shift in the middle of the eighteenth century, arising from what Kuhn delineates as the refusal of anomalies to conform to a general rule.[4] Although it is, as Kuhn's critics have noted, often difficult to specify precisely when an event or object is recognized as an anomaly, in part because this recognition may well postdate the first notice of the event or object in question, Trembley's individual discovery can be understood as such from the moment he described it to other naturalists (if not from the actual moment of its discovery). Not only did the polyp's "novel spectacle" push hard against extant paradigms both natural and theological but it expressly violated botanical as well as zoological expectations for what Ritvo identifies as the eighteenth and nineteenth centuries' "enterprise of classification."[5] By calling into question the "systematic flexibility" with which extreme atypicality might be accommodated, the polyp successfully manifested a point of crisis from which only a radical transformation of ideas could result.[6] For these reasons, the polyp acts as a target organism, an exemplary anomaly with which to examine the likewise aberrant—and often abhorrent—valuations of the vermicular. Its perceived monstrosity haunted the humans who studied it[7] as a result of its doubly soothing and galling state of being. It provided what Andrew Curran and Patrick Graille outline as a "benchmark," a monstrous organism capable of promoting a "rational study and understanding of the universe" coincident with the realization of the "overreaching regularity of organic life."[8] As what Aram Vartanian identifies as one such "radical biological phenomenon,"[9] the polyp quickly resonated with naturalists and litterateurs alike. From the subsequent worm investigations of Bonnet to the political and social satires of Voltaire to the thought experiments of Diderot, Trembley's polyp became a pivotal figure in the eighteenth century for thinking about and experimenting with the surprising nature of life.

In his work as a naturalist, Trembley not only mixed the so-called natural and artificial systems for organizing nature, resulting in what I regard as a therapeutic hybridization of raw taxonomic practices geared toward finding a place for his problematic polyp; he underscored the act and consequences of introducing something ostensibly new into every-day reality, of attempting to normalize that which proved subversive—even as it became increasingly (if disturbingly) comprehended as routine. Moreover, Trembley's descriptions of the polyp, the largely anthropomorphic rhetoric he used to characterize its structures and habits, and the operations he performed thereon all conspire toward an aestheticizing of the vermicular that, as I stated in my introduction, fruitfully combines the more classic repulsion with an inventive appeal to mutability, indeterminacy, and the irrepressibility of the organic. He relayed in minute detail what Darwin's *Temple of Nature* rendered in broad, dense strokes: an aesthetic imaginary symptomatic of the articulation of empirical study. He aestheticized the experiment at the same time that he promoted an experimental aesthetics. Just as he drew out what distinguished this nonconforming creature from the humans who studied it and from the organisms (plant and animal) against which attempts were made to classify it, Trembley implied crucial commonalities between them.

But before offering an in-depth examination of Trembley's dis-covery, its natural historical implications, and suggestive literary im-plications, it is important to acknowledge a crucial albeit pedestrian juxtaposition: any effective scientific discovery has at its foundation the clash of the new with the old. As Vartanian reveals, the polyp is a key element in the disruption of materialist thought; it helped to create a division among philosophers that traced the line of whether natural phenomena alone could explain the origin of living things.[10] The entrance of the polyp onto the scene of natural history study thus allows for a kind of contest between Cartesian mechanistic principles and materialistic determinism, refereed by the unstable (read "cutting edge"[11]) practice of taxonomy throughout the eighteenth century. As "perhaps the most fascinating single curiosity of natural history in the 1740s," the polyp became involved in what Vartanian recognizes as "speculations . . . ranging from the nature of the soul to the teleology of organic forms."[12] Its ability to regenerate, set against its deceptively simple form (which, by definition, lacked for the most part what Vartanian also notes are the senses and organs "proper to animals"), extended the polyp's philosophical reach for decades after concentrated scientific investigation into the material organism lapsed. La Mettrie's interpretation of the polyp's regenerative powers, for example, which deeply informed the pioneering *L'homme machine* (1748), led to what Vartanian cites as an attribution of "self-determination and 'design' to matter"[13]—thereby severing biology from theology for those followers of Cartesian concepts of automata.

When one currently accepted theory and one seemingly fantastic theory are made to rub against one another at a given time, the result is what Kuhn identifies as a "tradition-shattering complement to the tradition-bound activity of normal science."[14] This is what La Mettrie can be understood to have accomplished with his study of the polyp, to the fault of conceding any real impact of this organism prior to the adoption of it for his new materialism. "The polyp," further states Vartanian, "did not produce tangible philosophical results [before 1745], when La Mettrie seized upon earlier data and speculations afforded by Trembley's discovery."[15] Perhaps as a result of the rapidity with which the polyp's extraordinary characteristics were rendered all but standardized among a variety of vermiform invertebrates (occurring over a period of only four years or so), or perhaps because, once again, the organism in question produced an insistent and uncomfortable analogy between high and low forms of life, Trembley's work remains as relatively obscure(d) in today's crowded studies of eighteenth-century culture and thought as it did in its own era. It is therefore important to recuperate through a number of eighteenth-century naturalists what, according to Vartanian, La Mettrie first distilled into a comprehensive philosophical doctrine as well as to trace the critical approaches that have since sought likewise to reclaim the extensive impact of Trembley and/or the polyp. Doing so exposes how natural history has largely filtered out the discoverer from the discovery. It underscores mutability as an ironically more rooted trait—literally as well as metaphorically—in worms than in man, as the polyp takes on increasingly more symbolic characteristics against the relatively static figure of the naturalist.

There is only one extant modern biography of Trembley. Published in 1952 by John R. Baker, *Abraham Trembley of Geneva: Scientist and Philosopher* contains foundational source material not previously available—and has since been utilized as the standard copy from which any investigation into the life of Trembley might begin. According to Baker's research, which includes intimate correspondence with the descendents of Trembley still living in their native Geneva, a brief eulogy for Trembley was published two years after his death, in 1786, and the next year, Trembley's nephew published the first biography of his uncle (in fourteen thousand words).[16] Then, in 1902, Trembley's great-great-grandson, Maurice Trembley, gave "a preliminary account" to the Société helvétique des Sciences naturalles of some letters he discovered "in an attic in the ancestral home at Petit Sacconex, Geneva" between Réaumur and Trembley.[17] This was followed by a formal and extended version of this same account, under the title *Correspondence inédite entre Réaumur et Abraham Trembley,* which appeared after the death of Maurice Trembley in 1942. Regardless of what Vartanian and others view as the critical shortcomings of Baker's biography,[18] its presentation of Trembley as a student of life processes as well as its recounting of significant genealogies (familial, natural, historical, and literary) expands Trembley's interest in biology to coincide with the political, religious, and moral contexts in which he lived.

Over three decades after the appearance of Vartanian's critical essay and Baker's biography, Howard and Sylvia Lenhoff published *Hydra and the Birth of Experimental Biology, 1744: Abraham Trembley's Memoirs Concerning the Natural History of a Type of Freshwater Polyp with Arms Shaped Like Horns* (1986). This text brought into print for the first time an English translation of Trembley's definitive treatise on the polyp, *Mémoires, pour servir à l'histoire d'un genre de polypes d'eau douce, à bras en forme de cornes* (1744), complete with high-quality reproductions of Lyonet's original illustrative engravings. Divided into two parts, the publication opens with "Some Reflections on Abraham Trembley and His *Mémoires.*" This particular essay combines the Lenhoffs' shared expertise in biology and history to present a general and accessible introduction to the life of Trembley, the context in which he made his discovery of the polyp, and the discovery itself. It also provides a cursory glance at the various intellectual and cultural debates ignited by the polyp, laying claim to the wormlike "little machine" or "little monster," as it was alternately called throughout the eighteenth century. The second part of the text then produces the singular English translation of the *Mémoires* themselves.[19] Furthermore, the text works to position the polyp in terms of modern biological research, providing a "Twentieth Century Perspective on Trembley's Approaches to Biology." The Lenhoffs' continued work on Trembley and his polyp, which has now spanned over two decades and has produced a variety of separate works (some, like Baker's work, also a result of direct correspondence with the existing Trembley family of Geneva), remains the most prolific and dedicated example of contemporary Trembley studies.

As a testament to the gradual mounting of modern interest in the polyp, Virginia Dawson's 1987 publication of *Nature's Enigma: The Problem of the Polyp in the Letters of Bonnet, Trembley and Réaumur* offers a persuasive argument for why the polyp in particular "made the decade of the 1740s one of crisis"[20] and makes widely available the lengthy correspondences between Bonnet and Trembley; Bonnet and Gabriel Cramer (a mathematician from the Academy of Calvin, in Geneva, where both Bonnet and Trembley received their formal educations); Bonnet and Réaumur; and Trembley and Réaumur.[21] The critical bulk of the text works to demonstrate how these letters "support the view that the discovery of the polyp was substantially due to the independence of the Genevan scientific tradition from that of the French."[22] In particular, Dawson argues that "the unfolding of the discovery of the polyp through the Trembley–Réaumur letters demonstrates not Réaumur's influence, but rather their differences in interpretation of the discovery."[23] Consequently, this study is based on the primary tenet that Réaumur's role in the history of the polyp has been given too much weight. And so *Nature's Enigma* continues the recuperative work seemingly endemic to Trembley studies;[24] it presents a calculated effort to reinstate Trembley to his discovery at the same time as it makes clear their inevitable disassociation.

Especially significant to my project, Dawson extends her discussions of the polyp to include what Réaumur had suggested to Bonnet would be the comparable properties found in "all insects of the vermicular form."[25] To this end, she devotes an entire chapter to "Bonnet's Response to the Discovery [of the Polyp] and His Worm with Two Tails." "Regeneration," she argues, "led to the metaphysical impasse" of questioning the necessity of the soul within matter if matter itself were granted an organizing principle distinct from that of the Creator.[26] Dawson's argument highlights the interchangeability of the polyp and worm as figures of revolutionary potential and gestures toward how the worm ultimately surpassed the polyp in this role—leaving the former to act as the titular representative of this potential in a multitude of "vermicular form[s]."

Much as the worm overtook the polyp as an enunciative trope for the regenerative properties of lower invertebrates during the second half of the eighteenth century, the polyp overtook the naturalist who discovered it to the point where any direct focus on Trembley is rare in much of the modern scholarship that cannot deny his influence. Both Lorin Anderson and Shirley Roe, for example, have written articles centering on the decade of the 1740s, yet they neglect Trembley's role in this history. In "Charles Bonnet's Taxonomy and Chain of Being," Anderson discusses how Bonnet, through his 1768 metaphysical treatise *Contemplation de la nature,* presented the notion of a continuous, "hierarchic and static arrangement of all the manifestations of nature" so that "nothing—not a rock, tree, dog, or man—remained outside this all-embracing continuum."[27] Despite Anderson's several discussions of the lower forms and their impact on understanding this static classification system, Trembley himself is never mentioned, not even when the polyp briefly appears. Not surprisingly, then, the final Foucauldian claim of the article, which states that Bonnet was not interested so much in the nature of life but "with classifying," so that "life entered only as another category in this process,"[28] ironically elides Trembley from the very process he helped to defіne.

Similarly, Roe's later article, "John Turberville Needham and the Generation of Living Organisms," mentions the polyp only tangentially, and Trembley not at all, with regard to the "several significant discoveries [made in the 1740s] in biology, among them the freshwater polyp, parthenogenesis in aphids, and a number of unusual phenomena in the microscopic realm."[29] Although she situates her argument in the exact era of Trembley's discovery, the article itself is more concerned with one of the many effects of the polyp on eighteenth-century thought: that the naturalist and Roman Catholic priest John Needham desired to uphold a "moral science through the defense of the preexistent germ theory and the Cartesian hypothesis of innate ideas."[30] While this article treats singularly the material that Roe's own earlier publication, *Matter, Life, and Generation,* presented with broader treatment, an insistent elision of Trembley remains. Perhaps, then, the best way to read Trembley against the natural history he helped to construct and the science he later influenced is to liken him finally to the very idea of the polyp that consumed him. He is a fortuitous instigator of change, able to produce a multitude of investigations from a single discovery, and himself regenerated unseen into seemingly disparate contexts.

Today Trembley's polyp is one of the standard types of regenerative organisms introduced to students of biology, medicine, and agriculture. Marc Ratcliff most recently devoted an entire chapter to Trembley and the polyp in his 2009 *The Quest for the Invisible,* reevaluating the effect Trembley's discovery had on Enlightenment microscopy and the communication of scientific innovations. Furthermore, both Trembley and the polyp have lately appeared in articles ranging from a consideration of stem cell research to a reprisal of literary evidence for the regeneration of Napoleonic France.[31] My argument accounts for how Trembley's discovery sets a kind of vermicular standard from which mutability and the constancy of anomaly might emerge as constructive tropes beyond the confines of natural history.

## On the Order of Wonder

The son of a Genevan military family fallen on hard times,[32] Trembley began his career as a naturalist in 1737, during his employment as a tutor to the sons of Bentinck's father-in-law, Count d'Aldembourg of Varel, Germany. Here Trembley read the early volumes of Réaumur's work *Mémoires pour servir à l'histoire des insectes* and narrowed his field of study to those natural objects that he could find in his immediate environs. As Baker notes, Trembley found in Réaumur "a scientific outlook that was in accord with his own character. Réaumur was one who observed accurately, described simply what he saw, and avoided hypothesis."[33] After reading Réaumur's *Mémoires,* Trembley began preliminary studies of beetle larvae and moths that he found feeding on woolen materials and also first turned his empirical eye toward freshwater ponds and ditches. It was 1739, and he was now employed at Bentinck's summer mansion of Sorgvliet, only a mile and a half from the center of the Hague. While working for Count Bentinck in Holland, Trembley had also become friends with several of the University of Leiden's distinguished professors, among whom were Gravesande, professor of mathematics and astronomy and chair of philosophy; Albinus, professor of anatomy and surgery; and Allamand, first tutor to Gravesande's children and editor of his collected works, and later professor of philosophy. Significantly, both Albinus and Allamand would be among the first to confirm Trembley's imminent discovery not just of the polyp itself but of the polyp's astonishing ability to regenerate from cuttings. The intimate intellectual circle in which Trembley found himself began a lifelong interest in the broad landscape of scientific pursuit. It took far less than a lifetime for Trembley's polyp to alter irrevocably the natural historical record—but not before another insect prepared the way with its own astonishing reproductive behavior.

Anticipating by one month the freshwater plant collecting that would lead Trembley simply to notice the polyp (thus preceding any actual communication of the find), fellow Geneven naturalist and cousin to Trembley, Charles Bonnet, had proven the parthenogenesis of aphids, or plant lice. He had been asked by Réaumur to confirm what was then suspected to be the aphids' ability to reproduce without male fertilization. Prior to Bonnet's findings, Leeuwenhoek had concluded that aphids were viviparous, able to give birth to live offspring directly from the female. In the first place, this contradicted what was then understood to be the egg-laying habits of insects, making the aphids more akin to mammals and hence more readily comprehended—and perhaps more discomfiting. In the second place, because Leeuwenhoek could not adequately distinguish male aphids, he believed that the aphid itself was an hermaphroditic organism. Réaumur, however, disagreed. Because he could not find any males in the aphid population he studied, and because he operated from a strictly empirical perspective (throwing aside the general rule for observable proof), he suggested that either no males existed or copulation occurred before birth.[34] Not until the meticulous and repeated experiments of Bonnet, therefore, was parthenogenesis confirmed as an exceptional case of insect generation.

By establishing that aphids did in fact reproduce without male fertilization, Bonnet successfully overturned the general law of coupling thought to be intrinsic to the generation of all animals, thereby making "the humble aphid . . . an ideal warning against overconfidence in taxonomic reasoning."[35] This tiny creature became a kind of prelude to the larger questions that the still smaller creature, the freshwater polyp, would open for eighteenth-century taxonomers and philosophers. The polyp's apparent structure and manner of multiplication, for example, would throw into question the distinction between plant and animal and even briefly reopen the spontaneous generation debate thought to have been closed in the previous century. Bonnet's discovery significantly irritated the surface of accepted explanations of animal generation, unwittingly making eighteenth-century taxonomic practice vulnerable to what Trembley's polyp would cement as the regular irregularity of nature. "[Nature's] works may be extraordinary," argues Corcos, "but never irregular."[36] The impossible ideal of man's need to create an all-inclusive system for classifying the objects of nature would seem pathological if it were not for the fact that the natural world continually offered up the empirical evidence for its logical existence.

Given Trembley's relation to Bonnet, his interest in the work of Réaumur, and his regular correspondence with both men, it is not surprising that immediately following Bonnet's discovery, he was asked to reconfirm the validity, and hence regularity, of parthenogenesis through his own series of experiments. Once Réaumur had read the results of Bonnet's work to the Académie des Sciences in Paris, it was agreed that "a single experiment, however well performed, was not sufficient to remove all doubt, since the conclusion was contrary to a law that had seemed to be generally established by the unanimous concurrence of all the facts previously observed."[37] Consequently, when Trembley, in combination with his friend and colleague Pieter Lyonet (Dutch naturalist and engraver), did confirm Bonnet's discovery, the positive results made Trembley wary of imposing general laws onto the particulars of nature. He grew suspicious of what Dawson articulates as "the complacent Cartesian assumption that all of nature would eventually be comprehended under a few simple laws."[38] Thus, while Trembley was busy with his novice research into the polyp, he was also performing what is the hallmark of scientific study: the replication of experiment. This method of corroboration, backed by a community of naturalists across Europe and Great Britain, which shared research and materials (even down to the sending of sample organisms by horseback or boat, for example, should none be readily available in one's native setting), would prove as indispensable a testimony to the polyp's strange habit of regeneration as it did to parthenogenesis in aphids.

Although other contemporary discoveries, such as the sensitive plant as well as the aphid, had shaken taxonomic practices, the discovery of the polyp more fully typifies the controversial polymorphism of "scientific systematizing" on which Ritvo expounds and the process through which Kuhn envisions scientific revolution to be achieved: "continual competition between a number of distinct views of nature, each partially derived from, and all roughly compatible with, the dictates of scientific observation and method."[39] It marks an upheaval of eighteenth-century epistemology as it attempts both to account for and to reflect the minute particulars of a nature in flux.

Like Bonnet's aphid, Trembley's polyp exhibited strange reproductive habits; unlike the aphid, the polyp was a practically unknown inhabitant of nature's landscape. Indeed, so easily overlooked was the polyp that Trembley initially thought that he was the first to discover it—a fact that, while wrong, helps to underscore the kind of blind simultaneity of detection needed to ignite a conceptual revolution. Consequently, while Trembley must certainly be credited with the careful study and identification of the polyp, the actual discovery of this organism is more complicated and multiplicitous than what he alone found in the ditches at the Sorgvliet. In fact, the polyp had already been detected by the turn of the eighteenth century. But the polyp was not a polyp—yet. Loosely called an "animalculum," simply because it was tiny and displayed apparent motility, this creature had been caught up in the collecting nets of Leeuwenhoek and an anonymous Country Gentleman from England.[40] Also prior to Trembley's discovery was that of the French naturalist Bernard de Jussieu. Jussieu himself, however, never published on the subject. He had only drawings made, which he communicated to Réaumur for the sixth volume of *Mémoires pour servir à l'histoire des insectes*.[41] All three men nonetheless called attention to the unstable identification of an organism so odd as to merit what can only be understood as its fourth and effectively publicized discovery nearly forty years after its first detection.

Although Trembley recognizes in his own *Mémoires* that "other people saw polyps before [he] did" and that "many more inquisitive individuals would have chanced upon them in the course of investigating plants or aquatic animals,"[42] it is important to preserve the initial ignorance with which he began to pursue his study of this creature. Without it, Trembley would perhaps not have taken so much care in his research, particularly considering what came to be the astonishing discovery of regeneration definitively made by him. Even his own commentary considering both Leeuwenhoek's and the Country Gentleman's role in the developing history of the polyp supports the idea that he felt he had something new to offer in what he realized only later was a previously trod field of discovery. Both in his original 1742 letter to the Royal Society and in his *Mémoires,* Trembley points out what he sees as the great "consistency between the observations [of Leeuwenhoek and the anonymous Country Gentleman]. Both noticed one of the most remarkable characteristics of the polyps, that is, their natural mode of multiplying. They were struck by it and certainly would not have failed to study it further had they possessed a substantial number of polyps. Leeuwenhoek, however, was able to find only a few, and the anonymous Englishman but a single polyp."[43] From this it is evident that Trembley felt he had found a suitable niche into which to insert his original empirical agenda.

Significantly, Trembley's recognition that his discovery was a later and separate arrival at some of the same ideas espoused or suggested by his predecessors reaffirmed both his belief in empirical work to unveil the mysteries of nature and his distrust of determinate principles of knowledge. As "an index both to the strongly traditional nature of normal science and to the completeness with which the traditional pursuit prepares the way for its own change,"[44] the community of discovery encompassing a Dutchman, an Englishman, a Frenchman, and a Genevan reveals an underlying, even intrinsic consistency in man's approach to the natural world. Scientific novelty inevitably goes the way of natural anomaly, absorbed into the vastness of a landscape untethered from myopic prejudices to reveal that *all that can be is.*

In his aptly titled 1742 letter "Observations and Experiments upon the Fresh-water Polypus," which effectively launches the brief but intense study of the polyp in the 1740s, Trembley spares no introductory remarks. The letter is first headed by one of Lyonet's illustrations of a single polyp (see Figure 3.1), and only then is it followed by a practical decription of "the Animal in question":

> The Animal in question is an aquatick insect. . . . It is represented in the Figure annexed. Its Body *A B.* which is pretty slender, has on its anterior Extremity *A.* several Horns *A C.* which serve it instead of Legs and Arms, and which are yet slenderer than the Body. The Mouth of the *Polypus* is in that anterior Extremity; it opens into the Stomach, which takes up the whole Length of the Body *A B.* This whole Body forms but one Pipe; a sort of a Gut, which can be open'd at both Ends.[45]

Presented first under the broad category of "Animal," only to be immediately specified as "an aquatick insect," Trembley describes the

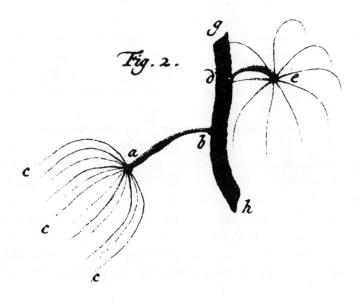

FIGURE 3.1. Abraham Trembley, "The Figure of the Fresh-water Polypus, Sticking to a Twig," illustrated by Pierre Lyonet. Courtesy of Howard and Sylvia Lenhoff and Boxwood Press.

polyp *("Polypus")* against what his readers would most readily identify with: themselves. By delineating the "slender body" of this new organism, equating its "Legs and Arms" with "Horns," and identifying a "Stomach" or "sort of a Gut" to signify its "whole Body," Trembley establishes an image for this new creature through a largely anthropomorphic (or, at the very least, biomorphic) rhetoric. The polyp, if not directly analogous to man, is certainly ascribed the structural characteristics of those more complex organisms reading about its discovery.

Conspicuously absent from this initial description, however, is the polycephalism most readily attributed to the mythic hydra. Instead, Trembley recognizes just a single "Mouth" and identifies "Legs and Arms" where the many "heads" of the hydra would be located. Additionally, he chooses to articulate these appendages through the less antagonistic anatomical analogy of "Horns" (only later referring to such protuberances as the collective "head" of the organism). On one hand, these such "Legs and Arms" directly reflect their purpose, used as they are for both the polyp's motility and its ability to grab prey. On the other hand, the deployment of this particular diction veers away from any immediate monstrification of the polyp, favoring instead a construction of utilitarian wonder.

The remaining pages of the letter continue to enumerate the polyp's myriad characteristics, but as Trembley develops in brief these anatomical comparisons, he becomes increasingly uneasy about their implications. He describes the variable "Length of the Body" and the uneven "Number of Legs or Arms," particularly with respect to the organism's ability to contract or extend itself to "any Degree imaginable"; its strange manner of moving and eating; and, most significantly, its surprising reproductive or multiplicative behavior. As Trembley would later state in the opening of his full-length treatise, "the little creature whose natural history I am about to present has revealed facts to me which are so unusual and so contrary to the ideas generally held on the nature of animals, that to accept them demands the clearest of proofs."[46] Understandably, then, Trembley approached his initial letter to the Royal Society like an advertisement, providing only a cursory and provocative glance into what he would later understand as the polyp's vital ability to generate by budding and to regenerate from cuttings. He used this letter to announce his forthcoming "History of the Polypus, which I am now at work upon"[47] (his *Mémoires*) and to urge study of these organisms independent from his own. Stating, "I am ready to impart to every one who shall desire to make Observations on these Animals, all the Means and Contrivances I have used; to enable them to practice the same, and to judge of them,"[48] Trembley strategically introduces a new organism through his insistence of shared investigation. In short, he promotes a method for making the unfamiliar familiar, the anomalous somehow normative—while yet maintaining the extraordinary character of the polyp itself.

First attracted by the polyps of "a pretty green color," Trembley initially identified these particular polyps as plants simply because of their visible likeness to surrounding flora. Owing to their shape, their

green color, and their seeming immobility, the polyps were likened to
bits of grass or the tufts of a dandelion seed.[49] Once under surveillance
in his powder jars,[50] however, the polyps displayed two properties that
served immediately to destabilize this preliminary classification: the
extension and contraction of its "arms." They appeared to Trembley
to move not in effective response to the agitation of the water in
which they sat but according to some internal cause. So he "jogged
ever so slightly the vessel holding the polyps" to see "how the ensuing
movement of the water would affect their arms":

> I expected to see their arms and even their bodies merely shaken
> or dragged along with the motion of the water. Instead I saw the
> polyps contract so suddenly and so forcefully that their bodies
> looked like mere particles of green matter and their arms disap-
> peared from sight altogether. I was caught by surprise. This surprise
> served to excite my curiosity and make me doubly attentive.[51]

In fact, for Trembley, this movement recalled the crawling action of
"snails and other creatures that contract and extend."[52] It suggested,
in other words, the vitality of what was then attributed to insects,
leaving Trembley to suspect that what he first assumed to be tiny,
parasitic water plants might instead be a kind of fauna.

Nonetheless, he could not ignore the empirical evidence provided
by the shape and color of the polyps. These previously observed
properties told him to set the animated forms incongruently into
the plant kingdom. At first, Trembley "thought it not impossible
that they might be sensitive plants," leaving their "contraction and
extension" to be "no more extraordinary than the response of such
plants to touch."[53] Doubt, however, had settled into the matrix of his
studies as he considered what he recognized as the existence of disparate properties in a single form, which, in combination, crossed and
recrossed the supposedly fixed boundary between plant and animal.
Consequently, Trembley determined to continue his investigation
"until new observations would resolve the issue."[54]

With Trembley neglecting the role of taxonomer for observation
itself, shifting from the tasks of "description and classification" to focus

on a study of life processes through observation and experimentation,[55] it is no wonder that he operated under an assumed prejudice against artificial systematicity. His guiding curiosity suggested instead that the setting for an accurate relationship between the forms of nature and their representations must occur unaffectedly in the mind of man. Thus it was only after watching the polyps "advance [step-by-step] along the walls of the vessel, like inch worms and various aquatic insects," that Trembley was persuaded (albeit not permanently) of their animal nature.[56] Their deliberate, calculated movements from one surface of a powder jar to another, particularly in what Trembley would later realize was their response to changing light, clearly demonstrated that these animals moved not, like a sensitive plant, according to external agitation but as a result of a willful mechanistic motility (see Figure 3.2).

Following what Trembley believed was a decisive observation, he suspended his study of the polyp. Having "intended no more than to learn whether they were animals,"[57] he was content to realize the polyp's place in the natural world. What this reveals, in turn, however, is that at the same time that Trembley distrusted the categorical constructions of Linnaeus, he nevertheless remained influenced by a desire to ascertain an order in nature. His reluctance to prescribe an order therefore appears overridden by the very belief that there is in fact an operational order. Because Trembley began the subject of his study by chance; because he came to several hypotheses only after the empirical means were presented to him, and so permitted the classification to emerge, as it were, naturally; because he then followed up each hypothesis with additional observation; and because he understood each reflection to be only an infinitesimal portion and reflection of a larger design, he exposes the epistemological paradox that plagued materialist thought: whereas on one hand, nature is believed to contain its own order of things, which only needs disclosing by man, on the other hand, man himself must put into language that larger design whose system, as a result of man's place being somewhere within it, can never be fully realized. The classification of even the smallest organism, then, is tantamount to setting yet another piece of an immeasurable puzzle, which has as its aim a determination of the

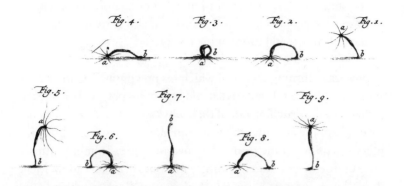

FIGURE 3.2. Lyonet's sketches of a polyp in motion, in Abraham Trembley, *Mémoires, pour servir à l'histoire d'un genre de polypes d'eau douce, à bras en forme de cornes.* Courtesy of Howard and Sylvia Lenhoff and Boxwood Press.

nature of life itself. But inasmuch as the polyp was just such a piece, its ability to continually catch Trembley "by surprise" destabilized any notion of categorical fixity—and suggested that the immeasurable puzzle is also always unsettled.

After a month had elapsed from what he felt was the defining observation, Trembley once again chanced to notice his polyps: several of these organisms that remained captive in the powder jars in his study had gathered on the side of the jar facing daylight. While this observation did nothing immediate to change Trembley's understanding of the polyp as an insect–animal, it did excite his curiosity again, this time engendering active experimentation to complement his passive observation:

> Recall now that my glass vessel had been placed on the inside sill of a window. . . . I turned the jar halfway around so that the large cluster of polyps was on the least bright side of the jar, and only a few polyps were on the side facing the light. Then it was a question of seeing whether the mass of polyps would pass from the poorly lit side to the best-lit side. . . . The next day I found a number of them already there. . . . Once more I turned the jar and in so doing I repeated the same experiment and I witnessed

the same result. . . . From [this] moment on I resolved not only
to seek enlightenment on this matter, but also to try to examine
the overall natural history of the polyps.[58]

By physically turning the jar in which his polyps sat, Trembley turns
from being satisfied with the what and how of his polyps' structure and
behavior to the searching out of their whys and wherefores. Although
it would appear here that the taxonomic query was overridden by a
query touching on the principles governing life, Trembley himself
never quite emerges from wrestling with issues of classification. Metaphysical pursuits were better left to his cousin, Bonnet, whose failing
eyesight and belief in a kind of natural theology led to an exchange
of empirical observation for philosophical inference. "Not one word
relating to plastic forces, soul or metaphysical questions," cites Ratcliff,
appears in Trembley's initial letter to the Royal Society, his subsequent
*Mémoires,* or his myriad correspondences.[59] Trembley, then, only set
about to "examine the overall natural history of the polyps" by first
establishing the creatures' affinity with other widely known insects.

The discoveries of the polyps' predisposition toward light as well as
their demonstrated purposive activity were not altogether new. "Several
kinds of flies and nocturnal butterflies afford constant examples of
these phenomena on summer evenings. [And] few people are unaware
of the use made of candlelight and torches as lures to attract and
catch various aquatic animals."[60] What was new, however, was the
close attention Trembley accorded the polyp even after it manifested
a common pattern of behavior. Rather than again assigning it a category, resulting from its comparison against other similarly organized
bodies, his use of analogy suggests a plasticity inherent in systems
of classification—if not in the organism itself. Rather than placing
his polyps into a preexisting category, Trembley suggested that the
category itself be revised or reorganized, and even further specified, to
account for the polyps. Within the "various species of small aquatic
creatures" attracted to light, for example, Trembley cited "one kind
which, according to its structure, even should be classified among the
polyps."[61] By proclaiming that the structure of his green polyps is also
to be found in at least one other kind of aquatic creature, Trembley

calls into question the validity of then-current categories into which all aquatic creatures had been placed.

We cannot neglect the foresight of this implicitly plastic model because even within today's taxonomic ideals, organisms continue to defy the boundaries set to them. In the first place, the polyp of the eighteenth century has since been classified as the aforementioned cnidarian or coelenterate, an invertebrate animal categorized by its saclike internal cavity, radially symmetrical body, and agentic tentacles. (As previously alluded to, others in the modern phyla of Cnidaria or Coelenterata include jellyfish, sea anemones, and corals.) In the second place, new discoveries are still being made among the vermicular organisms with which the polyp resonates. For example, in summer 2004, scientists announced the discovery of the first whalebone-eating marine worms, found in the waters off the coast of California. *Osedax frankpressi,* or the bone-devouring tube worm, is able to digest actual bone matter of deceased whales and other dead organisms that have come to rest on the ocean floor, with the aid of an internal bacteria *(Oceanospiralles)* that breaks down the oil in the bones.[62] Whereas these worms (and their bacteria) exist at extremely cold temperatures, another aquatic worm had been previously discovered to exist in an environment thought devoid of life owing to extreme heat and toxic quantities of sulfur. *Alvinella pompejana,* or the Pompeii worm, discovered in the 1980s, is found only at the hydrothermal vents in the Pacific Ocean, primarily near the Galápagos Islands.[63] As far as is presently known, worms are the most temperature-tolerant animals on the planet and are found in practically every environment on earth. With this in mind, what Ratcliff determines as an absence of "plastic forces" from the thinking of Trembley, Deleuze might recognize— through Leibniz and alongside Bennett—as Trembley's unconscious articulation of the polyp's precise vitalism or strict organicism: he projects the machinelike over and above the mechanical in an effort to confirm its autonomous material existence.[64]

Although Deleuze's particular discussion looks to verify the composition of inorganic machines, I have employed it here to highlight how Trembley might be approaching the intrinsic organicism of his "little machines." Keeping in mind the Cartesian idea of a little machine, it is important to clarify that the use of the word *organism* in the eighteenth century—particularly by Réaumur, Bonnet, Trembley, Linnaeus, and the like—is distinct from its use in the nineteenth century. The first half of the eighteenth century universally accepted that animals were understood in mechanical terms, whereas the nineteenth century reflected the effects of eighteenth-century debates over the nature of life. Thus the latter century gave to animals more organic and sentient notions of organization, whereas the former century maintained what Réaumur, for example, understood as the "organized bodies" of animals, which called attention to their Cartesian structure. However, as Dawson reveals, "like the Newtonian arguments for gravity as evidence of God's continuing active presence in His Creation, the [developing] study of natural history provided an antidote to the Cartesian 'fiction' of a completely mechanical universe."[65] On one hand, this is what attracted Trembley and Bonnet, as they moved farther afield from Réaumur's strict antiteleological sentiments; on the other hand, neither Trembley nor Bonnet, nor, in fact, Réaumur, could fail to recognize the potential for their experiments to support the theory that "matter itself had organizing principles heretofore reserved for the Creator."[66] Such anti-Cartesianism was believed, in turn, by Buffon and Needham, and given definition in La Mettrie's *L'homme machine*. So while there indeed exists "not one word" present in the works of Trembley with regard to "plastic forces," these same works implicitly challenge and begin to dismantle the dominant suppositions of the nature of life's constructions—prompting the naturalist community at large, and Trembley, in particular, to deepen their studies of the polyp.

Having resumed his study of the polyp full time, and having recognized the organism's structure to be one of its defining properties, Trembley returned to his observations, looking closer at what he remarked was the polyp's odd physical organization: it had an unequal number of arms. Although this was not necessarily an unnatural variation, the variation itself was typically only found in plants—and so Trembley further compared the polyp's arms with branches and roots. This meant, of course, that what he had already surmised to be an animal he now "speculated anew"[67] to be a plant. While

Trembley concedes that thinking of the polyp as a plant was now the "less natural idea," he also admits the fortuitousness of once again considering this possibility:

> [It] made me think of cutting up the polyps. I conjectured that if a polyp were cut in two and if each of the severed parts lived and became a complete polyp, it would be clear that these organisms were plants. Since I was much more inclined to think of them as animals, however, I did not set much store by this experiment; I expected to see these cleaved polyps die.[68]

Reflecting the Cartesian tendencies of Bonnet and Réaumur, Trembley believed in the necessary functional unity of the animal.[69] And he had had experience with cultivating plants from cuttings. Thus, on one hand, his first invasive experiment on the polyp uncharacteristically contained a preconceived result, an hypothesis by which Trembley "did not set much store." On the other hand, Trembley's empiricism allowed for the experiment to dictate its own results—seeming aberration notwithstanding.

On November 25, 1740, Trembley sectioned a polyp for the first time. After being cut, using the delicate tool of a boar bristle, both pieces of the polyp immediately contracted. Within the same day, however, each piece extended out again, and the first piece (the anterior end) began to wave its arms. With this, Trembley already had before him two signs of animal life after the sectioning had taken place, that is, extension and movement. Although these signs remained conceivably within a Cartesian framework, given that it was the so-called head of the polyp that displayed an animated force, what followed in Trembley's experiment did not:

> It seemed natural enough to me that the half [of the polyp] composed of the head and a portion of the body could still live. I thought that the operation which I had performed had only mutilated the head part without disrupting its animal economy. I compared this first part to a lizard which has lost its tail and which does not die from losing it. Indeed, again supposing that

the polyp was an animal, I assumed that the second part was only a kind of tail without the organs vital to the life of the animal. I did not think that it could survive for long separated from the rest of the body. Who would have imagined that it would grow back a head![70]

Needless to say, rather than die, the polyp multiplied. One polyp soon became two complete, functioning polyps, leaving Trembley bewildered:

According to the original reasoning behind this experiment I would have to conclude positively that the polyps were plants, and moreover, plants which could grow from cuttings. Nevertheless I was very far from hazarding such a decision. The more I observed whole polyps, and even the two parts in which the reproduction just described took place, the more their activity called to mind the image of an animal. Their movement seemed spontaneous, a characteristic always regarded as foreign to plants, but one with which we are familiar through endless examples among animals. Everything I had done to extricate myself from doubt had served only to plunge me deeper into perplexity.[71]

With the question of the polyp's classification, as well as its general state of being, having now risen for the third time, doubt continued to act as a stimulus for the curiosity that led Trembley into series on series of experiments. It was also about this time that Trembley had successfully reared aphids according to Bonnet's (and others') hypothesis of parthenogenesis. Practically simultaneously, Trembley thus had before him two organisms whose multiplicative behaviors exhibited nothing like that heretofore seen in animals. Moreover, he soon discovered that in contrast to the artificial regeneration that he had engendered in the polyps, these organisms multiplied naturally in a manner "very closely akin to the way plants multiply when they give off *shoots* [namely, by budding]."[72] For Trembley, the polyp's natural mode of reproduction, which, as he describes, "occurs without copulation," acts as yet another confirmation of parthenogenesis, and so "the polyps again constitute an exception to an allegedly universal rule."[73]

Trembley was at a crossroads; his suspicion of generalizations had grown considerably more acute. "In particular, it increased [his] distrust of rules which would rank the two properties [he] had found in the polyps under two different classes of organisms, one characteristic belonging to animals and the other to plants."[74] As Dawson rightly observes, "the regeneration of the polyp into complete individuals after it had been cut up was both novel and disturbing. It did not fit easily into the preformationist explanation, nor did it jibe with the accepted concept of animal machine, a Cartesian legacy."[75] Instead, the polyp introduced evidence that denied the preexistence theory of germs, while seeming to support the theory of epigenesis—and even, at first blush, the theory of spontaneous generation. In consequence, Trembley compromised and began to think of polyps as "plant–animals, since they seemed to belong to a species midway between these two classes of organisms."[76]

Recalling what Linnaeus termed a zoophyte, an elusive form that bridges plant to animal (of which the sensitive plant was once thought to be an example), Trembley nonetheless felt that an actual designation of the polyp as a plant–animal was just as suspect as definitively choosing one form over the other. "I am all the more circumspect," writes a stymied Trembley to Réaumur,

> because the facts which the little bodies present are new. I suspend my judgment. I do not dare to give it a name, although this would be very convenient. That of *animal plant* or *plant animal* presents itself rather naturally. But it is impossible to decide anything anymore.[77]

Trembley goes on to remark that "even should no other exceptions be found than those furnished by the polyps whose natural history I offer, their natural mode of reproducing by shoots can teach us twice over that the so-called general rules, which are almost universally accepted, do not deserve that name."[78] For Trembley, then, his criticism of contemporary naturalists for their reliance on general rules and, in effect, for their blindness to the normality of the apparent abnormalities found in nature was well founded. However, this criticism did not preclude Trembley from continuing to pursue the polyp for its categorical determination, thereby revealing a naturalist's consuming anxiety over categories.

In March 1741, Trembley obtained the proof he needed to secure finally the polyp as an animal: not only did he see the polyps eat, "swallow[ing] worms as long and even longer than themselves,"[79] he also gained corroboration of his overall discovery from Réaumur. Whereas Trembley wavered between discrete categorical assignation, Réaumur "did not hesitate to classify [the polyps] as animals."[80] And it was Réaumur who finally gave the name "polyp" *(polipe, polypus)* to Trembley's discovery, thereby marking its resemblance in miniature to the larger sea polypus, or octopus, and emphasizing its animal nature—however rudimentary.[81] Réaumur, through his authoritative presence in the field of insect study, convinced Trembley that his polyps were indeed animals at the same time that the empirical evidence manifested to confirm this.

Consequently, Trembley went on to distinguish his *freshwater* polyp from that of the sea, owing to the "various other animals which could be included in [the class of the polyp]." Even this, however, "proved inadequate," and so Trembley further specified his found organism according to its "most obvious feature": the shape of its arms, or horns.[82] Thus he named such polyps (as stated in the title of his full-length treatise), *polypes d'eau douce à bras en forme de cornes* (freshwater polyps with arms shaped like horns). The freshwater polyp only took on the more familiar name of "hydra" after Trembley successfully caused multiple heads to be generated on a single vermicular body, and Linnaeus established the genus *Hydra* in 1746. According to Lamarck's *Philosophie Zoologique* (1809), the polyp was both imperfect and simple, and the animal biology he discusses accounts largely for the behavioral and structural information gathered by Trembley and his contemporaries. Nonetheless, the polyp's subgelatinous and regenerating body, with scarcely any faculties, continued to maintain this creature in a hazy space between plant and animal through to the end of the eighteenth century. Lamarck, however, began to divide into more specialized classes the category of insects in general, and vermiforms in particular, at the turn of the nineteenth century, paying special attention to the demarcations of body material, propagation, and the presence of willful movement. Within the Lamarckian system, therefore, the polyp was only less simple, less obscure, than the *infusiorians,* or internal parasitic worms. For Lamarck (himself responsible for coining the term *invertebrates* and caused to suffer the title of "professor of the natural history of insects and worms" at the newly reorganized Jardin des Plantes: Museé National d'Histoire Naturelle), and then for others, worms marked the beginning of structural complexity; they signaled the tendency seen in natural objects to establish an ever-increasing system of articulations.

Of course, what Trembley finally accepted as incontrovertible evidence of the animal nature of his polyps (i.e., the fact that they ingested insects) is not without its future irony. Almost twenty years later, in 1760, Governor Arthur Dobbs of Brunswick, North Carolina, discovered the "catch fly sensitive," later known as the Venus flytrap, which he merely described as a plant that closes up in response to irritation. But once specimens were sent to England, it was discovered that this plant was carnivorous.[83] A ready example for the advantage of a harbored skepticism, this latter discovery is in keeping with Trembley's idea that "it is more appropriate to suspend judgment rather than to make decisions which almost always are based on the presumption that Nature is as limited as the faculties of those who study her"—an idea also inhabiting William Blake's visionary art.[84] Moreover, Trembley relates the prescient statement that "independent of the evidence furnished us by the polyps, it is easy to see that we do not know enough about plants and animals to formulate general rules," thereby presenting a necessary loophole of indeterminacy in all empirical pursuits—"evidence furnished us by the polyps" notwithstanding.[85]

It was 1744 when Trembley published his *Mémoires* (his promised "History of the Polypous"). In its preface, he mentions that "knowledge of the remarkable properties of the polyps could bring pleasure to the inquisitive and contribute something to the progress of natural history,"[86] in much the same way that Réaumur's earlier *Mémoires* sought to communicate the wonders of the insect world at large to an enraptured public. Not only did the confluence of observation, experiment, and declaration appear to settle Trembley's fluctuating mind, it underscored the value and necessity of the replication of experiment. For Trembley, natural history study equated an essential curiosity that overwrote any repugnancy with pleasure, virtue, and progress, thereby granting epistemological advancement an undeniably coded aesthetic value.

During the intervening years from the polyp's discovery to Trembley's first dissertation on the subject, frenzied dialogues concerning this creature reverberated across national boundaries. Evidencing what Ratcliff calls Trembley's "strategy of generosity,"[87] a cooperative of naturalists carried out the observations and experiments articulated and/or inspired by Trembley. By combining wonder and order, and attracted by the disturbing proliferation of anomalous behavior in vermiforms, this international cooperative was instrumental in erecting first the polyp then the worm as symbols of categorical mutability, material as well as aesthetic, and for suggesting the imaginative possibilities in both.

## Vital Replication

Laying one such suggestive foundation were what Trembley tellingly described as the "operations [he] performed on the polyps."[88] Begun with the cutting up of the polyps described earlier, these "operations" exposed the seemingly indefatigable vitality of these minute organisms. Not only did Trembley slice the polyps transversely into all manner of pieces, so that he once ended up with fifty animals "out of a single one,"[89] he also cut into them lengthwise to create those polycephalic monsters in miniature:

> The reader may well imagine that after I had succeeded in making some Hydras, I was not content to stop at that. I cut off the heads of the one that had seven, and a few days later I beheld in it a prodigy hardly inferior to the fabulous Hydra of Lerna. It acquired seven new heads; and, if I had continued to cut them off as they sprouted, no doubt I would have seen others grow. But

here is something more than the fable dared to invent: the seven heads that I cut from this Hydra, after being fed, became perfect animals; if I so chose, I could turn each of them into a Hydra.[90]

While the creation of this "natural" hydra was the result of Trembley's artificial manipulations of the polyp's facility to regenerate, it is also important to note that both he and Bonnet compared these manipulations to the polyp's own ability to generate by budding. During this process, one "mother" polyp could project several buds, and these buds could in turn project several others, all without having fully detached from the parent form. The parent form then manifested what both naturalists understood to be a kind of genealogical tree, giving the appearance of a many-headed organism or hydra (when in fact it was a contiguous branching of several generations of individuals). In this way, Trembley's "operation" re-created in kind what nature already produced. The polyp's continued ability to live and do well in nature after such an operation thus subsumed monstrosity under biological possibility. As such, nature could be understood to present not anomalies or extant aberrations per se but rather a series of particulars in which nothing remained outside its purview.

From the success of his initial operations on the polyp, Trembley continued to create what he affectionately called his "little monsters," which, after first having resulted from division, were soon realized to result also from reuniting the disconnected parts. Just as he cut the polyps to multiply their population, he also successfully grafted one polyp onto (or, more accurately, into) another, thereby reducing the overall population by doubling single polyps.[91] In effect, Trembley at once implied and disavowed what would become known as the Malthusian threat of exponential increase; his manipulations of the polyp's capacity to regenerate projected a crucial diplopia of being that was as thrilling as it was repugnant. Finally, Trembley performed the meticulous operation of turning the polyp inside out to determine precisely how the skin of the polyp functioned in relation to the organism's overall intake of nourishment.[92] He arrived at the idea to invert artificially what he found to be three distinct species of polyp from what he had observed naturally in just one species: the "tufted polyp," which, "incapable of contracting" like the green and brown polyps, would withdraw instead into a transparent case or tube. From this, Trembley observed that the "skin of [this] polyp is attached to the opening of the case in such a way that when the polyp moves inside, that portion of the skin cannot follow. Thus the skin remains attached by its lower end to the opening of the case which the polyp enters by turning itself inside out. The tuft, which holds by its base to the upper end of this skin, enters with it and ends up lodged in the tube formed by the skin when the skin has entered completely and is completely inverted."[93] Not only, then, did the polyp challenge categorical fixity with regard to eighteenth-century taxonomic practices, it brought to the fore questions concerning the principle of life—namely, where does this principle reside? How malleable is it?—and the relative hierarchy of the chain of being. In sum, while Trembley himself did not venture beyond the confines of a naturalist's empirical task, he did provide the agar out of which metaphysical contemplation and material speculation grew. His discovery of the polyp's strange habits of regeneration, coupled to the polyp's capacity to survive in any number of configurations, fueled the widespread philosophical debates over the nature and organization of life itself.

Trembley's belief in the scientific community and the importance of replicating experiments allowed his work with the polyp to be quickly and openly appropriated—both empirically and philosophically. Proclaiming that "any person in *England* . . . desirous to make Observations on the *Polypous,* and to repeat [his] Experiments" need only ask,[94] Trembley rightly anticipated the obvious "need [for] more than one eyewitness" to uphold his account of the curious behaviors of his discovered creature.[95] As a result, he painstakingly sent his polyps to all the "intellectual centres of Europe," as well as to any "who desired to repeat [his] experiments,"[96] carefully circulating actual polyps along with "their environment and proper food, and the instructions both for the conservation of the system and the reproduction of experiments."[97] Naturally, he sent his first samples to Bonnet and Réaumur, who both produced the same results as Trembley. Bonnet, however, also admits to his having turned to the more ubiquitous earthworm to initiate his investigations.[98] Not able to find any specimens of the polyp in his native environs, and impatient to uncover the details that Trembley left out of his cursory 1742 letter to the Royal Society, Bonnet essentially found an appropriate stand-in. In fact, as others also repeatedly determined (including Trembley's friend and engraver, Lyonet), Bonnet rightly assumed that any organism of the "worm-kind, whose general Organization being simple, and consisting chiefly of only one strait Gut, or Passage, from the Mouth to the Vent" (of which the polyp was surely one and the earthworm another), manifested "that strange Prerogative of being multiplied, as it were, by Cuttings."[99] Stafford calls these organisms "comic cavorters." She writes,

> Abraham Trembley's notorious experiments with the fresh water polyp during the 1740s had set the biological world agog. In defiance of reason, he demonstrated that an organic chit or speck could regenerate into a whole and healthy organism. Scientists subsequently engaged in a frenzy of amputation: segmented earthworms, horned slugs, footed snails, limbed toads and frogs were variously lopped to test their regenerative capacities. . . . These unruly and colorful fragments were thus responsible for making a new aspect of the invisible visible.[100]

Thus was regeneration quickly, perhaps chaotically, found to be a common vermicular trait. It consistently underscored the extraordinary, if "unruly," nature of nature in contrast to any singular anomaly.

Across the English Channel, and soon after the publication of Trembley's 1742 letter, then president of the Royal Society Martin Folkes and fellow naturalist Henry Baker also received samples of the polyp. The latter forestalled Trembley's 1744 *Mémoires* with his own 1743 treatise, *An Attempt towards a Natural History of the Polype*. But this publication merely provided an account of Baker's repetition of Trembley's experiments. While this action displeased (like unsportsmanlike conduct) many naturalists on both sides of the English Channel, namely, Folkes and Réaumur, Trembley himself continued to furnish Baker with both information and specimens.[101] This unflappable quality of Trembley's "strategy of generosity" is perhaps the leading reason for Trembley's characteristic displacement from his own discovery.

Given the rapidity and openness with which information concerning the polyp was exchanged, the polyp itself, like its discoverer, possessed only a fleeting—albeit impressive and influential—fame. Trembley recognized that "in two years' time," the phenomenon of the polyps' regeneration had "become widely known, so that the facts which at first seemed beyond belief, [had] been proven true of a variety of animals differing not only in species, but even in genus."[102] Likewise, in a 1745 letter from Peter Collinson, elected member of the Royal Society, to Cadwallader Colden, an American colonial statesman from Scotland generally known as the author of the first scientific works published in the colonies, Collinson writes, "The Surprising Phenomena of the Polypus Entertain'd the Curious for a year or Two past but Now the Vertuosi of Europe are taken up In Electrical Experiments, and what can be more Astonishing than that the Base rubing [*sic*] of a Glass Tube Should Investigate a person with Electric Fire."[103] It is apparent from both Trembley's *Mémoires* and Collinson's letter that what was once thought of as exceptional was after "a year or Two" found to be pedestrian among a variety of lower organisms and accepted as a matter-of-fact mechanism for their survival. Collinson's letter highlights instead the sweeping effect with which "Electrical Experiments" would attract the attention of scientists and the general public in the latter half of the eighteenth century (and on into the nineteenth). This shift from natural history to electrochemistry further occluded the record of Trembley's investigations. Perhaps as a result of the ease with which many naturalists could replicate Trembley's findings, or perhaps owing to a presiding discomfort toward an organism that at the outset manifested "attributes" seemingly "independent of rational plan,"[104] the polyp itself faded quickly from the gaze of natural history. In contrast, the ideas suggested by its ability to regenerate effected a perennial germination in man's imagination.

One letter, submitted to the Royal Society in November 1742 by J. F. Gronovius, a friend, peer, and patron of Linnaeus, presented the first of many practical accounts calling for a full dissertation of Trembley's experimental sectioning of the polyp—not from Trembley, however, but from Réaumur. To this letter is added a long note outlining the early communication history and confirmations of Trembley's discovery. Beginning with a full account given by Buffon to the Royal Society on October 29, 1741 (from his letter dated July 18, 1741), concerning not just the polyp but also the aphid, this history traces the correspondences between Buffon and Folkes, and Folkes and Count Bentinck, ending with a recuperation of Leeuwenhoek's earlier discovery. In the letter itself, Gronovius further accounts for the confirmation of the polyp's regenerative habits through the repeated experiments of Albinus and Allamand (two of Trembley's friends from the University of Leiden, previously noted). Added to this is the first introduction of the polyp into the arena of natural history study, from which Buffon constructed his own subsequent letter to the Royal Society of London: Réaumur's reading to the Académie des Sciences in Paris a letter sent him by Trembley. Thus, within a single year, all before Trembley's original 1742 letter appeared, news of the polyp had crossed from Holland to France and on to England. Such communications of Buffon, Réaumur, and Baker, for example, despite the lion's share of the attention they received, were not at all anticipations but rather derivations of Trembley's work.[105] The consistent displacement of Trembley from his discovery, revealed as it is through the convoluted publication and reception history of the polyp in the early 1740s, emphasizes at once the excitement, unease, and sometimes invention with which the polyp was approached.

While waiting for Trembley's authoritative dissertation, Gronovius did not hesitate to submit his own thoughts on an organism he neither saw nor experimented on. He thinks, for example, that the polyp is not "a perfect Animal, but a kind of the *Uvæ marinæ, Holothuria* or *Zoophyta,* which really are living when they are first catched," though quickly dead and thus unmoving thereafter.[106] With this, Gronovius suggests that a blurring of the line between animate and inanimate translates into a blurring of the line between animal and plant and thus leaves the polyp suspended in both. In contrast to Trembley's exacting observations, Gronovius offered unsubstantiated conjecture that would nonetheless maintain the polyp as part of—rather than apart from and thus a potential destroyer of—a general system of classification (namely, Linnaeus's *Systema Naturae*). Whereas Trembley concerned himself with what Stafford distinguishes as "a sensuous, pleasurable, or merely 'curious' *watching*," which in turn led to his precise, if disruptive, observations, Gronovius assembled "rational, tasking, language-driven *observations*"[107] that sought to defeat exception as a possible call for reorganization—direct evidence notwithstanding. Given, however, that a Linnaean approach to taxonomy concerns itself with the structure of the insect, the discovery of regeneration in insects continued to prove a particularly sticky problem. When, for example, Gronovius cites "what is [this] most surprising" property of the polyp, he begs the question of how the structure of the organism should be defined, that is, before or after the cutting?[108] He recognizes in the polyp a characteristic capacity to dodge even the most unfounded attempts to secure its taxonomy within existing categories.

Accordingly, an anonymous Cambridge gentleman, writing from Paris, submits not just a practical accounting of "what has lately been reported concerning the Insect mentioned on Page 218 of this Transaction" (referring to the extract of Gronovius's letter mentioned earlier); he also explicitly registers the instability of categorical definition at this time. The author is more concerned here with exposing an underlying regularity that goes against "the general Metaphysical Notions we have formerly learned"[109] than with emphasizing a taxonomy of the visible by recapitulating the structure and habits of the polyp. He recognizes in this creature "the very thing quite common" to plants that "*Monsieur Réaumur's* Memoir is said to give a rare Example of in the Animal."[110] Following this, the Cambridge author ruminates on the "great Probability . . . of a scale of Nature," which, in turn, leads him to suggest the far-reaching potential for disclosing all of nature while at the same time recognizing an apparent impossibility of doing the same.[111]

The anonymous Cambridge gentleman claims that rarity and exception are merely traits of a nature as yet unseen but not inexistent. The polyp, then, must be understood as essentially new to contributors to eighteenth-century natural history and their audience but prosaic to the natural world. The organism itself continues to exist as it always had, but everything changes in the recognition and representation of its existence. In this sense, the discovery of the polyp did not present a new organism, it more accurately represented a new idea. "Discovery," says Kuhn, "commences with the awareness of anomaly, i.e. with the recognition that nature has somehow violated the paradigm-induced expectations that govern normal science."[112] Thus, for "the man who is striving to solve a problem defined by existing knowledge and technique," "unanticipated novelty, the new discovery, can emerge only to the extent that his anticipations about nature and his instruments prove wrong."[113] This is the inestimable value of the polyp; as a material instance of what was before unseen and unknown, the polyp suggests a wider set of possibilities: it not only rationalizes the fantastic through empirical investigation but it also allows for logical association, speculation, and even invention. It draws attention to the slippery agency of man's approach to nature and the pathetic fallacy with which nature as a totalized entity has been endowed. Had nature "somehow violated" our "expectations" with the discovery of the polyp? Or was it our "expectations" that "somehow violated" the natural world? It follows that what made the polyp exceptional soon moved inexorably (and paradoxically) toward a general rule when demonstrated by a ubiquitous population of re-generating insects. As such, the discovery of the polyp's regenerative properties can be said to have come not from first acquiring the rules to perform the necessary science but from doing the science itself.[114]

Clearly any attempt to construct a universalized representation of the natural world, in accordance with the evidence offered up by its minute particulars, brings with it the interpretive machinery of analogy. But what happens when that analogy extends finally from man to worm, demonstrating affinities and frustrating hierarchical differences? The anonymous Cambridge gentleman, for example, put forward exactly that conceptual claim to compare the simple polyp or worm to the more complex being of man. Not only does he relate the polyp-as-hydra to "some very remarkable Monsters that have ap-peared in the World, where even some of the most essential Parts of Two [human] *Fœtus's* have been seen wonderfully united in One and the same Body," he also details "the Difficulty of killing some of the Tribes of Insects and Reptiles" and the relative plasticity of form. He cites how such plasticity decreases against the increasing complexity of form on the chain of being as well as how the human, as a singular organism, reflects this equation as it develops from *"Embryo"* through "infancy" to the adult form of "our own Kind."[115] In comparison to the polyp, then, humans appear fragile and prone to mortal accident; we, as the more "perfect Animal," die with greater ease than the more imperfect. Yet, while the author bemoans the imprisonment of the human animal in so vulnerable a complexity, he also exalts it because it manages to survive at times in so monstrous a state (e.g., conjoined twins). This elicits a twofold consequence to doing the science that led to the discovery of regeneration in animals: a kind of collapse of the chain of being, which raises the ontological concern that man is more in accord with the insects than in conflict, suggests, in turn, that anomaly and monstrosity might serve as common translations for the diplopic patterning of nature and the experiments seeking to represent it.

## Vermicular Man

In keeping with some of Trembley's closing remarks from his 1744 *Mémoires,* eighteenth-century novelists such as Henry Fielding, Tobias Smollett, and Oliver Goldsmith, as well as the satirist Voltaire and the encyclopedist Diderot, typified a reliance at times on the experience of natural history to cement their imaginative fabrications.[116] But they also manifested what were more latent figurations in the natural historical record. The polyp was used, for example, as a figure for political and economic satire, for the derogation of natural history study (particularly in those writings aimed critically at materialism), and even as a marker of naïveté. Fielding wrote a satirical skit on the multiplicative properties and influence of money after reading about the polyp in the *Philosophical Transactions,* garrulously titling his piece "Some Papers Proper to be Read before the R——L Society, Concerning the Terrestrial Chrysipus, Golden-Foot or Guinea; an Insect, or Vegetable, resembling the Polypus, which hath the surprising Property, That being cut into several Pieces, each Piece becomes a perfect Animal, or Vegetable, as complete as that of which it was originally only a Part" (1743). Smollet published *The Adventures of*

*Peregrine Pickle, in which are included, memoirs of a lady of quality* (1751), within which he voiced his contempt for the polyp, for what he understood was an animal with no economic significance. And Oliver Goldsmith offered similarly biting criticism in "The bee, being essays on the most interesting subjects" (1759) and in *The Citizen of the world; or letters from a Chinese philosopher, residing in London, to his friends in the east* (1762). Voltaire, however, presented what amounts to fairly unsophisticated critiques of the polyp's ever being considered an animal, as collected in *Œuvres complètes de Voltaire* (1819).[117]

But of the writers mentioned, all neglected to consider what Denis Diderot did: he saw that the material properties of the polyp could be a positive trope with which to reimagine life and the place of humans within it. Coincident with his writing of the entry for the polyp in the *Encyclopédie*, Diderot's *La Rêve de d'Alembert* (1769), through its speculative application of regeneration as an intrinsic human property, presents just such a consideration. Inventing on Diderot's own materialist epistemology, this work executes a logical transgression of the boundaries between insect and human, life and death, general and particular, to produce a thought experiment that explores living matter in its seemingly indeterminate yet irrepressible mutability.

Presented as a three-act play, or conversation in three parts, *La Rêve* rehearses the generation and classification debates of the period as an aesthetic form free from the strict empiricism with which Trembley presented the matter of the polyp. With the historical figures of Diderot himself, Jean le Rond d'Alembert (mathematician), Théophile de Bordeu (physician), and Julie de l'Espinasse (salon hostess) making up its cast of interlocutors, *La Rêve* reveals what l'Espinasse incongruently calls the pleasurable yet "abominable tastes" of the human mind for speculative philosophizing.[118] Both she and Bordeu, for example, consider in the second part of the text what Diderot and d'Alembert had conjectured in the first: a purely physical and mechanical nature. Denying God a role in the natural world, both conversations ultimately attract more questions than they answer.[119] Covering such topics as the origin of life, asexual and sexual reproduction, crossbreeding, and the manipulation of genetic inheritances, *La Rêve* manages to overturn conventional moral and psychological codes of eighteenth-century sensibility in favor of normalizing aberrant sexual behaviors and transgressive generative practices. However scandalous, such "abominable tastes" of the human mind emerge as a positive aesthetic sense in the text; they elicit the pleasure of imagining ostensibly transgressive implications of a purely material nature.

One of the most striking abominations in *La Rêve* appears when the freshwater polyp is exponentially transformed by a dreaming d'Alembert. It is changed into an ameliorative figure for what I discussed earlier was the low survivability of the human. By questioning Diderot ("Mr. Philosopher") about the possible "existence of polyps of all kinds, even human ones," d'Alembert quickly arrives at what he teasingly identifies as "Human polyps in Jupiter or Saturn!":

> Males splitting up into males and females into females—that's a funny idea. . . . Man splitting up into myriads of men the size of atoms which could be kept between sheets of paper like insect-eggs, which spin their own cocoons, stay for some time in the chrysalis stage, then cut through their cocoons and emerge like butterflies, in fact a ready-made human society, a whole province populated by the fragments of one individual, that's fascinating to think about. . . . If there is a place where man can divide himself up into myriads of microscopic men, people there should be less reluctant to die, for the loss of one man can so easily be made up that it must give rise to little regret.[120]

Overheard by l'Espinasse, and then communicated to Bordeu, this portion of d'Alembert's dream projects what May Spangler calls the material privilege of regeneration from polyp to human.[121] Spangler recognizes in the polyp the "malléabilité extraordinaire de ce petit être" (the extraordinary malleability of this small being), which she transposes from Trembley's material discovery to Diderot's literary invention—or "spéculation scientifique" (scientific speculation)—that marks off the intellectual difference between poet and philosopher. Whereas the poet's argument, continues Spangler, takes up the implications of "une espèce de polype" (a species or type of polyp), that of the philosopher uses the polyp as "un squelette" (a skeleton or framework) of ideas.[122] By privileging the polyp's regenerative habits, Diderot thus effectively turns the polyp into that viable trope of mutability capable of challenging not only man's egocentric view of the natural world but also his role within it.

D'Alembert's dream-construction of the human polyp follows after a discussion between l'Espinasse and Bordeu, in which Bordeu fills in some missing cognitive threads of the first part of the dream that l'Espinasse had recounted to him. Stating that the "real polyp can be destroyed only by crushing," Bordeu goes on to make the distinction between "ordinary animals, such as ourselves or fish," and "worms, serpents and polypous creatures" one of ascending vitality.[123] Related to the organization of an organism, this vitality appears in either a contiguous form (e.g., "ourselves"), which, if cut to pieces, quickly expires, or a continuous form, which, like the polyp, is not only capable of living and doing well again after such an operation but is able to multiply its kind ("populated by the fragments of one individual"). In this way is the human confirmed as a more vulnerable organism than the polyp. The latter notion is what shapes d'Alembert's rapid assimilation of man to the polyp's reproduction-by-budding ("males splitting into males and females into females") and the reduction of man to "the size of atoms" and his resulting likeness to a collection of "insect-eggs." The effect of this extended simile is to relegate man to a category simultaneously inferior and superior to the one he is said currently to inhabit. In other words, this simile actively destabilizes the taxonomy of a being who is himself wrestling with the challenge of taxonomic certainty in the lower organisms in an effort to emancipate himself from his own organic vulnerability.

Not only is man compared to that lesser life-form, the insect, but this insect demonstrates capabilities that surpass those of man. As a result, the human polyp, existing extraterrestrially on Jupiter or Saturn, represents a type of organism that conflates evolutionary potential with this potential's origins. Just as it could be the product of "an inconceivable interval of successive centuries and modifications," the human polyp is also indicative of the "rudimentary state" of the selfsame adult form: "It is beginning at the wrong end," says Bordeu, "to observe and study the mature animal. You must go back to its rudimentary state, and it is relevant to strip yourself of your present bodily organization and return for a moment to the time when you were simply a soft, fibrous, shapeless, *vermicular* substance."[124] D'Alembert's construction of the human polyp allows for the "mature animal" to appear paradoxically in its own beginnings as a type of a worm. It is "a funny idea" that nonetheless captures the continuous relationship between seemingly contiguous organisms.

With what Vartanian claims is *La Rêve*'s "synthesis of biology and technology," which leaves the polyp to act as "a symbol of the recombinant potential of living matter,"[125] d'Alembert's dream of the human polyp speaks to the hypothesis that "nothing that exists can be against nature or outside nature."[126] Instead, "given time, nature brings about everything that is possible, she will sooner or later produce some such strange composite."[127] And in the *Encyclopédie*, Diderot similarly comments that "the discovery of the polyp, the hermaph-rodite aphid, and so many others of this kind, are in the eyes of the observer so many keys to nature, which he may use to more or less advantage according to the breadth or narrowness of his view."[128] But rather than assume that d'Alembert's speculations be read as science fiction prototypes or the prophetic vision of genetic engineering,[129] the privileged status of the polyp in Diderot's text calls attention to the more immediate consequence of a nature freed from the cat-egorical limitations of general rule yet exposing a unifying principle in which "there is no such thing [as individuals]; no, no such thing. There is but one great individual, and that is the whole."[130] Forced to incorporate what Curran recognizes as "mutating worlds, monsters, and an elaborate view of animal generation into [an] understanding of the human species,"[131] d'Alembert, l'Espinasse, and Bordeu treat the polyp as an exemplary figure with which to get at the "matter of real things."[132] It represents living matter at once mutable and inde-structible, anomalous and routine, anticipating as it does Darwin's principle of "organic happiness" with which a representation of the development of the natural world might be structured.

Like "insect-eggs" trapped "between sheets of paper," d'Alembert's human polyp is ultimately an aesthetic fabrication literally caught up in the pages of *La Rêve*. As such, this invented organism has been identified as "un monstre textuel, ou monstre de papier" (a textual, or paper, monster).[133] It achieves materiality only insofar as it emerges as a mounting literary representation of categorical breakdown. Not only does it collapse the taxonomic structures meant to separate insect and human but the polyp (human or otherwise) alludes to a permeable boundary between living matter and dead matter that likewise relies on a realization of the individual's absorption into the whole. Thus does d'Alembert proclaim that "to be born, to live and to die is merely to change forms."[134] It is the polyp, then, that helps to reposition man not solely as an interpreter or taxonomer *of* nature but as precisely that "imperceptible worm"[135] that continues to need definition *in* nature.

# 4

# "Art Thou but a Worm?" Blake and the Question Concerning Taxonomy

Man is a worm wearied with joy he seeks the caves of sleep / . . . in his Selfish cold repose —*The Four Zoas*

If thou chuse to elect a worm, it shall remove the mountains. —*Milton*

She cries: The Human is but a Worm —*Jerusalem*

The cut worm forgives the plow. —*The Marriage of Heaven and Hell*

the / eternal worm / Crept in the skeleton. —*The French Revolution*

& in each wrinkle on that face / Plant worms of death to feast upon the tongue of terrible curses —*Tiriel*

That an Eternal life awaits the worms of sixty winters —*Europe a Prophecy*

To teach mortal worms the path / That leads from the gates of the Grave. —*The Song of Los*

thundering / Around the wormy Garments of Albion . . . / Time was finished! —*Jerusalem*

EVEN A GLANCE at David Erdman's *A Concordance to the Writings of William Blake* makes unmistakably clear the fact that the worm attracted Blake as a rich literary trope. Give or take a few repetitions, there are eighty-eight "worm" references in Blake's textual oeuvre. They range from *earthworm, glowworm, silkworm,* and *tapeworm* to the more generic *worm* and its adjectival derivative, *wormy.* But this number doesn't account for the myriad mentions of polyps and caterpillars, maggots, flies, butterflies, and other related insects. Nor does it recognize the copious visual depictions of all such organisms and behaviors found throughout Blake's illuminated works. Eighty-eight thus corresponds to a relatively low calculation, a mere point of departure from which the significance of the vermiform in the work of Blake might be addressed.[1]

*Worm* also enjoys its own multifaceted entry in S. Foster Damon's *A Blake Dictionary,* in which it is defined primarily as "the lowest and weakest form of animal life, a simple alimentary tube without any means of self-defense."[2] Although copacetic with any superficial biological characterization of a vermiform, this definition serves as an almost misleading introduction to, if I may, the Blakean worm and its kaleidoscope traits. As Damon goes on to note, the worm is recognized in Blake's work to be (1) "like all other living things," that is, "of divine substance"; (2) "an emblem of [human] mortality," stemming from "Bildad's announce[ment] that man is a worm (*Job* xxv:6)"; and (3) directly involved in "the mystery of generation."[3] Just as the general definition resembles early (and thus incomplete and unstable) descriptions of, for example, Trembley's polyp, the additional explanations caution us against any maintenance of such a deceptively simple designation. Understanding the Blakean worm, in its varied and variable applications, therefore suggests a fluidity of form and sense working against reification while yet depending expressly on it. It exposes one insistent example of what Denise Gigante identifies as the "occasionally" inscrutable "symbolic units of design and poetry" with which Blake populated his works,[4] and it acts as an aesthetic lure, drawing attention to the imprisoned—albeit revolving—state of matter that must nevertheless perform as the site of "Imagination & Vision."[5]

From depicting an actual creeping creature to symbolizing the developmental stages of both human and nonhuman life,[6] to representing the eternal being simultaneous to the phenomenal or generative,[7] the worm arguably inhabits the full spectrum of Blake's mythos—and in doing so elides any sense of a formal taxonomy in favor of more abstract portrayals. But aside from the many cursory glosses to be found within Blake scholarship, which more often than not catalog the worm's appearance as a psychological symbol for "man's latent possibilities,"[8] as well as for its suggestive iconography of the phallus, this organism has heretofore been paid little critical attention as a vital (de)composer of Blake's visionary project. Only recently has such a biological form been looked to for its formal artistic influence on Blake, helping to reveal what Gigante calls an "epigenesist poetics" in response "to the pressing contemporary question, 'What is life?'"[9] Prior to this, David Lashmet's "Unfurling the Worm" and Koriko Kawasaki's "Form and Worm in William Blake" mark the only other Blake scholarship to draw on the worm specifically (and substantially) to mount their arguments. However, just as Lashmet's essay exists as part of a graduate student conference on Romanticism held at Emory University in 1996, Kawasaki's work endures as part of an essay collection from the Association of English Romanticism in Japan; to my knowledge, neither essay has ever been taken up into the larger canon of Blakean criticism. For an organism *at least* as seemingly pervasive and mutable in Blake's poetry as it is out in the natural world, the worm clearly remains largely overlooked by literary critique. So it is my goal to produce here a concentrated study of particular worm sightings in Blake—worm sightings which, while not exhaustive, are meant to inspire continued investigation into the significance of vermiforms for this early Romantic mind.

Needless to say, the plethora of Blakean worms and worminess, in text as well as image, easily warrants an extensive examination independent of the current study. I, however, have chosen to focus primarily on two illuminated works: *The Book of Thel* (1789) and "The Sick Rose" (*Songs of Experience*, 1794).[10] Together, these familiar poems readily employ the worm as a diplopic device, one that envisions the nature of nature as a purposive system of recycling: corruption is always suggestive of renewal, just as generation consistently gives way to decay. In each poem, the worm appears as the previously mentioned aesthetic lure, guiding the reader (and, as in *The Book of Thel*, the protagonist) toward an understanding of mortality as a necessary, even if undesirable and hence vile, element of organic happiness. This scheme resonates, in turn, in other such early illuminated works as *Visions of the Daughters of Albion* (1793) and *The [First] Book of Urizen* (1794) as well as in the emblematic work of *For the Sexes: The Gates of Pardise* (1793/circa 1820) and Blake's final epic prophecy, *Jerusalem: The Emanation of the Giant Albion* (1804–circa 1820). Read collectively, these works provide a way into this apparently hermetic, yet nonetheless holistic, design; they display worm work in its revolutionary potential to recast Romantic experiments in representation. In concert with the very mutability of its form, the worm can singularly transmit the contraries of innocence and experience, death and rebirth, life and nonlife, so that this organism-cum-trope reveals an essential unity underlying such confluences of Blake's poetic vision.

### "This World Is a World of Imagination & Vision"

When Darwin placed man into phylogenic relation with the worm and ant ("survey thy kindred forms, / Thy brother Emmets, and thy sister Worms!"), he collapsed cold taxonomic boundaries in favor of reflecting his cooperative view of the web of life. But he also succeeded in highlighting the permanence of distinction by explicitly juxtaposing simple organisms and the most complex (which, as I highlighted in my introduction, DiscoveryNews recently recaptured by analogizing a ragworm to the human cerebral cortex). By overlapping classificatory collapse with its construction, Darwin suggested that man revisit his own notions of superiority when faced with an immutable system of mutability, founded in shared decay. His memorable paraphrase from the book of Job[11] implied that the minutiae of nature might be read as epistemological models for man's perception of the natural world and the role he plays within it. Such a particular reading of a macrocosmic nature through microcosmic means is likewise trackable in Blake's emblem book, *For the Sexes: The Gates of Paradise,* an expanded revision of the earlier-wrought *For Children: The Gates of Paradise.* But in Blake's case, the macrocosmic nature under investigation is less about the natural world than it is about the precocious character of Man.[12]

"The Catterpiller on the Leaf / Reminds thee of thy Mothers Grief"—preceding the first of sixteen lyrical "Keys" to accompany (and decipher) the revised *Gates of Paradise,* this couplet immediately reflects the figures and landscape pictured in this work's frontispiece (see Figure 4.1). With what appears to be a hungry caterpillar hovering ominously, set atop what is depicted as the dark underside of an oak leaf, the plate quickly draws our attention to the distinctly lighter, veined leaf—on which lies a curious figure. This figure's tranquil human face is appended to the segmented body of a worm, recalling at once the posture of a swaddled (read newborn) child and the very organism representative of the putrefying dead. The infant–worm not only literalizes the bringing of man into close (perhaps too close!) relation with the worm but it also exposes generation and decay, life and death, as inextricable, operative contraries. Furthermore, when this figure is perceived together with the leaf on which it sits, the picture unfolds to butterfly effect. With the leaf acting the part of wings and the worm-body that of a butterfly's thorax and abdomen, the face of the child suggests an innocence trapped in the ephemeral experience of metamorphosis. This, in turn, transforms the infant–worm also into a representative for the chrysalis stage, anticipating imminent change.

Of course, this is all not to neglect the arguably more static (though no less threatening) figure of the caterpillar arched over the infant–worm, as if a natural canopy, with the whole of the image set against an open sky. Thus, when the accompanying verse articulates "the Catterpiller on the Leaf," it seems likely that it is directing us to this explicit caterpillar and hence to the idea that life carries with it its own threat of dissolution. But just as the caterpillar is poised to devour the leaf it inhabits, and so eat away and simultaneously produce a kind of basis for its being, the infant–worm, an apparently more promising image, must also consume such matter if it is to change

FIGURE 4.1. William Blake, *For the Sexes: The Gates of Paradise,* copy D. "What is Man! / The Suns Light when he unfolds it / Depends on the Organ that beholds it. / Published by WBlake 17 May 1793." Reproduced with permission of the Pierpont Morgan Library, New York. Gift of Mrs. Landon K. Thorne, 1973. PML 63936, Frontispiece.

forms. "Thy Mothers Grief" therefore evokes both inevitable death and emergent life, an imminent loss of innocence and the progenitor of experience, so that the "Catterpiller" finally emerges as transient a reference as it is an organism.

Such transience, moreover, allows this already composite symbol to speak paradoxically to a singular and enduring quality of man. Exclaiming "What is Man!," the inscription directly on the frontispiece advocates for a perceiving of the human in and through all things—making, of course, the infant–worm as apt an image as it is discomforting. Because, as the frontispiece goes on to state, "The Suns Light when he unfolds it / Depends on the Organ that beholds it," Blake proposes that perception and insight are defined by the strength or weakness, keenness or indifference, of the human eye. "I know that This World Is a World of Imagination & Vision," writes Blake to John Trusler in 1799. "I see Every thing I paint In This World, but Every body does not see alike. . . . As a man is, So he Sees. As the Eye is formed, such are its Powers."[13] Blake's anthropomorphism, therefore, must be understood as a complex interplay of human and nonhuman points of view, each representative of the "confined natu / re of bodily sensation" and each demonstrative of how "Poetic Genius [is] adapted / to the weakness of / every individual."[14] And yet, because on one hand, "Man by his reason- / ing power. can only / compare & judge of / what he has already / perciev'd," while on the other hand, "Mans percepti- / ons are not bound / -ed by organs of / perception, he per- / -cieves more than / sense (tho' ever / so acute) can / discover,"[15] the anthropomorphized image of the infant–worm reproduces exactly this tension of experience and vision. It inscribes our entrapment in "The same / dull round"[16] as a passing stage (albeit infinitely so) toward the Eternal or *un*-adapted Poetic Genius.

Just as *The Gates of Paradise* opens with worm imagery, so does it close.[17] Directly illustrative of Job 17:14, and anticipating Darwin's "sister Worms" couplet from *The Temple of Nature*, the final emblem-plate includes the caption, "I have said to the Worm: Thou art my mother & my sister." The accompanying image then depicts a human figure, hooded and crouched on the ground of a forested (yet defoliated) landscape most likely that of a graveyard on the other side

of "Death's Door"[18] (see Figure 4.2). This ungendered figure, light
against the dark backdrop, stares open-eyed at the viewer, holding a
staff upright with the right hand (gently grasped by its lowest end).
Encircling this seated figure is a segmented worm, most readily recognized as the common earthworm. Part of the worm's body rests in
front of the bent knees and draped clothing of the human figure, while
another part coils around this same figure's left arm and flat-resting
left hand—as if to suggest some kind of connection or even bondage
between human and worm as well as between an idea of "life" and
its terrestrial environs. In addition, there is one clear human head
(possibly accompanied by others), partially exposed, emerging from,
sinking into, or simply embedded in the ground, set to the reader's
right of the human–worm entanglement. This suggests further that
the human figure is crouched atop a tomb or earthly grave. "The
implication of the designs as a whole," surmises John Beer, "is that
once one considers the agonies of mortal existence, as opposed to the
delights of Eternity that can be glimpsed in experiences of Vision, the
experience of death may be awaited without fear and seen simply as
the passing through a gateway, with the graveyard worm not consumer
but friend—even a relation."[19]

Although the final plate in the emblem book clearly speaks—
through both text and image—to *some kind* of "relation" between the
"graveyard worm" and man's "experience of death," Beer's idea that
the worm has moved from "consumer" through "friend" to arrive at
this "relation" implies a unilateral valuative shift from negative to
positive, from corruptor to comforter. I'm not so sure such a definitive shift occurs. I recommend instead a more disinterested approach
to render meaning, a kind of tilling of the symbolic import through
its material icons. Existence is as existence does. In its cultivation of
what Robert Essick identifies as Blake's dialectical thought, in which
"innocence and experience, heaven and hell, order and energy" reveal opposition to be the true friendship in Blakean contraries,[20] the
worm, itself depicted as enormously disproportionate to—and thus
somehow in greater equilibrium with—the human figure it borders,
can be read as both agent and outcome of "mortal existence." Emphatically *un*-anthropomorphized, and indisputably actualized, the

FIGURE 4.2. William Blake, *For the Sexes: The Gates of Paradise,*
copy D. "I have said to the Worm: Thou / art my mother & my
sister / Published by WBlake 17 May 1793." Reproduced with
permission of the Pierpont Morgan Library, New York. Gift of
Mrs. Landon K. Thorne, 1973. PML 63936, Plate 16.

outsized worm rests against and around the human figure, a token of
the vital alliance between being and nonbeing, humanity and perpe-
tuity. This essentially vermicular reading then sets the stage for what
in Blake's *Milton* appears as "Four-fold Man," against whose "vanity"
the "Lord" might "chuse to elect a worm, [for] it shall remove the
mountains."[21] Such action of worms is thereby elevated against what
his epic prophecy, *Jerusalem*, correspondingly casts as "the cradled
Infancy" of "Eternal Man," who "fell beneath his instruments of
husbandry and became / Subservient to the clods of the furrow! the
cattle and even / The emmet and earth-Worm are his superiors & his
lords."[22] As a capable contrary unto itself, the worm enacts a great
leveling just as it allows for a necessary ascendancy; it aids in what
the final plate of *The Gates of Paradise* intimates as the generation of
Eternal Man, which simultaneously emerges from and leads us (back)
to what the frontispiece revealed as the harmony between development
and decay. Thus does the final textual Key to *The Gates of Paradise*,
by performing in lyric what the emblem relates in image, necessarily
return us to "thy Mother's Grief"—only now the vision comes from
within (in the first-person point of view, "my") rather than from
without (in the second-person point of view, "thy"):

> And the Worm Weaving in the Ground
> Thou'rt *my* Mother from the Womb
> Wife, Sister, Daughter to the Tomb
> Weaving to Dreams the Sexual strife
> And weeping over the Web of Life[23]

Literally emblematic of a *turning in* to Blake's visionary project, the
capacity of the worm to represent diplopically the contrary states of
generation and decay, "order and energy," erodes strict classification
in favor of emancipatory abstraction and identification. Ultimately
against the idea "that there was nothing in the universe that could
not be perceived by the five senses,"[24] Blake effectively dismantled
boundaries to construct meaning. He opposed conceptual limitations
set by the materialism of Bacon, Locke, and Newton, for example,
instead choosing an irrepressibly (always "Weaving in the Ground")

animate nature through which to filter the desires and aptitudes of man reaching into Poetic Genius.[25] In this way does the worm serve to anchor and preserve what the prologue to *The Gates of Paradise* initially divulged: "Mutual Forgiveness of each Vice / Such are the Gates of Paradise."[26]

## An Elemental Process

Given that each element, or Key, to these "Gates of Paradise" was rendered not only textually but visually, at length printed in black ink on woven paper and bound with calfskin over marbled boards,[27] it bears revisiting here Blake's celebrated processes of etching and engraving that led to the unique existence of these and other illuminated prints. It bears revisiting because the practice of relief etching, developed by Blake in novel response to the intaglio process in which he had been trained, both produces and is produced by what I have been arguing is the diplopic paradox necessary for "the doors of perception [to be] cleansed / [so that] every thing would appear to man as it is, in- / -finite—":[28]

> . . . the notion that man has a body
> distinct from his soul, is to be expunged; this
> I shall do, by printing in the infernal method, by
> corrosives, which in Hell are salutary and me-
> -dicinal, melting apparent surfaces away, and
> displaying the infinite which was hid,[29]

More than a reference by Blake to his own profession, this oft-quoted passage from *The Marriage of Heaven and Hell* (circa 1790–93) calls attention to the metaphoric inversion intrinsic to the practice of relief etching, asserting what Essick describes as "the importance of method when imagination addresses itself to life through art."[30] Just prior to his fifteenth birthday, Blake became an apprentice to James Basire, engraver to the Society of Antiquaries as well as to the Royal Society,[31] with whom he studied for seven years (1772–79). This apprenticeship began Blake's lifelong career not as the revolutionary

etcher–painter–poet[32] we often think of him today but as a journey-
man laboring to produce over 380 commercial prints and occasionally
commissioned to provide his own illustrations to the works of other
poets.[33] For example, through the recommendations of Henry Fuseli
and Joseph Johnson, Blake was commissioned to make engravings
for Darwin's *The Loves of Plants*. This work has since provoked Blake
scholars to note some dominant parallels between Darwin's complete
*Botanic Garden* and Blake's *The Book of Thel*, particularly considering
these works' shared personifications of flora and fauna.[34]

Under Basire, Blake mastered the practical techniques of engraving
and etching, such as the preparation of the copper plate, the process
of counterproofing (the transfer in reverse of a drawing or print onto
the bare copper plate), and mirror-image writing. Working primarily
within the intaglio technique, "a negative process in the sense that the
material (both ground and copper) is removed to create the incised lines
that receive ink," Blake learned moreover the delicate yet aggressive
practice of "biting" the plate with acid to effect the desired design.[35]

It is out of this background, combined (perhaps somewhat conten-
tiously) with his desire to be an original artist, whose "never-ending
labors . . . struggle[d] to harness matter in the service of spirit,"[36]
that Blake invented relief etching.[37] Unlike intaglio, this is "a positive process, for the artist adds material to delineate the image. The
copper is then removed from the surrounding areas not covered by
the image."[38] Thus must the artist "draw his design in an acid resist
[directly] on the plate," leaving the remaining raised surfaces to receive
the ink for printmaking.[39] The emphasis on the integral topography
of each plate made both image and text appear similarly sculpturelike:
laden with form to produce content. It provided his poetry with an
unmistakable materiality, substantively constructive in its corrosive,
"infernal method." Additionally, owing to the softness of the copper
plates, Blake would have had to correct flattened inversions and other
corruptions of form over and again to make up for their unavoidable
degradation. As an etcher, then, Blake was fully aware of the challenge and influence the material posed in the production of his art.
His relief etching, in itself a second reversal and more labor-intensive
process than intaglio, sought to expose what was hidden beneath the

surface of the plate—making his art what W. J. T. Mitchell describes as "a curious compound of the representational and the abstract."[40]

Just as matter must decay to generate (i.e., reveal) its eternal form, freed from the imprisoning senses, so must Blake, in effect, destroy the integrity of the copper plate to create his visionary art. Although etching as a general practice relies on this destruction–creation formula,[41] Blake's relief etching presupposes the revelation of form in a way intaglio cannot. Because Blake manipulates the ground *around* the form he wishes to produce, rather than inscribing the form itself, he suggests a kind of *emboîtement* for artistic creation: the form appears to preexist its development, leaving Blake himself to disclose and release what the Eternal (Poetic Genius, we might say) had set before him. Thus does it track when Essick notes that Blake's "revolt against the [artistic-commercial] system manifests itself in three imaginative forms: separate plates and book illustrations designed and executed for aesthetic purposes beyond the commercial, relief etching, and prophetic narrative in which the abstracting processes of reproductive engraving become basic metaphors in a myth of creation, fall, and entrapment."[42] Blake's engraving practices, inclusive of his application of image to text or text to image, undoubtedly helped to inform what I have identified as his effective imaginative diplopia. His applied ideas of reversibility and reflection manifest the contrary states that make up many of his works' visionary inversions, with the worm often invoked as a double agent in their transmission.

### Under Threat of Decay

*The Book of Thel* boasts a straightforward plot, but with convoluted, even contradictory effects, which are further underscored by its illuminations (copy J). The poem follows Thel, the youngest of Mne Seraphim's shepherdesses, as she interacts with four anthropomorphized objects from the natural world. In "the secret air," "Down by the river Adona,"[43] Thel encounters the Lilly of the Valley, who in turn hands her off to the Cloud, the Worm, and the Clod of Clay, all in what initially reads as Thel's search for purpose in an organic world. But even the opening line, "The daughters of *Mne* Seraphim led round their sunny flocks,"[44] highlights the need to tread carefully through a text seemingly transparent in its productions. Beyond any possible spelling error occasioned by the etching process (namely, "Mne" vs. the abbreviated "Mme."), several studies of *The Book of Thel* have noted the promising significance of the scripted name of "Mne Seraphim": her name "suggests a hybrid of the classical mother of the muses Mnemosyne and the angelic, inspirational Seraphim of the Bible."[45] The visual likeness of "Mne" to the polite abbreviation of Madame, however, also turns this hybridity into a significant pun, wherein Mnemosyne, or Memory, appears as a mature individual intimately linked to a plurality of the highest-ranking angels in the Christian canon. Memory as Muse thus acts, in effect, to address another more collective form of itself (i.e., Seraphic enthusiasm), both of which are positioned in the role of mother and guardian—thereby suggesting a double image of visionary inspiration to be the very type of perception through which to access both Thel's "gentle lamentation" of "O life of this our spring!"[46] and her pursuant investigation of the same.

Given this twofold prelude into Thel's quest, the quest itself might be viewed through an equally doubled aspect. Leaving what Damon defines as "a place of primal innocence,"[47] only to return "unhinderd" when met with her own aspect of death, Thel apparently carries her innocence through the experience of "her mortal day."[48] She conveys what Mitchell emphasizes as the "state of innocence and pastoral unity [in which] human beings can converse directly with natural creatures [without] conflict between life and death."[49] But she also conveys the potential to suffer from an "alienated, divided consciousness,"[50] one that ultimately condemns her to realize rather than simply borrow from the consequences of mortality. At once motivated by, yet somehow distinct from, mortal existence, Thel appears to occupy the states of Innocence and Experience simultaneously, until Thel herself might be understood as both human and something altogether not. Thus can the poem be read as a prolonged lament, projecting the mystery of existence to question not only the purpose of life but also who or what Thel is that she can finally refuse its dissolution.

It is significant that Thel's quest and character deny any fixed taxonomy, pointing instead to a flexibility of form and mutability of meaning to match those natural objects with which she converses. Thel herself has been defined as both a young virgin on the cusp of puberty and the personification of Desire itself, with the latter suggested in large part by the multiple source associations of the name "Thel."[51] She has been discussed "as a real person, fully fleshed," who must grow from "child to woman" and who represents "the entrance of the soul into a mortal body."[52] She has been recognized "as a figure of innocence facing experience, a being still retaining her visionary nature, but contemplating descent into the materiality of the world—including entry into the human form."[53] As these and other descriptions suggest, Thel is exceptionally adept at slipping between symbolic registers. In fact, because Thel is initially described "*in paleness . . . / To fade away* like morning beauty from her mortal day," yet no less a denizen of "eternal vales,"[54] she is introduced as being *already* inculcated into a temporal system while yet enjoying perpetual existence. Her ambiguous yet dynamic presence in the poem, guiding the reader just as she herself is guided, implies that the poem as a whole deals in certain uncertainties, or mutabilities, of sense and form. Like the worm exposing decay as the matter of generation, Thel releases the constraints of being from any restrictive dichotomy. Whether innocent *in* existence or innocent *of* existence, Thel's ability to carry the poem's content across the boundaries of life and death, notions of living and nonliving—to confront, as it were, what would be the inevitability of her own demise without actually succumbing to it—leaves her experiential mode in vital question.

With this in mind, Thel's eventual interaction with the Worm, as the only natural object with which she converses that is also indicative of an indeterminate taxonomy ("Art thou a Worm?"[55]), becomes the key instance through which to read Thel's movements through (and experience of) "the materiality of the world." This simple vermiform exemplifies her ability to partake in decay without being consumed by it and to ingest the knowledge of selfless sacrifice as an essential tenet of the natural world without being destroyed by it.

Following the pastoral overture of "all but the youngest"[56] of Mne Seraphim's daughters, *The Book of Thel* relies on a tight series of similes to project its protagonist into "the secret air" of transient existence:

> Ah. Thel is like a watry bow. and like a parting cloud.
> Like a reflection in a glass. like shadows in the water.
> Like dreams of infants. like a smile upon an infants face.
> Like the doves voice, like transient day, like music in the air:[57]

Such similes allow Thel to effectively try on the trappings of relative ephemerality; they provide rhetorical connection to the otherwise divided state of Thel's arguably "primal innocence." In so doing, they also betoken Thel's lament at her own perceived purposelessness ("to flourish in eternal vales"), which she curiously compares to "a faint cloud kindled at the rising sun: / I vanish from my pearly throne, and who shall find my place."[58] This unconscious slip from eternal to ephemeral markers marks out the very problematic within which Thel resides. Her perception of existence, any existence (including her own), is always already twofold, as if the temporal were an aspect of permanence not unlike Darwin's idea of immutable mutability. Thus can Thel take up and refuse in sequence the related roles of the Lilly, the Cloud, the Worm, and the Clod of Clay, while yet determining her own (lack of) purpose alongside them.

Ostensibly unable to enact the role of the Lilly, which, by "Giving to those that cannot crave," "nourish[es] the innocent lamb," "Revives the milked cow, & tames the fire-breathing steed," Thel moves quickly on to liken herself to that "faint cloud" who "in one hour . . . fade[s] away."[59] But this, too, she quickly realizes is an unsustainable comparison, asking, "Why thou complainest not" against her own "yet I complain."[60] Initially, then, she rejects any analogy between herself and the beauty, pleasure, sustenance, and unity for which the Lilly and the Cloud stand. She assumes instead that she has no place (for "who shall find" it?) within the schema in which the Lilly exists, and she disavows any connection to the "unseen" yet no less restorative role with which the Cloud is credited, announcing in turn that "I fear that I am not like thee."[61] From the Lilly, a "watry weed" of the "lowly vales," to the "hovering and glittering" Cloud,[62] Thel's first two interactions leave her to bemoan what she understands would be her virtual lack of impact, imprint even, on any feature of a natural system. That Thel might dwell in, but not contribute to, such a system simply accentuates her own sense of purposelessness, leading her to insist that she is "without a use": "or did she only live. to be at death the food of worms."[63]

But it is in this last exasperated articulation that Thel arrives at a declaration (however inadvertent) of her own purpose within a system with which she knows no communion. As the Cloud declares, "Then if thou art the food of worms. O virgin of the skies, / How great thy use, how great thy blessing; every thing that lives, / Lives not alone. nor for itself."[64] Although Thel concedes that unlike the Lilly and the Cloud, she does not exist to nourish the flora and fauna in her own vales of Har,[65] she nonetheless stumbles on a like purpose. Characteristic of what Fuller designates as Thel's passivity, the conflict between consciousness and the actuality of purpose keeps Thel "unaware, not engaging with what is essential for growth."[66] By and large, Thel is an observer, a "pensive queen"[67] only asking questions to which she rejects the answer. However, when she invokes the worms, followed by the Cloud's responsible calling on the "weak worm from its lowly bed" to confront her,[68] Thel is stripped of her passivity. The distance between a mere awareness of mortality and her own engagement with it closes, enfolding her directly into its organic processes. And so she begins to hear what Nichols designates as a kind of biological message: "living things reach their fullness and die after preparing the way (organically and reproductively) for new living things, new forms of organic life."[69]

To unknowingly recognize herself as worm food is finally to align herself with the nourishing roles performed by the Lilly and the Cloud and, by extension, the whole of the natural world. In her innocence, she has sacrificed herself to worms, making experience that which happens whether or not she realizes it. But rather than fade or vanish into pastoral scenes of cultivation, the idea of Thel's consumption ultimately stirs up an image of gross corruption—with which she is directly met in the closing scene of the poem. Reflective of the construction as well as dissolution of Thel's found use value, the worm is figured as a positive image that nonetheless casts Thel as the vile site on which her fear of decay (and hence death) materializes.

The poem, however, delays this morbid materiality by presenting the Worm as an "image of weakness," "helpless and naked"[70]—like that encountered in the frontispiece to *The Gates of Paradise*. This preemptive sketch draws Thel toward the unpleasant mechanism of her own purpose by making it palatable, even pitiable to her: the Worm appears "like an infant wrapped in the Lillys leaf"[71] (recalling Thel's reliance on simile to compose relationships). Rising from "its lowly bed," mute yet weeping, the Worm is laden with diminutive qualifiers. Like dressing up a wolf in sheep's clothing, Thel's introduction to the Worm overwrites this organism's material function and traditional symbolic import with an inviting aesthetic formulation associated with a vulnerable innocence, suggestive not of decay but of procreation,[72] not of separateness but of what Nichols defines as a "powerful connectedness that unites all living things."[73]

Not surprisingly, the illuminated plates of the poem emphasize and help to define this reevaluation. Plate 6, for example, represents the Worm as the named "infant" of the text; it lies exposed atop green grasses, cradled by "the Lilly's leaf" (see Figure 4.3). Given its position in the center of the plate, set at the bottom of the illuminated top portion and just above the actual text of the poem, the Worm lies on a narrative threshold of text and image—just as it inhabits that of life and death. Thel, too, occupies a similar threshold. In this plate, she stands upright, over the Worm, her arms outstretched to mirror the figure of the exiting Cloud in the upper left corner. Signifying what Mellor and others interpret as an open, even cruciform posture, Thel "welcomes her responsibility to be 'the food of worms' with arms spread in delight over the tiny infant resting on the ground. Her eager acceptance is accentuated by the draperies that swirl around her feet as she rushes toward the child."[74] While this so-claimed eager rush might be overstating the astonishment with which Thel viewed this figure of the Worm, as it occludes the sense of hesitation and surprise through which Thel inquires after the organism's identification ("Is this a Worm?"[75]), her drapery of dress indeed emphasizes an intimate connection between the two. It weights her figure to the very ground in which the Worm usually dwells. Likewise, just as Thel's dress blows left, in concert with an oncoming darkness (far right), the Cloud's gossamer drapery trails right, thereby revealing a

## III.

Then Thel astonish'd view'd the Worm upon its dewy bed.

Art thou a Worm? image of weakness. art thou but a Worm?
I see thee like an infant wrapped in the Lillys leaf:
Ah weep not little voice, thou canst not speak. but thou canst weep;
Is this a Worm? I see thee lay helpless & naked: weeping,
And none to answer, none to cherish thee with mothers smiles.

The Clod of Clay heard the Worms voice, & raisd her pitying head;
She bowd over the weeping infant, and her life exhald
In milky fondness, then on Thel she fixd her humble eyes.

O beauty of the vales of Har, we live not for ourselves,
Thou seest me the meanest thing, and so I am indeed;
My bosom of itself is cold. and of itself is dark,

But

FIGURE 4.3. William Blake, *The Book of Thel,* plate 6, Keynes copy H/Bentley copy J. Lowell EC75.B5815.793va, Houghton Library, Harvard University. Reproduced with permission.

contrasting wind blowing in from the left. Together, these directional variations designate a shift in the already tenuous thresholds of appearance and signification. They call attention to the Cloud's exit as a decisive contrast to the Worm's entrance. But as "neither worm nor cloud," Thel appears as a "being suspended between earth and'air,"[76] as if awaiting her specific assignment in the poem's humanized topical system. It is no wonder, then, that Thel is indeed "astonish'd"[77] at the Worm's innocuous appearance and so driven repeatedly to question its taxonomy—thrice asking, "Art thou a Worm?"; "art thou but a Worm?"; "Is this a Worm?"[78]—in an effort to reconcile function to formulation. In fact, unlike the other beings populating the poem, Thel must consciously choose her assigned purpose (as the etymology of her name might indicate) rather than passively accept it. As a result, she also rejects the explanations of these beings in favor of entering with "virgin feet" directly into "the couches of the dead,"[79] nudged (not forced) to experience the consequences of mortal existence through an innocent descent into the environment of the Worm.

Plate 7 subsequently draws Thel into a closely seated posture, her downward gaze pointing us to the personified Worm (and its guardian, the Clod of Clay)—and thus to the bottom of the plate (see Figure 4.4). Thel is enclosed by what Erdman has identified as "the colorless monotropa or corpse-plant, which lives without green tissue," and she is portrayed as Mitchell describes her, with "the flowers and leaves which formerly curled at Thel's feet now ben[t] over her, as if she had shrunk in scale in order to converse with the lowliest of creatures."[80] Positioned beneath the text of the plate, this image insinuates a kind of underground or cavelike scene, in which the corpse-plant survives without exposure to sunlight and both the Worm and the Clod of Clay exist in familiar (if usually hidden) entanglement. Given Thel's tentative, if not wholly passive, approach to her own purposiveness, the position of her body, the direction of her gaze, and her proportional relation to the landscape all appear apt as she progresses toward the matter of her dissolution. At once timorous and protective, Thel anticipates, on one hand, what Northrop Frye identifies as the "mental cowardice" seen in such recurring Blakean figures as Theotormon, Urizen, and Los.[81] On the other hand, she calls to mind what Mitchell

But he that loves the lowly, pours his oil upon my head,
And kisses me, and binds his nuptial bands around my breast.
And says; Thou mother of my children, I have loved thee.
And I have given thee a crown that none can take away
But how this is sweet maid, I know not, and I cannot know,
I ponder, and I cannot ponder; yet I live and love.

The daughter of beauty wip'd her pitying tears with her white veil,
And said. Alas! I knew not this, and therefore did I weep;
That God would love a Worm I knew, and punish the evil foot
That wilful, bruis'd its helpless form: but that he cherishd it
With milk and oil, I never knew; and therefore did I weep.
And I complaind in the mild air, because I fade away,
And lay me down in thy cold bed, and leave my shining lot.

Queen of the vales, the matron Clay answerd: I heard thy sighs,
And all thy moans flew oer my roof, but I have calld them down:
Wilt thou O Queen enter my house, tis given thee to enter,
And to return; fear nothing, enter with thy virgin feet.

FIGURE 4.4. William Blake, *The Book of Thel,* plate 7, Keynes copy H/Bentley copy J. Lowell EC75.B5815.793va, Houghton Library, Harvard University. Reproduced with permission.

reads as the Virgin Mary's adoration of the infant Jesus, with Thel as the Madonna, the Worm as Jesus, and the Clod of Clay as John the Baptist.[82] Read as such, this scene acts as an implicit reminder of the contraries collecting around the figure of the Worm. It echoes what appears in Blake's "Annotations to Lavater's *Aphorisms on Man*": "God is in the lowest effects as well as the highest causes for he is become a worm that he may nourish the weak."[83] This is also what Thel herself comes to learn:

> That God would love a Worm I knew, and punish the evil foot
> That wilful, bruis'd its helpless form: but that he cherish'd it
> With milk and oil, I never knew[84]

The divinity with which Blake repeatedly contextualizes this organism secures the principle of Thel's quest alongside her growing knowledge of a material purpose, once again setting the essential contraries of the ephemeral and the eternal to view. Thus, when the lowly infant–worm is presented with arms extended in open welcome, it not only carries over Thel's gesture from the previous plate but it beckons Thel to the very context of her elected purposiveness through a striking combination of iconic imagery and natural activity.

Through the "eternal gates" and into "the land unknown; / . . . where the fibrous roots / Of every heart on earth infixes deep its restless twists," Thel finally arrives at "her own grave plot."[85] This eternal space, suggestive of phenomena in a "restless" and hence paradoxically renewing state of decay, marks the Worm as a diplopic device through which to comprehend matter's immutable mutability. Furthermore, in an hypothesized meeting between Thel and "the maggots or worm-babies [to] whom she . . . would eagerly give her body (first the milk of her breast and then her entire body) to feed and nourish this life cycle," Mellor calls for the juxtaposition of reproductive generation to consumptive decay.[86] By conflating the productivity of vermicular processes with the vermiform's symbolic value of both vile corruption and holy veneration, the Worm in Blake's poem transmutes meaning, just as it does matter, to provide Thel with an exemplary means to preserve her innocence in the context of experience.

As the lure with which Thel is drawn down into her individual seat of death ("& there she sat down, / And heard this voice of sorrow breathed from the hollow pit"[87]), the Worm presages with mute acceptance the contrastingly mournful queries of a self already fulfilling its putrid purpose. Vulnerable and open to destruction, Thel's "own little piece of nature—its senses and sexual drives,"[88] provides her the opportunity to observe (or, at the very least, to hear of) the effects of her living "not alone. nor for [her]self." But rather than glorify a community of recycling forms, counted as holy by a system that blesses "every thing that lives,"[89] anointing even the "lowly" worm with "milk and oil," the performance of Thel's sacrifice emphasizes the more sinister aspect of such a system. It condemns her to the "same dull round," imprisoned by senses that expose the limitations—not the liberties—of perception and experience: "Why cannot the Ear be closed to its own destruction? / Or the glistening Eye to the poison of a smile! / . . . Why a Nostril wide inhaling terror trembling & affright / . . . Why a little curtain of flesh on the bed of our desire?"[90]

Because Thel is visiting herself, a self already the "food of worms" and so (being) absorbed into the patterns of nature, she gains a distinctly doubled perspective of her state of being: as both external witness and internal agent, Thel experiences the consequences of materiality by seeing herself as precisely that unprotected site where her fear of dissolution materialized. It is a perspective altogether liberating *and* limiting, compelling Thel once again to make a choice: "The Virgin started from her seat, & with a shriek. / Fled back unhinderd till she came into the vales of / Har."[91] Whether this choice act relays pity, fear, or panic at "the prospect of being consumed in the grave by worms," or a more willful and affirming rejection "of what she has learned,"[92] the fact remains that Thel ultimately negates the specific work of the worm. She rejects one register of a purposive though all too vile existence in favor of (re)turning with "virgin feet" to the pastoral innocence of her native vales. In doing so, however, Thel openly allows the state of Experience to pass likewise "unhinderd" *through her.* Complicating any "static self-preservation,"[93] therefore, the final lines of *Thel* reveal that of all the organic forms Thel encountered in the poem, she finally accepts the changeful vermiform for its protected ability to transmute both substance and meaning. In the end, Thel, if not willing to partake in her vision of the natural world, is reconciled safely to its memory through a vermicular reading of Experience.

## Promise in Putrefaction

In contrast to *The Book of Thel,* "The Sick Rose" (King's College copy) begins rather than ends in the seat of decay.[94] From the opening line, "O Rose thou art sick,"[95] we are given to recognize a lamentable shift that occurred anterior to the poem. The Rose has already lost the vitality of a healthy and delicate nature to sickness and imminent destruction. The immediate result of this anteriority is a(n) (un)settling of the poem onto the figure responsible for this changed state: "The invisible worm."[96] As an insidious contaminant, the worm destroys the life of the Rose from the inside out, making the Rose an apposite replacement for Thel. This Rose serves ironically as the blessed site of corruption, within which the worm can finally work at the decomposition denied it in *The Book of Thel.* Such destruction, however, also carries with it the suggestion of accusation, as if to implicate the Rose into its own degraded–degrading state. With the word *sick* already burdened with several meanings in Blake's time (e.g., "ill," "pale," and "wan" as well as "corrupt through sin or wrongdoing"),[97] any material reading of the relationship between the worm and the Rose slips easily into a sexual as well as spiritual one. With the Rose calling its classical symbolic values of innocence, purity, and beauty into the text,[98] the presence of the worm, although markedly unseen ("invisible"), has a deleterious connotation equally in line with its own traditionally corruptive significance: with its "dark secret love" penetrating the Rose's "bed / Of crimson joy,"[99] the worm represents either the ruin of Innocence or a poisoning of the innocent pleasure of sexuality.[100] Consequently, whereas Thel arguably explores "the limits of Innocence" when she "fails to engage with [experiential] constrictions,"[101] the Rose can be read to engage directly, even fundamentally, with these same constrictions in an effort to display the cost—be it physical or spiritual—immediate to living forms: "Does thy life destroy."[102] Add to this the possible reading of "The Sick Rose" *not* through the perspective of its eponymous subject but through that of its antagonistic corollary ("The invisible worm") and the poem's sense shifts from being rooted in decay to flourishing with (re)production. The figure of the worm thus provides in large part for what Fuller argues is the poem's presentation of "a vivid experience of nature's vital forces."[103]

While the worm undermines the vitality of the Rose, the Rose nourishes the life of the worm, making the site of decay in the poem also that of generation—and the worm a symbol of variable development intrinsic to nature's recycling means. Blake alludes to this perspectival exchange in the way he articulates the worm in the text of the poem:

> The invisible worm.
> That flies in the night
> In the howling storm:
>
> Has found out thy bed[104]

Once again Blake asks his reader to attach an anterior reading to his presented text (which is aggravated by the stanza gulf we are made to traverse in this eight-line poem). The worm's imperceptibility coupled with its nocturnal flight, both of which have led already to its having "found" a suitable host, suggests that in fact this worm is a moth—a mature, adult form of a vermiform. Furthermore, because a moth will seek out an appropriate plant within which to deposit its eggs, the ambiguous "worm" here signals at once the end and the beginning of its life cycle. Without the adult form having first laid its eggs in the bud of the Rose, no hungry pupae would then emerge to devour with healthy appetite this conversely sickening flower. Thus, by conflating a juvenile worm with its parent form, and so suggesting in turn that progeny and progenitor exist together as a single creature, Blake not only represents in lyric the (re)generative properties of insects discovered by Bonnet and Trembley, for example,[105] but he also reimagines metamorphosis as an epigenetic simultaneity, a diplopic rendering of the emergent stages in the vermicular life cycle. Moreover, the so-called invisible worm could recall the spontaneous generation debates that resurfaced in the late seventeenth and eighteenth centuries,[106] leaving this organism to evoke as perplexing an origin as it does a definition against its patent vitality and mutability.

While textually the worm acts as a site of compression, reducing into a single mention the varied forms and inferences of the worm, its multitiered depiction on the illuminated plate loosens this interpretive strain. The plate presents visual markers that expand the text and guide the reader through the poem's representations of organic happiness, replete with its attendant irony. Unlike *The Book of Thel,* whose illuminations function most readily like transcriptions of the text, presenting the worm visually, for example, in the same way it is described textually ("like an infant wrapped in the Lillys leaf," an "image of weakness"), the illumination of "The Sick Rose" discards this one-to-one ratio of representation, along with the worm's ameliorative disguise, in favor of utilizing image as an elucidation and amplification of text.[107]

Just as the text of the poem inscribes the worm as "invisible," which in itself serves paradoxically to underscore (and thus manifest) what is supposed to remain unseen, the illumination includes a definitively visible, segmented worm at the bottom middle of the plate (see Figure 4.5). This representative earthworm or possibly magot encircles the waist of a female figure, often understood as the humanized form of the Rose, whose own outstretched arms are reminiscent of both Thel and her guiding Worm—and indicative of terror or supplication, acceptance or even veneration, of the natural cycle in which she is now inescapably implicated. As this figure protudes from the flower's drooping, open blossom, ambiguous as to whether it is exiting from or being drawn into the Rose, perhaps by the worm itself, the presence of the worm exacerbates this ambiguity just as it helps to define how an Innocence in bloom translates into the withering appearance of Experience. By visually entangling the literal and figurative modes of the poem, decay and experience appear to result always from generation and innocence—just as the latter must always paradoxically result from the former. Corroborated by the heterogeneously sexed forms of the worm ("*his* dark secret love") and the woman–Rose, this

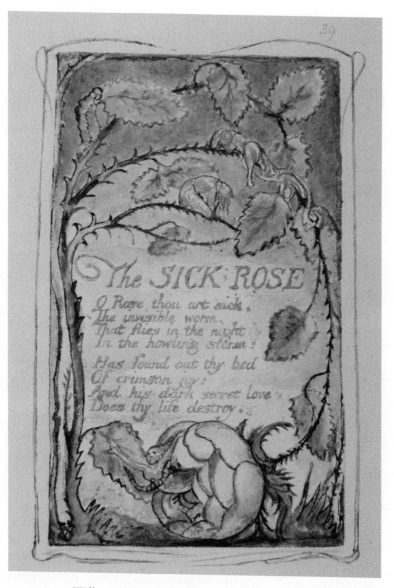

FIGURE 4.5. William Blake, "The Sick Rose," plate 39 in *Songs of Innocence and of Experience*. Reproduced with permission of the Provost and Scholars of King's College, Cambridge.

doubled or doubling representation of the poem's only named characters brings high and low, complex and simple organisms once again into close relation.

Playing with similar conditions to those encountered in both *Thel* and *The Gates of Paradise,* "The Sick Rose" relies as much on the interrelation between text and image as it does on the proportionality of figure to landscape and figure to figure. Like the final plate in *The Gates of Paradise,* the size of the worm in "The Sick Rose" appears equal to that of the human form, thereby emphasizing an allegorical kinship.[108] However, the worm's size is also in appropriate proportion to that of the Rose, which is itself in relative dimension to the pictured plant as a whole. This designates the female figure as a miniature, all but consumed by the comparatively large flora and fauna on the plate, which, by extension, insinuates a similar sense of humility to that later prescribed by (as now just one example among many) Darwin's "sister Worms."

Of course, such humility is only further emphasized by the fact that the heavy blossom of the Rose, within which all of the textual action of the poem conceivably takes place, actively collects the reader's gaze to drop it down to the bottom of the plate. In doing so, the poem as a whole appears physically anchored to its lyrical foundation of decay, with the text literally resting on the crowded, entropic image of the Rose. Meanwhile, the extended figures of worm and woman, suspended between the interior and exterior of the flower, and likewise floating in an intermediary space between air and earth, keep this gaze from sinking wholly into the fetid ground. Instead, these dynamic figures move the eye slightly upward and to the left. The woman's own left-oriented gaze and outstretched arms, paired with the worm's pointed shape, point toward the thick, thorny stem of the rosebush rooted to the bottom left of the plate, only to then reach up and around the same, like a frame. Such an arrangement orchestrates a clockwise motion through which the eye is made to traverse the plate's metamorphic landscape. With the bloom of the Rose as the point of visual as well as lyrical entry into the poem's wormy content, its stem then acts as a conduit between this content's expression of decay and its suggestion of generation and renewal. Moreover, the stem delimits the space—and thus contains the natural objects therein—needed to display such activities.

Following the plant stem up the left side of the plate, the eye is met with three branches, each supporting one image of the three emergent stages of the worm textually condensed into "The invisible worm." The first image is that of a caterpillar or, better perhaps, an inchworm.[109] Set into the uppermost left corner of the plate, with the lower half of its body clinging to a thorny branch, as its upper half reaches up (possibly to chew on a leaf), this particular worm reflects in manner, if not in type, the ground-dwelling earthworm or maggot: it, too, draws generation from the site of decay. But because it sits alone, noticeably positioned atop, rather than within, the thorny frame, the inchworm opposes the ostensibly undetectable and confined nature of the "invisible" earthworm—intimating imminent metamorphosis rather than decomposition. The potential for this organism to change from worm to winged insect directly aligns it with the moth integral to bringing about the action of the poem and so alludes to the poem's cycle as an ephemeral—though fixed—representation of an eternal cycle (again, like the frontispiece to *The Gates of Paradise*). In addition, with the vegetative borders reflecting the restricted perception of purely materialist conceptions of nature, the inchworm implies a way out of this "same dull round"; it consistently transcends the limits of its own referent, but not without exposing the intrinsic unity of contraries as that which keeps the life cycle in infinite repetition.

In addition to this inchworm, the illuminated plate of "The Sick Rose" portrays two supplementary figures to complete the picture of potential metamorphosis: two miniaturized female forms, each placed on her own thorny branch extending across and down the top of the plate. Reflective, on one hand, of the Rose's blighted bud and, on the other, of the worm's causative behavior, these languishing figures bring the reader's gaze full circle. They not only draw the eye back down toward the central Rose; they render decay and generation as a totalized system hinging on the sense of vital infestation from which the plate as a whole suffers.

The lowermost and most defined figure kneels in the middle of the upper half of the plate, on the first main branch extending from the Rose bush's stem. Bent over in a contracted position, facing right with her hair draping down toward the rotten flower, she both mirrors the bud of the large bloom (though less developed and thus more tightly closed) and is reminiscent of the compact energy of a chrysalis.[110] Her bodily position, together with its placement on the plate, indicates an intermediary stage in the life cycle of a vermiform. The second female figure, situated above and to the right of this chrysalis form, can be read, like the body of Thel in plate 6 of *The Book of Thel*, as apparently suspended between two emergent states. Lying prone, with one leg hanging over the branch on which she sits and her head, facing left, still wrapped in the protective covering of her arm, this figure gives the impression of a moth newly emerging from its cocoon. Moreover, by pointing away from the downward pull of the plate, her body's left-facing orientation interrupts the eye's clockwise rotation back toward the sick Rose to evoke an ascendant alternative like that suggested by the feeding inchworm. But this same figure nonetheless continues to project imminent dissolution, with the drapery of her dress unfurled and worming its way down the parent stem of the Rose toward the site of decay. Considering such a division of interpretation, this latter figure endorses the full form of the Rose as an essentially diplopic construction: able simultaneously to point toward generation and decay, while yet suspended to view in its transmutative state.

In the illumination of "The Sick Rose," Blake constructs a kind of barbed *tableau vivant* of the experiential mode. By unpacking and redistributing the unstable material identity of the worm across the landscape of the plate, the worm itself becomes a visual trope capable of representing the point at which decay gives way to generation and generation turns to decay. It is significant, then, that any potential to transcend this system is held always *in potential*, captured finally by a second rose stem rooted just to the left of the one thus far discussed.[111] This additional plant, only intermittently visible within the material confines of the plate, effectively frames the central frame of the poem. Weaving in and out of the physical boundary, it appears first in the lower left corner, then extends part way up the left margin to disappear, until it arcs back in at the upper left corner, only to disappear again, until, finally, a fragment of its thorny branch comes into view in the lower right corner of the plate. As a result of this double framing, the uppermost worm suddenly seems as trapped as its lowermost counterpart, thereby highlighting the imprisoned state of matter against its latent metamorphic capacity. Together, the inchworm and earthworm reveal that to enter into nature's cycle of decay and generation is the curse of organic matter; yet not to enter (as Thel chose) is to deny organicism—and thus to deny, finally, organic existence. Thus can the curse or threat of Experience also be its blessing, proving accordingly that there is always and again promise in putrefaction.

Even a glance at the title page–frontispiece of *The Book of Thel,* in direct comparison with the illuminated plate of "The Sick Rose," brings such diplopic promise into acute visual focus (see Figure 4.6). Centered not on a rose but on the pasqueflower, or *Anemone pulsatilla,* the illuminated title page of *Thel* displays miniature figures similar in behavior and implication to those of the woman–Rose and earthworm–maggot in "The Sick Rose." The willowlike tree rooted in the bottom left of the plate, extending clockwise with entwined vines up and around the relative limits of the plate, echoes the tangle of rose stems framing "The Sick Rose."[112] Add to this the clearly epitaph-like engraving of the poem's title and *The Book of Thel* appears like a tomb, visited by the figure of Thel, who is portrayed with shepherd's staff in hand and a curious, though detached, visage.[113] Because the totality of this image bears a striking resemblance, in both its represented objects and patternistic flow, to the etching of "The Sick Rose" (and, by extension, to the final plate of *The Gates of Paradise*), it likewise imparts a more emphatic trace of the grave—and hence of an aesthetic of decay—onto the vital composition of both works. In *The Book of Thel* and "The Sick Rose," Blake dismantles what Mellor describes as "the benevolently closed world of Innocence—which realizes the fusion of God and man,"[114] to expose nature's material processes as a positively corrupt and segmented reflection of the Eternal. Producing an ouroboric effect in which nature generates and consumes itself, each complementary poem exhibits a world emerging from and collapsing into a decay inclusive of both physical and spiritual registers. The worm is thus reliably positioned as the crucial trope through which such representative bifurcation can be holistically (re)inscribed.

## "Visions of Eternity"

In lieu of a protracted accounting of all the worm sightings in Blake, the preceding study is meant to define a pattern through which the effect of Blake's worm work might be read. In keeping with such an aim, I close this chapter as I opened it, with several additional—though no more exhaustive—passages in which the vermiform appears to illustrate the productive tension between the ephemeral and the eternal:

> Does not the eagle scorn the earth & despise the treasures beneath?
> But the mole knoweth what is there, & the worm shall tell it thee.
> Does not the worm erect a pillar in the mouldering church yard?[115]

> Ask the blind worm the secrets of the grave, and why her spires
> Love to curl round the bones of death![116]

> If Theotormon once would turn his loved eyes upon me;
> How can I be defild when I reflect thy image pure?
> Sweetest the fruit that the worm feeds on.[117]

> When Enitharmon sick,
> Felt a Worm within her womb.
> 4. Yet helpless it lay like a Worm
> In the trembling womb
> To be moulded into existence[118]

> Many sorrows and dismal throes
> Many forms of fish, bird & beast
> Brought forth an Infant form
> Where was a worm before.[119]

Just as both *Visions of the Daughters of Albion* and *The [First] Book of Urizen* (as excerpted here) rely on the worm as a destructive though ultimately regenerative figure, capable of preserving wisdom and populating worlds, the comprehensive *Jerusalem* submits the worm as an unexpected yet suitable palliative for a world suffering its own existence:

FIGURE 4.6. William Blake, *The Book of Thel,* title page, plate 2, Keynes copy H/Bentley copy J. Lowell EC75.B5815.793va, Houghton Library, Harvard University. Reproduced with permission.

Why wilt thou give to her a Body whose life is but a Shade?
Her joy and love, a shade! a shade of sweet repose:
But animated and vegetated, she is a devouring worm:
What shall we do for thee O lovely mild Jerusalem?[120]

. . . but thou shalt be a Non Entity for ever
And if any enter into thee, thou shalt be an Unquenchable Fire
And he shall be a never dying Worm, mutually tormented by
Those that thou tormentest, a Hell & Despair for ever & ever[121]

Encompassed by the frozen Net and by the rooted Tree . . .
I walk in affliction: I am a worm, and no living soul!
A worm going to eternal torment![122]

Let the Human Organs be kept in their perfect Integrity
At will Contracting into Worms, or Expanding into Gods[123]

To read Blake's visionary project filtered through such a persistent trope demands that we revisit the worm for its loathsome, maybe quaint, but definitively conventional significations as a mere agent of corruption. As a fundamentally progressive, potent, even enchanting symbol of organic happiness, the worm should lose what Beer describes as "its horror" to become "emblematic of a whole process by which human beings adorn themselves with the emotions expressed in their human garments (made in some cases by the industry of silkworms) rather than allowing themselves to be eaten alive by the destructive passions that turn into the deathly constrictiveness of winding sheets."[124] It should propel us to follow Oothoon's direction and "Take thy bliss O Man!"[125] It should convince us of our own significant place and purpose, at the same time releasing us into the prophetic visions attendant to it.

This, finally, is what the image of the title page to *Jerusalem* signifies. As a ready diplopia of man and worm, its scripted subtitle reads almost like a palimpsest, with *The Emanation of the Giant Albion* also revealing *The Emanation of the Giant Worm* (see Figure 4.7). As a result of italicized lettering and added gold leaf, the seemingly windswept and diaphanous background coloring, and the close proximity of figure

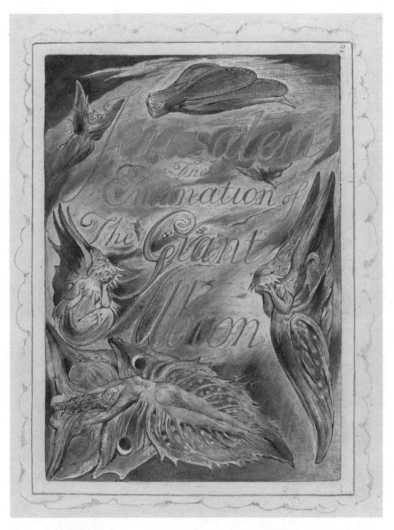

FIGURE 4.7. William Blake, *Jerusalem: The Emanation of the Giant Albion*, title page, copy E. Courtesy of Yale Center for British Art, Yale University.

to letter, "Albion" easily slips into "Worm." The first letter, "A," loses its left slope to the airy folds of both the cloudy sky and the seated, mothlike creature to its left. Out of this dissolution, the right slope of the "A" combines visually with the simple "l" and the stem of the "b," looking now like a capital "W" outlined at its bottom by the lowermost moth figure's expanded wing. From here, the protrusion of the "b" turns into an "o," the "i" into an "r," and the "on" into an exaggerated "m."[126] As such, the Worm appears to cast up its eternal image at the site of what we can only understand as the ephemeral (read decaying) empires for which Albion stands: Man, Britain, Western society. At the same time, however, Albion must also be understood as always coming to be (the "Great Polypus of Generation") against the contracted image of the Worm.[127] Together, both ideal forms, presented through the visual overlap of symbols (words), negate any hierarchy of development in favor of perpetual process.

Clearly as a result of its unequalled length, *Jerusalem* reads visually as well as textually as the most densely vermiculated text in Blake's illuminated canon. From the image of a female form wrapped by a giant worm in the middle of plate 63 to the likewise (though more ambiguously) enmeshed forms of human and worm climbing up the right side of plate 80 to the single, thin, extended worm creating a similar border on plate 82 to the snail, frog, spider, moth, and worm banner set at the bottom of plate 98, not to mention the more ethereal vermiform representations folded into Blake's characteristically "animated and vegetated" motifs, virtually every page contains some kind of wormy illustration. But so, too, do even the shortest of Blake's illuminated works. Blake thus succeeded at illustrating a vile yet recuperative vision by using the worm as a prophetic key. Through his comprehensive mythos, he exposed decay as the matter of generation for both the material world and the Romantic imagination. He proved that "Living Form is Existence" and that "the worm shall tell it thee."[128]

# 5

# A Diet of Worms; or, *Frankenstein* and the Matter of a Vile Romanticism

> I saw how the fine form of man was degraded and wasted; I beheld the corruption of death succeed to the blooming cheek of life; I saw how the worm inherited the wonders of the eye and brain.
>
> —Victor Frankenstein

ON APRIL 15, 2010, the *Boston Globe* reported that "British civil aviation authorities ordered [Iceland's] airspace closed, due to a cloud of ash drifting from [its] erupting Eyjafjallajökull volcano. The volcano ha[d] erupted for the second time in less than a month, melting ice, shooting smoke and steam into the air and forcing hundreds of people to flee rising floodwaters. The volcanic ash ha[d] forced the cancellation of many flights and disrupted air traffic across northern Europe, stranding thousands of passengers."[1] While this recent geological aberration is most often recounted for its widespread negative impacts on human health, habitat, and air travel, the 1815 super-colossal eruption of Mount Tambora almost two hundred years earlier, in Indonesia, has since been granted a more constructive effect—at least in literary circles. Boasting what was then "the largest volcanic eruption in recorded history,"[2] Tambora's nineteenth-century outburst altered the atmosphere and hence the climate of earth's northern hemisphere for at least three years.[3] Much of Europe, eastern Canada, and the northeastern United States suffered cataclysmic effects such as crop failure and livestock fatalities, famine, seasonal temperature inversions, and the death of over seventy-one thousand people. In what came to be known as the

"Year without a Summer," 1816 saw "mid-summer frosts in New York State and June snowfalls in New England and Newfoundland and Labrador."[4] Notably, Geneva, Switzerland, experienced that same year what Mary Shelley described rather plainly as a "wet, ungenial summer";[5] its unusual rainfalls and cooler temperatures effectively kept the famous party of Lord Byron, John Polidori, Percy and Mary Shelley, and Shelley's stepsister Claire Clairmont confined indoors at the Villa Diodati. Such circumstantial confinement has in turn been added to discussions outlining the confluence of forces that led to the realization of Shelley's first published novel, *Frankenstein; or the Modern Prometheus* (1818).[6] Thus what overwhelmingly appears as a catastrophic episode, marked by an acute environmental abnormality, can also be read as the selfsame anomaly responsible in part for one of the most enduring literary creations of the last two centuries.

I open this chapter with what amounts to a kind of ghastly weather report in an effort to illustrate how the work of a Romantic imagination might emerge from and reflect certain incongruencies experienced in the natural world. Moreover, by tracking *Frankenstein*'s inception back through its suggestive stimuli, to include geological and climatological conditions alongside the oft-rehearsed biographical, sociocultural, literary, and scientific inspirations of the text, we as readers continue to increase our understanding of "how [Shelley], then a young girl, came to think of, and to dilate upon, so very hideous an idea"[7] as that of Victor Frankenstein's creation of the creature. It is as if by uncovering the influences on Shelley's imagination, we might likewise disclose those on Victor's[8] and hence gain insight into the machinations of Shelley's fictive productions. We might glimpse how anomaly can at once set off, readjust, and result from organic as well as epistemological and aesthetic patterns.

The singular text of *Frankenstein*, spawning countless variations across an ever-growing field of media, was affectionately described by Shelley as her own "hideous progeny . . . the offspring of happy days"[9] spent in the company of friends and loved ones. And yet the story, as the now twice-pronounced adjective *hideous* suggests, comes to light as the fleshed-out "transcript of the grim terrors of [her] waking dream."[10] The apparent juxtaposition between process and product, between "happy" and "terror," between the context(s) in which the novel was born and the resulting story that the novel presents, parallels in turn the tension between Victor's method of experimentation and its consequences. Like Shelley, Victor authors his own "hideous progeny" and sets it loose on the world (although he distinctly does not, as Shelley does in her novel, "bid [it] go forth and prosper"[11]). The creative act and its resultant object therefore slip from the world of the litterateur into that of the scientist; novel and creature, respectively, beg the question of their own existence. But whereas the former has been largely answered by Shelley's added introduction to the novel in 1831, as well as by its original preface and the extensive research continuously published on the lives and works of both Mary and Percy Shelley (as well as their predecessors and peers), the latter retains a certain mystique with regard to precisely how Victor brought life out of death. In other words, no do-it-yourself manual for making man is included in the novel. In fact, Victor directly counteracts this possibility by remaining "impenetrable" to Walton's questions concerning "the particulars of the creature's formation."[12] Nevertheless, Victor also insists that his "tale conveys in its series the internal evidence of the truth of the events of which it is composed."[13] So why should this evidence not extend in some fashion to the creature's being-in-existence? Why is the discovery of such a technical explanation so important in a novel that announces its desire—moreover, its necessity—to hide it?[14]

The last few decades have enjoyed a surge in scholars interested in recuperating literary criticism through scientific contexts, in general, and a concentration on delineating the type(s) of scientizing found within Shelley's novel, in particular. James Rieger's 1974 declaration that the chemistry of Victor Frankenstein is "switched-on magic, souped-up alchemy, the electrification of Agrippa and Paracelsus"[15] acted as a kind of call to arms for detailing at length what Samuel Vasbinder labeled two years later as the novel's "scientific attitudes."[16] In her 1989 essay "A Feminist Critique of Science,"[17] Mellor went on to claim for *Frankenstein* a twofold view of science:[18]

> [Shelley] distinguishes between that scientific research which attempts to describe accurately the functionings of the physical universe and that which attempts to *control* or *change* the universe

through human intervention. Implicitly she celebrates the former, which she associates most closely with the work of Erasmus Darwin, while she calls attention to the dangers inherent in the latter, found in the work of Humphrey Davy and Luigi Galvani.[19]

Here Mellor underscored what has become, in modern scholarship, the overwhelming attention given to electrochemical, galvanic, or otherwise shocking experiments to explain the existence of the creature. She appropriately opened her study with Erasmus Darwin, delivering a detailed and insightful discussion of the influence his treatises and poems had on *Frankenstein,* finally to connect questions of reproduction with notions of "animal electricity" and animation readily exhibited by the contemporaneous experiments of Davy, Galvani, and others.

Marilyn Butler continued this trend of privileging the chemical sciences in her own updated introduction to the 1818 *Frankenstein* (following Rieger's). In this essay, she devoted a section to "The Shelleys and Radical Science," adding the eighteenth-century surgeon and physiologist William Lawrence (1783–1867) to the litanies of influential scientists constructed by Vasbinder and Mellor. All three scholars likewise constructed their arguments primarily using biographical data culled from the journal entries of Shelley and her husband—both of whose journals contain detailed reading lists across a good number of their entries, making it clear that scientizing was a public and popular activity in the Shelleys' intellectual sphere. Oftentimes, however, a conflation of voices occurs in these critical pieces that confuses (Percy) Shelley with (Mary) Shelley, as if to assume whatever science Percy studied, Mary knew as well.

I say this not to take away from the fact that Percy Shelley contributed greatly to his wife's exposure to the sciences and speculations of her day. Butler and others have written extensively and convincingly on Percy Shelley's fascination with and practice of chemical and electrical experiments as well as his intense industry in reading science—which husband and wife intimately shared.[20] Furthermore, the intellectual as well as professional input of Percy Shelley is undeniable in a novel that admittedly bears his preface;[21] however, I am more interested in the immediacy of what the novel presents than in an unraveling of the voices capable of presenting it.[22]

Consequently, my discussion in this chapter draws out what Mellor suggested Shelley only "implicitly celebrates" in her novel: "scientific research which attempts to describe accurately the functionings of the physical universe." I propose that in fact the novel extends this attempt into a fully realized account of nature's kinetic materiality—and its seemingly transgressive manipulations, both natural and synthetic. To do so, I concentrate my study of *Frankenstein* on a heretofore disregarded, if not discounted, aspect of the novel: its perhaps surprising reliance on worms and worminess to expose and effect anomaly in nature. As the material, literal evocation of what I will demonstrate is the novel's persistent yet variable trope of decay, worm studies act in the novel as the natural historical precedent through which to read finally Victor's creation of the creature. Worms foreground, rather than oppose, electrical intervention, transmuting decay into a kind of regeneration.

The very egregiousness of Victor's ultimate manipulation of dead matter draws the reader's attention to the powerful and disturbing feature of nature's processual existence and to the monstrosity possible within it. What Mellor's and others' presentations of the "scientific research attempt[ing] to *control* or *change* the universe through human intervention" largely neglect to consider, therefore, are the novel's importation of the popular vermicular experiments undertaken by naturalists like Trembley and Bonnet (incidentally, both Genevans, like Victor himself) throughout the eighteenth century. The reportings of these experiments were indeed either read directly by Shelley or reached her through conversations and letters,[23] and so they provide an indispensable context with which to reclaim a comprehensive account of the scientizing present in her literary creation.

Moving from the grand scene of climatological disturbance to the minute oddities of insect study, natural–historical research into Shelley's novel easily spans the whole of nature's schema. But like the transposition of the novel from "hideous progeny" to iconic progenitor, worm studies in particular present an untraced opportunity to revise inquiries into "the creature's formation" from "impenetrable" to comprehensible and to recast our understanding of Shelley's narrative plan as a whole.

Read, like Diderot's *La Rêve de d'Alembert,* as another such imaginative extrapolation of the experiments of Trembley and his contemporaries, *Frankenstein* draws on the worm as a literary figure that not only represents but replicates—at "eight feet in height, and proportionably large"[24]—the origin and progress of life. Similar to Trembley, Victor "discovered" an anomalous creature. Yet in Shelley's novel, this organism is not readily found in nature; rather, it is manufactured from organic bits. However paradoxical, I am not claiming that the creature replicates life itself. Unlike Trembley's polyp, the creature is not regenerated per se; its replication is of a different order: (re)animation. The creature is, overall, a factitious being, one that displays (and betrays) its own constructedness—and thus the constructedness of its being *in existence.*

Through the manner and mode of Victor's bringing his experiment to life, the creature exists as an exaggerated artifice of the role of decomposition in nature's organic cycle. As a result, the creature sticks out, separated—but not severed—from organic cycles so that it can operate beyond the likewise organic metaphor of Trembley's polyp or Bonnet's worms. It explodes taxonomic categories and natural–historical sensibilities, while yet throwing into relief the lasting desire (or anxiety) to classify all forms of animate life. The creature reveals monstrosity to be an inherent characteristic of the natural world; nature is no more static than the creature is normative, yet both fit diplopic patterns of attraction and repulsion.

In "Facing the Ugly: The Case of *Frankenstein,*" Gigante argues that "Shelley extracts the Creature from the crack opened up by the ugly in eighteenth-century aesthetic theory in order to posit him as that aesthetic impossibility: the positive manifestation of ugliness."[25] She identifies the ugly as a category of lack—literally without formal construction or, in the case of Edmund Burke, defined ambiguously as "not beautiful"—out of which the creature might be pulled as a figure of excess, "exceedingly ugly" and "universally offensive."[26] Interestingly, Gigante's argument gestures toward the crucial diplopia that results from the juxtaposition of lack and excess, making what is ostensibly ugly about the creature immediately vile: an aesthetic object uncomfortable yet grounded in its existence, pitiable on the grounds of contempt as well as compassion. This wretched state is, in turn, reflected by the creature's being a material composite of decay and (re)animation (not to mention a double of its own creator). Thus, rather than allow, as Gigante does, that the creature is "that which threatens to consume and disorder" (as a result of its ugliness) the subject positions of Victor Frankenstein and Mary Shelley,[27] the singular figure of the creature must be recognized inversely as that which defines and delimits these subjects through the paradox of double vision intrinsic to its vile, factitious form.

"All critics agree with Victor," writes Maureen McLane, "that the monster is a problem; how to describe the problem is a further problem."[28] In her study of Shelley's novel, McLane moves beyond aesthetic considerations to offer an "anthropological and anthropomorphic" reading that casts the creature as a "literate species" with a history constructed by and through literature. *Frankenstein,* she claims, constructs the humanities into "a remedy for the horrifying body which science has produced"; however, the resultant creature, "neither human nor inanimate," still "persists as a challenge to those who would build communities of affinity."[29] Conscious not to "resolve or categorize the problem of the monster" but rather to situate this creature within the discursive terrain of the human,[30] McLane's study provides an appropriate model for rethinking man against his inventions—organic as well as literary.

My study of the figure of the worm illustrates and widens the problem of taxonomic fluency that Gigante and McLane recognize, in different registers, as constitutive of Shelley's novel. The worm acts as a pointed rhetorical marker with which to elucidate Victor's shifting relationship to his experiment, from material project to aestheticomoral exercise. By tracking the worm's appearances and functions in the text, the reader can, in turn, track how Shelley constructs what I come to identify as the matter of a vile Romanticism.

## Unearthing the Principle of Life

Reminiscent of Erasmus Darwin, who claimed imagination's ability to "improve nature by the exertions of art,"[31] Shelley's protagonist attempts to improve nature by the exertions of science, thereby exposing an empirical methodology for what the imagination invents. Rather than showing a priori the parts making up the whole, as I illustrated in Darwin's *The Temple of Nature, Frankenstein* demonstrates a posteriori the whole according to its parts. In other words, whereas Darwin begins with a totalized notion of the natural world, and works strenuously in his poem to illustrate how such an existing yet ever-expanding organic whole came to be, Victor aims to reconstitute totality itself by fabricating a singular being. The resultant creature thus stands as a perverse example of diplopic paradox, in which dissection and reconstitution are mutually constitutive and decay and generation reveal a defining monstrosity literally built into the natural world.

According to Shelley's 1831 introduction, one of the "various philosophical" conversations between Byron and her husband at Villa Diodati tread on "the nature of the principle of life, and whether there was any probability of its ever being discovered and communicated."[32] As Shelley listened in, both men discussed in specifics "the experiments of Dr. [Erasmus] Darwin . . . who preserved a piece of vermicelli in a glass case, till by some extraordinary means it began to move with voluntary motion."[33] From there, both men turned to grander and more startling speculations such as the reanimation of a corpse or the manufacture of a creature "endued with vital warmth."[34] In like fashion, the preface to the novel opens with the assertion that "the event on which this fiction is founded has been supposed, by Dr. Darwin, and some of the physiological writers of Germany, as not of impossible occurrence."[35] Given Shelley's own admission that she relays here not "what the Doctor really did, or said he did, but, as more to [her] purpose, of what was then spoken of as having been done by him,"[36] the source for her "vermicelli" reference remains a debated topic focused largely on Darwin's *The Temple of Nature* for its answer.

Vasbinder, for example, suggests an aural similarity between *vermicelli* and what Darwin referred to as the *Conferva fontinalis,*[37] a type of freshwater algae often thought to generate spontaneously. King-Hele hears resonance between *vermicelli* and *Temple*'s vorticella whirls, or vorticellae, freshwater organisms known today as ciliates and also once thought to generate spontaneously.[38] Carlos Seligo submits *Vermis tenia,* or the tapeworm, as yet another possible reference point, in consequence of both its aural echo and visual similarity to vermicelli pasta and its abject status as a spontaneously generated parasite.[39] Finally, Nichols proposes that Shelley's "vermicelli" might have come from a "recipe" with which Darwin presents life emerging from a "paste composed of flour and water, which has been suffered to become acescent [sour]," and from which "even organic particles of dead animals may, when exposed to a due degree of warmth and moisture, regain some degree of vitality."[40] Each of these attributions remains possible, bringing to bear such related motifs as, clearly, spontaneous generation, the principle of life, and reanimation—all inculcated into Shelley's conceptual creation of the creature. Oddly, however, none of these proposals emphasizes the simple literal translation of "vermicelli": by thinking small, thinking of "little worms," the contrasts between what Victor intended to accomplish and what he ultimately did, and, by extension, what Shelley set out to produce—a mere ghost story—and the celebrated novel that exists today, dramatically increase. Such a tiny vermicular creature, in all its potential natural historical allusions, therefore sets a specific threshold of scale against which all of the productions in and of the novel can be evaluated.

From the first statement to its corroborated recapitulation, and through whatever quagmire of attribution, the novel openly establishes the surprising habits of reanimation in "little worms" as a defining stimulus for the imaginative vision of its author:

> I saw—with shut eyes, but acute mental vision,—I saw the pale student of unhallowed arts kneeling beside the thing he had put together. I saw the hideous phantasm of a man stretched out, and then, on the working of some powerful engine, show signs of life, and stir with an uneasy, half vital motion.[41]

Shelley's Diderotian-like conjecture of a "supremely frightful" creature of "imperfect animation"[42] easily recalls the published accounts of regeneration in the lower organisms together with those accounts of galvanically initiated motion in individual body parts and whole corpses (human, frog, or otherwise). Consequently, the creature stands as a fantastic extrapolation of not only the eighteenth and early nineteenth centuries' fascination with electrochemical experimentation but with this period's discovery of generation and regeneration in the vermiform. The creature's existence duly "speak[s] to the mysterious fear of our [human] nature"[43] by throwing into stark relief the very hallmark of Victor's trespasses into nature: the damning query, "whence did the principle of life proceed?"[44]

With vermicular experiments acting as a kind of flash point at which Shelley's invention "to mock the stupendous mechanism of the Creator"[45] ignited, the resultant creature begs the question of how man, one of God's creations, gained the power to create life in the first place. Not only can this question be answered in/by the text itself but the realized existence of the creature demands a likewise more tangible source for the "spark of being"[46] than both the oft-cited phenomenal combustion of Davy or the *electricitatis* of Galvani can supply.[47] The passing mention of a "spark of being," as ambiguous as it is contested, cannot fully justify the manifest empirical methodology with which Victor approaches his studies of "the human frame, and indeed any animal endued with life,"[48] nor can it substantiate Shelley's own storytelling means. To assume that the mysterious "spark of being" is that which alone can be read as the principle of life is to mischaracterize Frankenstein as "a petty experimentalist"[49] and Shelley as a mere teller of ghost stories, whose speculative fiction is no more grounded in the materials of nature than her protagonist's.

If we consider that the so-called hideous corpse was "looked upon" by its creator "as the cradle of life,"[50] then the contentious ghost in Shelley's story must shift from the creature itself to what the creature signifies: man's harnessing of the elusive "spark of being." As Janis Caldwell reminds us, "perhaps because the tale is familiar, we often forget how odd it is that *Frankenstein* began as an entry in a ghost-story contest. The monster, after all, is an unlikely candidate for a ghost—constructed by a scientist out of dead body parts into a grossly oversized, undeniably living organism."[51] But it is precisely *because* the novel began as a ghost story that the corporeal creature grows all the more haunting. The "spectre which had haunted [Shelley's] midnight pillow"[52] is not so much "odd" as an impetus for her ghost story as it is misleading. Understood appropriately as the intangible principle of life made flesh, the creature stands as the embodied pioneer of a beguiling and troubling idea. The ghost is no less grounded in natural history than the ghost story it helps to project—and inevitably surpasses.

Following Victor's "bold question" concerning the origin of the principle of life, he confesses that "to examine the causes of life, we must first have recourse to death."[53] According to Alan Rauch, Victor's "fascination with the concept of life is thus wholly dependent on a parasitic devotion to death."[54] But why assume an approach to understanding life's mechanisms according to their apparent inverse? Why invoke the "parasite," a lower organism (plant or animal) that is as dependent on the host as it is repulsive to it, to describe Victor's interactions with life's systems?

Shelley's text provides two explanations, which together supply the necessary foundation from which her protagonist inexorably becomes the "modern Prometheus" of her title. First, it is significant that when beginning his tale of "great and unparalleled misfortunes"[55] to a similarly beset Walton, Victor relates his own coming to be within the context of his father's eventual passing away. Second, the trajectory of Victor's education, beginning in a kind of teleological empiricism and culminating in a fateful combination of ancient and modern systems of knowledge, lends itself to the dissolution motif to which he was heir. Victor's education continues to invent on the pattern set by his father's motivation for creating life, and the product of this education betrays indisputably the decay that brought it to light.

Given that "it was not until the decline of life that [his father, Alphonse Frankenstein] thought of marrying, and bestowing on the state sons who might carry his virtues and his name down to posterity,"[56] Victor appears as an unwitting inheritor of a curious legacy. He is born as a result of his father's thinking on his own pending death. Like the moldering forms of the butterfly and mushroom previously explicated in Darwin's *Temple,* which, over time and by way of natural chemical laws, nourish "the microscopic plant" that will once again engender the life cycle, or the provocative—even parasitic—interplay between rose and worm(s) as discussed in Blake's "The Sick Rose," Victor, as the eldest son and thus "destined successor to" his father's "labours and utility,"[57] is portrayed as the new growth to emerge from his aging progenitor. He was born to continue a cycle at the point of its decay—yet nevertheless meant to preserve the Frankenstein family name and to generate future stock.

As we know all too well, however, Victor proves himself an abject failure in this role. By the end of the novel, not only is Victor's father deceased, but no possibility exists for Victor to continue the family name. Elizabeth, too, is dead—killed by the creature, for whom Victor now lives only to pursue. Although born as if to reproduce, Victor displays only impotence in his would-be role of progenitor. Yet it is his precise place in the family dynamic—caught, as it were, in the idealized Romantic (revolutionary) transition from old to new, inevitable death to anticipated life—that defines not only his existence but his discovery and execution of the principle of life itself.

The sense of decay from which Victor himself was produced defines in turn his pattern of education as well as his eventual method for understanding life and its force of being through the nature of death. Although Victor, alongside Elizabeth and Henry Clerval, was taught Latin and English, "that [he] might read the writings in those languages," his studies were "never forced."[58] And while he "did not read so many books, or learn languages so quickly, as those who [were] disciplined according to the ordinary methods," "what [he did learn] was impressed the more deeply on [his memory]" as a result of what he describes was a teleologic education: "by some means we always had an end placed in view" with which "we were urged to application."[59] Accordingly, when, at thirteen, Victor chanced on the writings of Cornelius Agrippa (incidentally, as a result of "inclement weather [that] obliged [him] to remain a day confined"), he discovered not only his "predilection for" the "genius" of natural philosophy but the desire to accomplish what Agrippa and others urged: "I entered with the greatest diligence into the search of the philosopher's stone and the elixir of life."[60] In addition to what Victor would later learn was the outmoded goal of such diligence, he recounts how "the natural phaenomena that take place every day before our eyes did not escape

[his] examinations."[61] He tells, for example, of a blasted oak tree, "reduced" by lightening "to thin ribbands of wood." He recalls his "delight" and "astonishment" at the storm's destructive force and the ensuing experiments with "a small electrical machine" and "a kite, with a wire and string" attached—both designed by his father to explain "the various effects" of electricity's power in nature.[62]

Taken in by the alchemical works of Cornelius Agrippa, Paracelsus, and Albertus Magnus, as well as a variety of experiments apparently able to capture and manipulate nature, Victor hovered between "exploded" principles of the past and pioneering systems of eighteenth-century natural history-turned-science. Because of what Rauch identifies as the "slow and step-wise process of science, of arranging facts in 'connected classifications' [toward a definitive goal], [being] too mundane" to hold Victor's attention, Victor himself lacked the "social context for his science"[63] that might have prevented the production of his creature. By the time Victor reached seventeen years of age, therefore, chance circumstance and his teleoempiric education joined to manifest the intellectual angle of his macabre birthright.

Akin to his familial position, Victor's natural philosophical perspective was built on ruins. As Professor Krempe would later enlighten him, he "burdened [his] memory with exploded systems, and useless names . . . as musty as they [were] ancient."[64] But as a result of this "scientifical" ignorance, Victor's "dreams" of "raising ghosts or devils" and discovering the "elixir of life" remained "undisturbed by reality."[65] As he states, "I could not entirely throw [the early philosophers] aside, before some other system should occupy their place in my mind."[66] By what amounts to a filtering of old philosophies through new theories, Victor's scientizing largely engages in what I have been discussing throughout this book as vermicular reading.

If, as Shelley states in her 1831 introduction, "every thing must have a beginning . . . and that beginning must be linked to something that went before," then worms (as we shall see) provide the appropriate fulcrum on which "the change from life to death, and death to life"[67] that Victor discovers balances. Vermicular reading, by extension, helps to reveal Victor's scientizing method working in tandem with the narrative structure of *Frankenstein*. Analogous to what Shelley describes are "the Hindoos [who] give the world an elephant to support it, but make the elephant stand upon a tortoise,"[68] Victor supplies his creature with the principle of life, in accordance with the action of worms, but causes this principle to be rooted in decay. The reflection between scientific and literary invention therefore "consists in" what Shelley relates as "the capacity of seizing on the capabilities of a subject, and in the power of moulding and fashioning ideas suggested to it."[69]

Just as Shelley might be said to have reconfigured the vermicelli experiment of eighteenth-century naturalists, giving it renewed life in a new form, Victor seized on the possibilities inherent in the discovery of the principle of life to animate his creature. Victor's apparent methodological reanimation of an exploded system of knowledge is what sets a theoretical precedent for the creature's practical (re)animation: both reveal in their construction that unlikely origin of ruins. In contrast to Krempe, then, who had belittled Victor's pursuit of alchemy, Waldman (the other named professor from Victor's time as a student) insisted on the necessity of using such principles to construct new systems. As Victor recounts, the process of scientific inquiry and experimentation involves rethinking and recasting earlier scientific thought:

> He heard with attention my little narration concerning my [past] studies, and smiled at the names of Cornelius Agrippa, and Paracelsus, but without the contempt that M. Krempe had exhibited. He said, that "these were men to whose indefatigable zeal modern philosophers were indebted for most of the foundations of their knowledge. They had left to us, as an easier task, to give names, and arrange in connected classifications, the facts which they in a great degree had been the instruments of bringing to light. The labours of men of genius, however erroneously directed, scarcely ever fail in ultimately turning to the solid advantage of mankind."[70]

While, as Vasbinder has noted, this paragraph compresses "at least two centuries of learning beginning with Galileo and ending with Davy,"[71] Victor significantly ignores Waldman's targeted caveat of "however erroneously directed" to describe the "labours" of Agrippa and the like—the "men to whose indefatigable zeal modern philosophers were indebted." This selective hearing, as it turns out, is ultimately how Victor is able to interpret his professor's homily as a kind of tacit permission to pursue his own track of study; his youthful desire "to discover the cause of generation and life,"[72] as suggested to him by the alchemists, seems sanctioned by the knowledge afforded him from his modern endeavors into chemistry. "Nearly [his] sole occupation"[73] during the two years he spent at university, chemistry soon led him into increasingly more specialized—and complementary—areas of study, especially once he became "as well acquainted with the theory and practice of natural philosophy as depended on the lessons of any professors at Ingolstadt."[74] "Determined thenceforth to apply [himself] more particularly to those branches of natural philosophy which relate to physiology," to the fault of any broader social context, Victor became closely "acquainted with the science of anatomy."[75]

Although Vasbinder goes on to argue that "a modern scientist would feel that Victor's investigation is rather crude, mixing chemistry with physiology irresponsibly and ignorantly," he rightly acknowledges that at "the time in which these experiments and observations were made the nice distinctions of the twentieth-century sciences" had only begun to form.[76] Thus Victor is not simply a student of natural philosophy;[77] he breaks down this knowledge into the fields of chemistry, physics, anatomy (or, necropsy), physiology, and so on, to become what Waldman calls a "man of science."[78] As I will soon demonstrate, however, these separations occur only to be stitched together, creating a diplopic paradox of disciplinary division and collusion with which Victor will accomplish the construction of his creature.

In the meantime, Victor's focus on the internal workings of living things, tied inextricably to decay, allows for him to observe how "bodies deprived of life . . . had become food for the worm"[79]—as if a *tableau mort.* "In the post-mortem examination," outlines Caldwell, "the interior pathological processes of the body were brought to the surface, exposed to the 'brightness' of the medical gaze. . . . Death permits the pathological anatomist to read the disease process backward in time, granting him the power of seeing and knowing the previously invisible and inviolable."[80] Because such bodies, however, merely lent themselves to static academic observations, frozen at the most corrupt stage in the dynamic of being, they left Victor wanting a more active representation of this corruption. For Victor, "the disease process" he wished to discover and overcome was exactly the death presented by the corpses he studied (and that suffered by his mother). To violate "the ideal bounds" of life and death was his goal.[81] Not satisfied, then, with passive anatomizing, Victor quickly exchanged the sterile performance of the anatomy theater for the rotting operations found in "vaults and charnel houses."[82] Using these gothic settings as his needed "recourse to death," Victor finally "examines the causes of life" by placing himself squarely within the habitat of decay—where he can watch precisely "how the worm inherited the wonders of the eye and brain."[83]

His sentinel-like observations of "the natural decay and corruption of the human body"[84] can in fact be understood as the material inspiration for his ability to (re)animate life. As Vasbinder notes,

> How such an effect [i.e., "bestowing animation upon lifeless matter"] is transmitted there are few hints. We know that its discovery was in "stages" that were "distinct and probable," and that its production had to be effected by means of scientific instruments. We also know that the spark of life must be transferred from a living animal to a dead one. Victor speaks of torturing "the living animal to animate lifeless clay." . . . Whatever the exact method used to impart life to the eight-foot corpse . . . the fact remains that it *is* imparted.[85]

Although Vasbinder, accompanied by Mellor and Butler, and George Levine and U. C. Knoeplmacher (and others), provides valuable information on the presence and use of science that critics like Rieger believed to be absent from Shelley's novel, all neglect to consider the "hints" provided by Victor's indisputable investigations into insects (e.g., worms) as that part of the natural historical record from which Shelley most concretely draws. While indeed no literal formula for (re)animation is articulated in the text, worm work serves as its closest exemplar—able to be witnessed equally within the novel as without it. Perhaps this curious oversight recalls the discomfort of placing man into close proximity with the worm, be it figuratively or literally, implying that any critical investigation into the worm as a vital figure must suffer its own (unconscious?) repulsiveness. But it also underscores the necessity of reading the worm as exactly that flash point at which material empiricism and the Romantic imagination ignite to generate an invention as abhorrent as it is engaging. Thus, once Victor turns his full attention not merely to the bodies that had, by their death, become "food for the worm" but, more important, to the specific actions of the infecting "minutiae of causation,"[86] he suddenly and ecstastically realizes the means with which to achieve his godlike goal.

Just as the external conversation about a naturalist's experimentation with "little worms" was responsible in part for stimulating Shelley's imagination, the worms within the novel are employed as figures for Victor's creative impulse at the same time as they are deployed as organisms empirically sound. Exemplifying "the cause and progress of decay," worms in *Frankenstein* are capable of performing in observable time the "change from life to death, and death to life" similar to that found repeated throughout Darwin's *Temple of Nature*. Telling Walton that he was able to witness "how the worm inherited the wonders of the eye and brain" grants Victor a pivotal twofold wisdom: not only do such "minute aspects of nature"[87] carry out their processes of decomposition and reproduction under his watchful eye, breaking down matter and transforming it into a nutrient-rich material with which to support new life (be it more worms or some other organism altogether), they simultaneously realize the figurative interpretation with which Victor's own "eye and brain" are infected. "Like a sudden light," the tangible image of productive decay presented by the worms to Victor's eye incites an epiphany "so simple" that it surprised him that "[he] alone should be reserved to discover so astonishing a secret."[88]

Not only do the initial references to worms in *Frankenstein* signal the principle of life, they map this principle's beginning in decay—replete with the worm's traditional symbolism of death and destruction imported by the text's gothic sensibility.[89] Worms then represent the simultaneity of an Aristotelian coming to be and passing away of being. They provide decay with the means of renewal. And, by extension, they engender the defining shift in Victor's methodology from observation to experimentation: "I succeeded in discovering the cause of generation and life; *nay, more,* I became myself *capable of bestowing animation upon lifeless matter.*"[90]

Victor's scientific methodology of discovery and Shelley's literary methodology of invention both rest firmly on "the materials . . . afforded."[91] Both indeed suppose that the "tale conveys in its series *internal evidence* of the truth of the events of which it is composed";[92] further, both enact Shelley's claim that one cannot "create out of void."[93] The wormy circumstance that grounds both Victor's and Shelley's work announces the role of animation and reanimation in the novel as a whole. While not discounting galvanism, or electricity, as a possible validation for the "spark of being" with which Victor ultimately animated his creature,[94] worms anchor this so-called life fluid in a firm material base. Given the conspicuous absence of any mention of actual chemical experiments in the vicinity of the creature's fabrication, the reader is left to assume electricity's role through implication and allusion.[95] By contrast, the text transparently reproduces the natural historical record.

By focusing on the worm's role in the decomposition of human bodies, Victor echoes many of the eighteenth century's investigations into insects as well as the natural histories of invertebrates composed by Réaumur and Lamarck. Like these real-life counterparts, Victor sought to unlock the principle of life using a vermiform key. "[Shelley] shows Victor, therefore, engaged in a process of examination of the human body in as minute detail as possible to get an ordered picture of the whole before he will be able to begin the process of creation in reverse order."[96] However, because Victor not only discovers but replicates this process, effectively exhibiting the principle of life as a motile yet unchanging body, he surpasses the empirical exercises of a naturalist in favor of assuming the mantle of God. As is well known, these divine reachings, coupled to his personal history with decay, ironically punctuate the inevitable argument for his own demise.

## An Aesthetic of Decay

It can be said that Victor (re)animated life—as if spontaneously—from the discarded pieces of other bodies (human or otherwise[97]) in much the same way polyps and worms had been witnessed to regenerate, like a plant, from their own cuttings. But by choosing the dissecting room and slaughter-house to furnish him with his materials,[98] Victor essentially picked up where those non-fictional naturalists left off. Whereas Trembley, for example, cut up the polyp in order to observe what nature would do in due course, Victor sutured together the fragments he collected pre-cut from various sources. Rather than passively wait for an engendering, Victor actively dictated the expected process of regeneration—thereby converting it into the diplopic method of (re)animation. Just as his education had prescribed, he "had an end placed in view" toward which all his efforts were bent, which in turn disengaged him from the more fluid, adaptable mode of chance observation or even hypothesis-driven (rather than dictated) experimentation. By infamously displacing the role of nature with that of man, as if to suggest peremptorily that the two are contiguous rather than continuous entities, Victor succeeded in manipulating the natural order not only by reassigning and reformulating the behavior of regeneration through the chain of being but also by determining exactly how and when this operation would occur.

For Victor, however, the challenge in producing a response to his query into the principle of life was not in its discovery and execution but in its application: "Although I possessed the capacity of bestowing animation, yet to prepare a frame for the reception of it, with all its intricacies of fibres, muscles, and veins, still remained a work of inconceivable difficulty and labor."[99] Of course, Victor ultimately succeeded at "giv[ing] life to an animal as complex and wonderful as man"[100]—but what he failed to recognize was the effect that these apparent manipulations would have on himself, his creation, and the world at large. "He thus conceives of life" with what Harriet Hustis labels as the "blatant disregard for its ('filthy,' 'hideous') specifics,"[101] suggesting a conscious denial of aesthetic affect. But Victor's reaction to his own creative act suggests perhaps a more unconscious or insensible neglect, obscured beneath his arduous application of the learned principle of life.

"His limbs were in proportion, and I had selected his features as beautiful. Beautiful!—Great God!"[102] The unmistakable irony recounted by Victor in his first visual confrontation with the creature betrays the significant incongruity between what he strove to create and what actually stood as "the accomplishment of [his] toils."[103] Moreover, it betrays Victor's "inability to see—quite literally—the parts for the whole"[104] by denying the Romantic ideal of organic unity. Rather than simply "renew[ing] life where death had apparently devoted the body to corruption,"[105] his experimentation in regeneration results in a complex being noticeably suspended between the "ideal bounds" of life and death. Underscored by the fact that the creature (re)animates in the very season of decay, "on a dreary night of November,"[106] its existence presents an empirical object that literalizes the ontoepistemological rationale for Victor's begetting from corruption.

Given what we know of as Victor's contrariwise approach to ascertaining the principle of life, so that death suggests life just as decay suggests renewal, it stands to reason that when Victor witnessed the worms' work to decompose a body, he imagined its opposing force: recomposition. And if we follow such reasoning through, the only way for Victor to re-create life after the image of "complex" and "wonderful" man is, in essence, to inhabit the place and behaviors of a more simple and reviled organism: the worm. In other words, he understands that to make an innovative ascension on the chain of being, he must first descend it (as if to recall the metaphysical inversion of Dante, who had first to travel down the body of Satan to rise up from hell through purgatory into paradise).

By "dabbl[ing] among the unhallowed damps of the grave" in an effort to "pursue nature to her hiding places,"[107] Victor was able to turn worm work on its head, filling his "workshop of filthy creation" with the fundamental "instruments of life."[108] As a result, Victor cemented the process of decay to generation and emphasized his inability to throw aside exploded systems, while yet relying on the insights of new ones. Plainly, Victor recast old material with the new, turning the worm into a motif signifying the productive dissolution and reconstitution of both matter and ideas.

With singular concentration, Victor approached his experiment through the diplopia of decay and generation. Inasmuch as this recalls the intense order of his youthful drive for application and his visionary dexterity, it also signals a more common *dis*-order, a learned aesthetic myopia that plagued Victor up to the moment the "dull yellow eye of the creature"[109] opened. Severe and dependent on detection for potential correction, this myopia serves at once to perpetuate and to terminate the diplopia responsible for the creature's existence. It confirms the creature as a (re)animated being, originally alive yet salvaged from/in the corruption of the once-lived, just as it invalidates the anticipated achievement of Victor's experiment. Accordingly, and perhaps in an attempt to itemize the "double existence" of a man both miserable and of "celestial spirit" with which Walton credits him,[110] Victor reassembles his creative process from its most nascent beginnings, injecting retrospectively a subtle aestheticism into his empirical, even stoical education:

> In my education my father had taken the greatest precautions that my mind should be impressed with no supernatural horrors. I do not ever remember having trembled at a tale of superstition, or to have feared the apparition of a spirit. Darkness had no effect upon my fancy; and a church-yard was to me merely the receptacle of bodies deprived of life, which, from being the seat of beauty and strength, had become food for the worm.[111]

Defined by his lack of sensitivity to all that would be cataloged under the label of sublime terror, Victor's aesthetic myopia leaves him open to the unrecognized dangers of his gruesome studies. Although Victor confesses that his empirical approach to discerning the secrets of the principle of life had fixed his attention "upon every object the most insupportable to the delicacy of human feelings,"[112] his actions bespeak a sensibility freed from any ghoulish associations. That he posits "beauty and strength" as analogies for life, yet provides death with only a clinical (or Thel-like) assessment of its turning life into "food for the worm," highlights a kind of Burkean ugliness, which falls short of any strong effect on the passions. Beauty, for Victor, dissolves into a purely material explanation. The only property of any immediate consequence is that of decay itself.

In fact, it is only in hindsight, with the retelling of his tale to Walton, that Victor is able to relay a sense of what Marie Hélène Huet calls the "aesthetic shock"[113] within which he worked and for which his creature inevitably stood. Clearly, then, the creature's coming to consciousness not only reveals Victor's aptitude for animating "lifeless matter" but also rends the veil of his aesthetic ignorance. His resulting aesthetic sense subverts the established categories of the beautiful and the sublime by displaying an aesthetic of decay that consumes his narrative of creating life. Just as he cemented an understanding of life's renewal to its preceding decay in the process of experiment, Victor synchronizes an accompanying aesthetic firmly to the material in the wake of his experiment's arguable success.

But again, because Shelley orchestrates the telling of Victor's tale as a retrospective, it is important to remember that Victor recounts his "expedition of discovery"[114] while dying on a ship confined by arctic ice. It is within this frozen and desolate environment that he is finally able to aestheticize his experiment. The curious shortsightedness he exhibited while working to complete his experiment is thus overridden not simply by any face-to-face confrontation between creator and created but by the very act of retelling the tale from within an unmoving, blank landscape. Furthermore, only when trapped, as it were, between life and death can Victor reflect clearly—beyond his cultured myopia—on his deeds and their consequences. Thus is his dormant aesthetic sensibility awakened at the moment of life's extinguishing, as if to parody the selfsame epiphany that occurred when the creature's life began. On the continuum of death and life, Victor realizes how the product of his imagination outstripped its process.

As the full title of Shelley's novel reveals, Promethean transgression is at issue. Not unlike the Titan Prometheus himself, who stole for man the fire of the gods and thus the light of intellect, Victor procures a forbidden knowledge to construct an ostensibly new species. Made again and again to "dabble in dirt" and "pour over the microscope," Victor's character is introduced into the text through its repetitive striving to "penetrate into the recesses of nature" or to grasp the Titan's secrets of an "invisible world."[115] Thus does he become the "modern Prometheus," trading enigmatic power for the empiric observations and creative theories of man. Consequently, where Prometheus provided for a lower being the ability to act as a higher one, Victor accomplished the reverse: by mimicking the behavior of regeneration in lower organisms, he gave an allegedly higher organism the ability to act in part as one lower, which, in his mind, improved on nature by subverting man's insurmountable mortality. What he, of course, fails to achieve is the characteristic vitality prevalent in those vermiforms he chose as his inspiration. Instead, he ironically makes the creature as impotent as its creator, unable to effectively procreate unaided. The creature exists only as a result of Victor's manipulation of certain cuttings but can conceivably reproduce only through intercourse with a female mate.[116] In this latter sense does the creature reflect rather than outstrip more complex organisms, just as the former sense firmly aligns the creature with those more simple. Victor therefore rescales the chain of being, if only provisionally, to enact a worm's more efficient survival mechanism of regeneration in the image of man—but in one of "gigantic stature."[117]

By producing this new species according to the characteristic ability of a worm, yet without endowing it with the capacity to replicate itself, Victor solidifies its wormy nature at the same time as he works to suppress and surpass it. Cheating death, so to speak, the creature's existence implies a movement up the chain, closer to God, and thus away from any wormy origin and beyond the place of man. Interestingly, Victor nonetheless assumes that this "new species would bless [*him*] as its creator and source,"[118] as if to suggest that he could be the god toward which he himself strives from within his own humanity. Clearly Victor's myopia extends from an aesthetic lure into the relationship between thought, action, and outcome as well as into that between creator and created. He no more understands the correlation of product to process than he recognizes the convoluted irony of his achievement. As diplopic object, the creature is both greater than and lesser than Victor, beyond the constraints of human existence yet held captive by them. The living creature therefore destabilizes the chain of being, conflating its categorical assignations just as it destroys them.

Similarly, the irony inherent in the creature's figure extends beyond the corruption of beauty to frame—or, better yet, freeze-frame—the process of decay as an aesthetic object. The creature personifies man's fear of becoming "food for the worm" by holding to view the process of decay in a suspended state. The therefore monstrous presence of the creature in the text upsets what Darwin laid out as the principle of immutable mutability in *Temple,* needed to realize nature progressing toward perfection (as the ironic intent–telos of organic happiness). The creature stands for change but cannot change himself. The now immutable *im*-mutability of the creature, who "from [his] earliest remembrance had been as [he] then was in height and proportion,"[119] causes a misfire of categorical application. "How dare you," warns the creature, "sport thus with life?"[120]

While Victor picked up where Trembley left off in the cutting up of polyps, it is also important to reemphasize here that whereas Trembley began his experiment with a whole organism and then cut it to bits, Victor started with these bits, so to speak, to (re)construct a whole organism. This manipulation or inversion of the natural order of regeneration had its origin in Victor's interpretation of how to become a "man of science." On Waldman's advice, Victor was drawn to the various disciplines making up natural philosophical study at the close of the eighteenth century, but, as I mentioned, he approached these studies independently, anatomizing knowledge in an effort to construct his own natural philosophy. His approach toward totality, therefore, whether in the form of the creature or his assembling of the knowledge that led him to it, begins with dissection. As a result of his piecemeal approach, no unity can exist within the constructed totality so that "instead of revealing a continuity affiliated with the coherence of the natural world, [the idea of unity] takes us into a discontinuous world of reflective irony and ambiguity."[121] The manufactured nature of Victor's natural philosophy is laid bare, and the "materials . . . afforded" are seen as plainly as the creature—but these materials can neither presage the "catastrophe" of creation nor "delineate the wretch" that remains. "How strange, [the creature] thought, that the same cause should produce such opposite effects!"[122]

As I have shown through the works of naturalists and poets alike in the preceding chapters, an approach to understanding and representing nature hinges on the assessment and application of a natural order. In *Frankenstein,* however, such assessment and application led to a perversion of the same because these practices allowed for man, specifically Victor, "to become greater than his nature [would] allow";[123] he created from and within nature itself a wholly novel organism. A challenge to the natural order, yet nonetheless wrought from it, the now-conscious creature exposes the monstrous proportions familiar to readers of *Frankenstein*:

> His yellow skin scarcely covered the work of muscles and arteries beneath; his hair was of a lustrous black, and flowing; his teeth of a pearly whiteness; but these luxuriances only formed the more horrid contrast with his watery eyes, that seemed almost of the same colour as the dun white sockets in which they were set, his shriveled complexion, and straight black lips.[124]

With the preceding description of the creature clearly identifying the "horrid contrast" between the creature's features, it is hard to imagine the perfection and beauty with which Victor intended his design. Moreover, it is clear that Victor no longer sees this creature as an improvement on the fragility of mankind; rather his reaction of abhorrence in combination with the ghastly epithets he is quick to throw ("wretch," "miserable monster," "demoniacal corpse") betrays an aesthetic contextualization of the creature previously nonexistent. Having "worked hard for nearly two years, for the sole purpose of infusing life into an inanimate body,"[125] Victor finally turns from being a myopic materialist to an empiricist vulnerable—albeit too late (for him and his familiars)—to the vile aesthetic consequence of his extrapolative approach to the natural world.

Unlike Bordeu and l'Espinasse from *La Rêve de d'Alembert,* whose wild inventions of human polyps on Saturn or goat men on Earth resided safely within their intellectual hypothesizing, Victor's hypothesis not only materialized in the "solitary chamber, or rather cell, at the top of the house" he rented in Ingolstadt;[126] it walked out into the world. Because he succeeded in both giving matter to his idea and animating it, Victor was forced to confront the very likeness of the "supernatural horror"—"more horrid from its very resemblance [to himself]"[127]—that he had been taught to view unfeelingly as "food for the worm." In contrast to the speculative imaginings in Diderot's text, which carried no actualized aesthetic weight beyond a fanciful discomfort and pleasure in thinking, this confrontation finally reveals to Victor his vile, or loathsome, act of perversion: "Now that I had finished, the beauty of the dream vanished, and breathless horror and disgust filled my heart."[128]

It is no coincidence that once the apex of Victor's labors was reached, and the creature "breathed hard, and a convulsive motion agitated its limbs,"[129] Victor himself dreamed of what many have argued[130] was the impetus for his so-called improvements on the nature of man: the untimely death of his mother, Caroline Beaufort. Having come to the aid of Elizabeth, who had taken ill with scarlet fever, Victor's mother contracted the fever herself and died just as Elizabeth recovered. Caroline's death thus served as an intimate illustration of the exchange from "life to death and death to life" that would characterize Victor's future observations of the worm. Victor's introspective dream of this episode underscores such an exchange with disturbing effect:

> I thought I saw Elizabeth, in the bloom of health, walking in the streets of Ingolstadt. Delighted and surprised, I embraced her; but as I imprinted the first kiss on her lips, they became livid with the hue of death; her features appeared to change, and I thought that I held the corpse of my dead mother in my arms; a shroud enveloped her form, and I saw the grave-worms crawling in the folds of the flannel.[131]

It is not enough that the images from the preceding dream juxtapose life and death ("the bloom of health" with the "livid hue of death"). The lurid transformation from Elizabeth to Caroline suggests further Victor's culpable role in effecting the very exchange he acquired in sense from the worms since it is after his intervention ("I imprinted the first kiss on her lips") that Elizabeth morphs into his dead mother, who, in turn, gives way to "grave-worms crawling in the folds of the flannel [shroud]." Here Victor's dream reflects the corresponding nightmare of his reality: the dream revisits and replays the creature's putrid beginnings against "the various links that comprise [Victor's] chain of existence"[132]—that is, his mother and his cousin–sister–wife. Such "dream-logic," argues Fred Randel, "supplements the literal narrative,"[133] which in turn makes the creature seem to arise, through the action of worms, from the very corpse of his mother. Just as Victor was literally born from his mother in life, the creature can be figuratively read as a production from the same mother in death—and so becomes the relative doppelgänger of Victor so often described.

While the rapid dream sequence certainly acknowledges Victor's myriad psychic anxieties over, for example, the loss of his mother, the love of Elizabeth, and the existence of the creature,[134] it is more to my purposes that this sequence remains consistent with Victor's practice of inversion. Just as the dead appears to produce living organisms, a dream cements the reality of the creature's existence "turned loose into the world."[135] Breaking through the boundaries of life and death, noumena and phenomena, worms consistently act in the text as the material markers of an intangible principle irrevocably embodied.

But if we consider further that the dream, in its recollection, is sandwiched in the narrative itself between overtly reactionary accounts of, first, the creature's physical description post-animation and, second, the selfsame revealing dream (from which Victor awoke in "horror"), then the insistent materiality mentioned earlier gains an indelible aestheticization from Victor's perspective—an aestheticization that, in turn, haunts the entirety of his retrospective narrative. With the aid of an exemplary dream, the consequence of Victor's trespass into nature is brought into the foreground. Set as catastrophe,[136] the creature inspires disgust and horror to become the text's oft-repeated "loathsome" representation of Victor's success-cum-failure: "A mummy again endued with animation could not be so hideous as that wretch. I had gazed on him while unfinished: he was ugly then; but when those muscles and joints were rendered capable of motion, it became a thing such as even Dante could not have conceived."[137] Thus does the problem persist of "how [to] delineate the wretch."[138] If, by its being "ugly then" (before animation), the creature's characterization "precedes and predetermines"[139] the monstrosity intrinsic to taxonomic challenge, then we would do well to follow Victor's vermicular example: we must realize the creature as an emblem for the anomalies through which prescribed categories are filtered and recast.

Furthermore, when Victor explicitly questions "how to delineate the wretch," he recalls the problem posed by eighteenth-century naturalists: what to do with an organism that apparently refuses classification. For the naturalists, the response was to crowd such entities into identified or identifiable categories—ambiguity notwithstanding. Such crowding, as I demonstrated in chapter 3, however, inevitably undoes or recalibrates the very structure it was meant to uphold. By consistently attempting to manage the unboundedness of nature with the production of categories, naturalists reflexively revealed anomaly to be the common ground of shifting (and continued) definition. For Victor, then, although the physical, animated countenance of the creature dispels his aesthetic myopia, the resultant monstrosity also remains without (or beyond) aesthetic definition. It pairs what McLane defines as the "biological anomaly"[140] of the creature with a likewise anomalous aesthetic sensibility: the creature is uncomfortable to confront, its vile countenance and loathsome acts make it at once shameful and shamed, so that there is literally no frame to fit the creature. Similar to the "muscles and arteries" that appear to leak through "his yellow skin," the creature eludes both material and aesthetic identification. But because the creature maintains a patently "*too* real"[141] challenge to categorical definition, its existence casts a long shadow; it reaches back to redefine the man who created it and transform the signification of the organism that inspired it (Victor and the worm, respectively).

### A Natural History of Culpability

"William is dead!—that sweet child, whose smiles delighted and warmed my heart, who was so gentle, yet so gay! Victor, he is murdered!"[142] In a cruel reversal of the natural order, the youngest of the Frankensteins is the first to die. Just as "[Victor] scavenges from the dead to create life . . . the creature, in retribution, attacks the living to 'create' death."[143] Notably, the commencement of the creature's vengeful deeds reflects the same inversive patterning utilized by Victor to first bring the creature into existence, thereby effecting a kind of transfer of power from maker to made. "About five in the morning," relates Victor's father in a letter, "I discovered my lovely boy, whom the night before I had seen blooming and active in health, stretched on the grass livid and motionless: the print of the murderer's finger was on his neck."[144] Though the immediacy with which Alphonse describes how death replaced the once "blooming . . . health" of his son William repeats in kind Victor's own dream of Elizabeth-turned-Caroline, it does not hold the dream's same wormy promise of renewal finally and paradoxically realized in the ghastly form of the creature. There is instead a significant absence of vitality in the description of William's death; the indelible "print of the murderer's finger" negates the possibility of reanimation in a boy portrayed as "livid and motionless." The print tells of an irreparable rupture[145] in the familial chain of existence and recalls the order of death as Victor had experienced it with the death of his mother. In this way, the death of young William allows for a kind of finality to reenter a narrative that had grown increasingly consumed by cyclical processes. But this such finality has more to do with the irrevocable (read continued) consequences of being than of merely being-in-existence.

Marking a shift in the narrative's focus from the physiology of a life rendered to life's principled responsibilities, William's death is highlighted by a textual transformation of the work of the worm from material composter to moral fertilizer, from its studied role in decomposing bodies to that of recomposing humanity. Victor's diet of worms, his deliberate, regimented, and uncompromising approach to achieve his goal through material means, not only results in the creature per se but reveals the mechanism of acknowledgment for Victor's being accountable for the creature's conduct and thus his own.

For Victor to take responsibility for the vile affects of his "painful labor," to acknowledge that the creature be read as a cutting of Victor, a kind of budding off from the parent organism, even if only announcedly through his recollections to Walton, he must first be manifestly confronted by "the events which [he] had until now sought to forget."[146] As we know all too well, Victor abandoned the creature at the moment of its coming to consciousness: "[The creature] might have spoken, but I did not hear; one hand was stretched out, seemingly to detain me, but I escaped, and rushed down stairs."[147] This ill-fated departure was followed by Victor falling into a "nervous fever," during which he alternated between thinking that the creature might be "alive, and walking about" and reflecting on his "good-fortune" that he had been "freed from [such a] hideous guest."[148] "I threw the door [to my room] forcibly open, as children are accustomed to do when they expect a spectre to stand in waiting for them on the other side."[149] In short, Victor succumbed to the very fears he had been educated against, which left him in a state of mad-seeming elation—"It was not only joy that possessed me; I felt my flesh tingle with excess of sensitiveness, and my pulse beat rapidly"[150]—before he returned to be "the same happy creature who . . . had no sorrow or care."[151] Although Shelley's use of the term *creature* here, in reference to Victor, is perhaps as innocently coincidental as it is suggestive, her representation of Victor's restored health, of his ability to once again appreciate the "delightful sensations" of a "happy, *inanimate* nature,"[152] reads as a calculated antagonism to raise once again the quite *animate* "spectre" of the creature:

> A flash of lightning illuminated the object, and discovered its shape plainly to me; its gigantic stature, and the deformity of its aspect, more hideous than belongs to humanity, instantly informed me that it was the wretch, the filthy demon to whom I had given life. What did he there? Could he be (I shuddered at the conception) the murderer of my brother? No sooner did that idea cross my imagination, than I became convinced of its truth.[153]

In awful proportion to the event "so beautiful, yet terrific" as the lightning storm "echo[ing] from Salêve, the Juras, and the Alps of Savoy,"[154] through which Victor traveled on his way home to Geneva to comfort his grieving family, and within which he was first and fleetingly reintroduced to the "filthy demon to whom [he] had given life" and unleashed onto the world, the creature itself presents a vile aspect that reaches beyond sheer sublimity. He is "gigantic" in "stature" and with a physical "deformity" that cannot help but inform his likewise disfigured morality. The creature repulses, just as he draws in, the gaze of Victor, inspiring disgust and contempt where perhaps there might have been wonder. Unlike a lightning storm, the creature is shocking not for his sudden, even chance and magnificent appearance but for the tragic immediacy with which he reveals what he is *not*. "Nothing in human shape could have destroyed that fair child. *He* was the murderer! I could not doubt it."[155] Saying this, Victor assigns unquestionably "the print of the murderer's finger" to a being that literally appears *without* humanity, lacking a certain compassion or mercy as well as the physical traits necessary to catalog it squarely as a species of man.

That the creature appears in the environs surrounding Geneva of course suggests to Victor something more than mere coincidence with the murder of William, but it remains the association, which Victor is quick to make, between the filthy physiognomy of the creature and the verity and horror of its murderous deed that secures at once the autonomous existence of his experiment and its gruesome reflection of Victor himself, as if the creature were "[his] own vampire, [his] own spirit let loose from the grave, and forced to destroy all that was dear to [him]."[156] By his own admission, therefore, Victor confronts the creature not merely as that familiar doppelgänger but as an aesthetic object capable of transmitting together the attributes of life and death.[157] Just as Victor had learned from the worm how to "bestow animation upon lifeless matter," the creature's existence, appearance, and behavior continue to recall such wormy origins—so much so that Victor adds "vile insect"[158] to the litany of epithets with which he labels the creature, in place (again and again) of giving it a proper name.

Distinct from the previously noted "wretch," "miserable monster," and "demoniacal corpse" (to name a few), the tag "vile insect" reflects Victor's rage and disgust through its implied debasement of the creature. By miniaturizing what is clearly greater than himself,[159] Victor's rhetoric attempts to readjust the chain of being he so irrevocably altered. Paradoxically, by employing such a traditional insult, such as that found in the spiritual and political writings of Edwards and Burke, Victor inadvertently inscribes the creature as part of the selfsame humanity from which he wishes to eject it. Because "vile insect" recalls the creature's ghastly origins, and, by extension, Victor's role in this creature's existence, such name-calling succeeds finally in replacing the mercy seat from which Victor assumed his work with the seat of blame and regret from which Victor must now recount it.

It is not until the unjust death of Justine Moritz, "dignified" servant to the Frankenstein family and accused murderer of William, that Victor acknowledges, finally, "I the cause!"[160] As the body count rises, so, too, do Victor's feelings of associative guilt. In the aftermath of Justine's wrongful hanging, Victor dramatically transfers his accusation of the creature to himself: "*He* was the murderer" now reads "*I, the true murderer.*"[161] Thus does the full weight of culpability take lasting effect, cemented in Victor's narration by the symbolic evidence of his now having "felt the never-dying worm alive in [his] bosom, which allowed of no hope or consolation."[162] Whereas the worm was introduced into Victor's narrative as the material marker with which to (re)animate life from death, the evocation of the worm here signals the semantic shift to an active metaphor of eternal ("never-dying") guilt—as was prefigured by the "grave-worms" appearing in Victor's dream. The worm's presence is now "felt" to be constant and consumptive in its psychological effect, just as it had been observed, examined, and emulated for its mechanical properties.[163] Worms, then, are the very "minutiae of causation"[164] that enact a decisive transition in the narrative's content from material to moral decay.

It is important to highlight that while Victor appears to take responsibility for the creature's transgressive acts following the death of Justine, he keeps this acceptance to himself. For fear of making the "declaration . . . of a madman,"[165] Victor tells no one of his experiment and so can be said to have allowed by negligence the loss of William and by silence that of Justine. Likewise does the worm-as-symbol remain hidden, buried in Victor's "bosom." In contrast to the actual worms that Victor openly witnessed at work on the bodies of the dead, the figurative, invisible worm exemplifies and recalls the blind depravity of character that had been so quickly attached to the façade of the creature. Thus can the worm at once reveal and conceal the vile nature of man.

While Victor's tacit culpability effects a slow turning of the empirical gaze from experiment back to experimenter, which, for example, succeeds in naming Victor the same "wretch"[166] as his creature, this turn is made complete when the object of experiment inhabits the position of subject and becomes capable of defining itself against its creator. According to Barbara Freeman, "the very notion of showing is . . . bound up with, indeed a synonym for, monstrosity" so that "an investigation of monstrosity might demonstrate something about demonstration."[167] Owing to what Freeman outlines as the host of English words that reflect a conjunction of "something huge or enormous" with "a demonstration or proof, something shown or exhibited" (e.g., *monstrable, monstrance, to monstrate*),[168] the protracted confrontation between Victor and the creature is what allows finally for the creature to effect his own experiment, namely, to stand in judgment of Victor and, by extension, humankind.

Not until Victor acknowledges—however mutely—his role in the deaths of William and Justine does the interaction between himself and his creature move from a passive to an active state. Furthermore, as if in recognition of what McLane identifies as an "aesthetic revulsion" that "precludes social interaction,"[169] the creature conspires to kill with the firm purpose of drawing Victor out. In this way, the initial contact that reconnects the created to its creator, being transitory and solely visual, is replaced by the direct communication, even guileless declaration of a second meeting. "Listen to me, Frankenstein," demands the creature. "Hear my tale. . . . On you it rests, whether I quit for ever the neighborhood of man, and lead a harmless life, or become the scourge of your fellow-creatures, and the author of your own speedy ruin."[170] This commanding demonstration of agency, hyperbolizing Thel's own accepted agency in *The Book of Thel,* and revealing the creature's desire for "a harmless life" against his tale of maturing into wretchedness, causes what Gigante recognizes as a shift in "the site of aesthetic experience": "from physiological subject, the 'work of muscles and arteries' that register sensation, to the subject's fleshed-out representation of the object."[171] Because the creature's own narrative forms the center of an ever-expanding (or collapsing) narrative frame,[172] the creature's remonstrance of Victor acts as a pivot point around which the variable conceptual relations between subject and object, the material and the aesthetic, animate and inanimate, life and death, rotate. It acts like a decisive climax, disclosing a diplopic scene in which the creature must not only judge but be judged for the destructive creation of Victor's—and now his (the creature's) own—experiment.

Presaging the frozen and desolate arctic in which Victor finds the voice to confess his trespass into the system of nature, the glacial barrens of Montanvert, near Chamonix, set the scene in which the creature verbalizes what he had learned as a result of his being the living proof of this trespass:

> To be a great and virtuous man appeared the highest honour that can befall a sensitive being; to be base and vicious, as many on record have been, appeared the lowest degradation, a condition more abject than that of the blind mole or harmless worm.[173]

In this striking pronouncement, the creature registers its putative if also contested alignment with lowly life-forms. The "blind mole" and "harmless worm," elevated above the "more abject" nature of man's cruelty, form a revealing parallel with the creature and place Victor's metaphor of guilt into a larger context. Just as the worm performs its rotten work as part of a greater natural system (and so, we must say, does the verminous mole), the creature eventually positions his own acts of murderous vengeance as contingent on the nature of his creator. It shows, as Caldwell notes, that while his "mind arises from his material body, but matter does not in turn accurately express his mind," he has nonetheless been "coerced into a life he [would] regret."[174] The same "harmless" qualifier that the creature attaches to the worm crops up again and again when the creature talks about his own condition of existence, such as his aforementioned declaration that Victor is responsible for whether he (the creature) will "lead a harmless life" or when he again pleads with Victor to "render me harmless."[175] This latest enunciation follows close behind the creature's insistence that Victor create him a mate "of the same species," with "the same defects," so that "one as deformed and horrible as [himself] would not deny herself to [him]"[176]—as if to impose ex post facto an innocence of character and deed through the potential to empathize with as well as gain empathy from another.

The creature recalls how it had inhabited a hovel adjacent to the cottage of the DeLacey family, where it had listened to Felix instruct Safie from Volney's *Ruins of Empires*. From this text in particular, the creature acquired "insight into the manners, governments and religions of the different nations of the earth" and "heard details of vice and bloodshed" that caused it to "turn away with disgust and loathing."[177] In other words, it came to hear of the relative wickedness of man in relation to his propounded integrity, to wonder if man could indeed be "at once so powerful, so virtuous, and magnificent, yet so vicious and base."[178] The creature's repeated expression of man's twofold "condition" not only calls attention to his own struggle to classify the nature of both himself and the "sensitive being[s]" into whose society he had been blindly thrust (and out of which he had been hatefully driven); it secures the analogy of man : worm as the construction through which such diplopic definition can be achieved.

As a sublimated figure of culpability, one who "forces the society to articulate and redefine its understanding of 'human' and 'native'— and the practices proper to humanity—against the anomaly,"[179] the creature, like the "harmless worm" that engendered him and toward which he aspires, reiterates the abject quality against which Victor sinks into baseness. Consequently, as a "product of scientific experiment fueled by Romantic ambition,"[180] the creature outstrips the worm's disinterested existence with prejudiced acts and reflections to unseat man from his supreme position: "Remember, thou hast made me more powerful than thyself."[181] Going on to proclaim that the "increase of knowledge only discovered to me more clearly what a wretched outcast I was,"[182] the creature demonstrates his existence as more than mere figure. He reaches beyond representation to establish himself as a personification of definition, "a filthy mass that moved and talked."[183] Therefore must we recognize the creature as now immune to the more material work of the worm yet highly susceptible to its corruptive metaphor. It literalizes the "harmless worm" by projecting decay as a deferred process on its body at the same time that it discloses a body of evidence to transmute such coveted harmlessness into the immediacy of condemnation. The creature's "repeated attempts to make his 'self' into a rational being," proposes Anjana Sharma, "both create and deny in one stroke his place amidst humanity. Encountering himself as a monster, he sees the 'self' through the eye of the 'other.' His attempt to destroy his creator and every single relationship that [Victor] cherishes is nothing but his final act of self-effacement. He becomes a monster even as he tries to flee from himself."[184] Ultimately, then, the creature projects decay, both in his physical form and in his intellectual development, even as he strives toward generating his own improvement. Able to define man as the very heartless monster he, the creature, is doomed to embody, the creature comes to identify the vile nature of Victor to comprehend his own: "I pitied Frankenstein; my pity amounted to horror: I abhorred myself."[185] Thus can the "harmless worm" be read as the invocation through which to measure culpability and, as a consequence, justify the creature's continued existence as the very worm to gnaw at Victor's conscience.

## Modern Ouroboros; or, the Matter of an End

First William, then Justine, next Clerval. As merely a prelude to the vengeance killing[186] that would result from Victor breaking his promise of a mate to/for the creature, the strangulation of Clerval carries a more significant impact than perhaps the episode initially suggests. Although the creature's murder of Clerval pushes Victor back into a passing nervous fever, only to be followed by the same calamitous negligence of his last one (i.e., after the creature came to life), it first forces him to acknowledge aloud the culpability outlined for him by his creation.[187] Exclaiming, "Have my murderous machinations deprived you also, my dearest Henry, of life? Two I have destroyed; other victims await their destiny; but you, Clerval, my friend, my benefactor—,"[188] Victor exchanges mute metaphor for open confession. He exposes the fact that he himself does not die as others do—from excess of grief or guilt. Instead, Victor is "preserved [in] so miserable and detested a life," free from being "a prey for the worms" and thus reluctantly shielded from "the decay of the tomb."[189] Using these now familiar turns of putrefacted phrase, Victor not only equates his own existence with that of his creation's; he brings the trope of the worm full circle by inscribing the organism's material purpose onto himself. Yet he notably negates its functionality.

Worms appear in this episode as if to mock Victor in life with the "forgetfulness and rest"[190] they promise through their decomposing acts, as called on when Victor eulogizes Clerval. They are invoked by Victor here to have the same lack of effect displayed by the body of the creature. Worrying after the state of Clerval's existence now that his friend has died, Victor asks, "Does it now only exist in my memory? No, it is not thus; your form so divinely wrought, and beaming with beauty, has decayed, but your spirit still visits and consoles your unhappy friend."[191] Reminiscent of the Blakean notion that the spirit is trapped by the senses, and thus entombed in the body, Victor's lament suggests that without decay, the contingent freeing of one's spirit cannot occur. This seeming preservation foreshadows the arctic conditions under which Victor himself eventually dies and highlights the (lack of) wormy conditions that help recast our reading of *Frankenstein* as a Romantic text.

Just as Victor began by looking at bodies that had become "food for the worm" to conduct his experiment into the principle of life, he wishes to partake in this process himself when, "more miserable than man ever was before,"[192] he is faced with widening despair. But because the death of Clerval does not kill him, it is as if he is barred from the very natural order that he so egregiously manipulated and extrapolated into the creature. When he does finally sink beneath the weight of his existence, dying aboard Walton's icebound ship in the arctic, it is not surprising that he remains impracticable as "prey for the worms." Given that the arctic locates Victor, along with Walton and the creature, in "the seat of frost and desolation,"[193] worms and their vitality (insofar as eighteenth-century insect investigations lack any record of them in this region) exist in this environment no more than the decay associated with their presence. The body of Victor is conceivably preserved under these conditions; his body actualizes the deferred decay of his now-eclipsed regretful survival, implying a suspension from the natural order and indeed making him the very creature of his own creation. Moreover, because the remaining narrative wants in both the appearance and actions of worms, making the death of Clerval the last literal iteration of the worm in *Frankenstein,* a proposed respite from corruption emerges—which is also to say that renewal does not necessarily take its place.

In contrast to Victor, both Walton and the creature can be plausibly understood to effect a return to their respective "native wood[s]" at novel's end: Walton turns back to England, and the creature, by planning "to consume to ashes this miserable frame,"[194] exchanges the now ineffective work of the worm for the consuming flames of the pyre. Choosing to break down in total the organic matter from which his body was originally composed, the creature successfully reinserts himself into the natural order from which he had been exiled. So can the creature's death become a discernible stage in what Erasmus Darwin would identify as nature's progress toward perfection, inasmuch as the anomalous creature can be read as a necessary element against which to read organic happiness and determine the slippage of categorical fixity. Such complete decomposition of the creature functions at once to prove the matter of the creature's being-in-existence and to prohibit his "remains" from inspiring "any curious and unhallowed wretch" from repeating the transgression responsible for him.[195] As Huet affirms, "the generation of monsters remains Nature's ultimate secret, never to be shared and impossible to reproduce."[196] The final actions of both Walton and the creature effectively suspend discovery and hence its ruinous potential, echoing a more principled reprieve from corruption than that found at the site of Victor's body.

With the disastrous leanings not only of the creature but also of Walton neatly tied off by the novel's close, and Victor's dissolution put, as it were, on hold, any threat of regeneration in kind appears to be thwarted. Walton, the adventurer, relinquishes his quest; with "hopes blasted by cowardice and indecision, [he] come[s] back ignorant and disappointed," his purpose unfulfilled.[197] No creature is left to promote wretchedness or to reproduce, with Malthusian horror, "a race of devils . . . propagated upon the earth."[198] And Victor leaves neither kin nor protégé. Again, however, Victor does leave behind his body, and it is on this preserved ruin that I submit the whole of the novel finally depends. Like Victor, who has been shown to have built his creature from the decayed remnants of both material bodies and bodies of knowledge, Shelley, in turn, constructed her novel on the static remains of Victor. Like the creature, Victor's body is invented by the narrative. Unlike the creature, Victor's body is positioned in *Frankenstein* as the lasting material reflection of narrative itself. The arctic freeze rejects the perverter, not the perversion, of nature, making the matter on which the narrative depends ultimately read as monstrous as its character.[199]

But Victor is no monster per se. He is not anomalous in the same sense as the creature he created. He is the absolute Other, unable to experience resolution for his trespass into nature and incapable of being reconciled to a text that is itself a "hideous progeny." He remains unchanged and unchanging in his incompatibility, as exemplified by his conflicting deathbed appeals that Walton "undertake [his] unfinished work" and put an end to the life of the creature (that "instrument of mischief"), while yet imploring him to "seek happiness in tranquility, and avoid ambition, even if it be only the apparently innocent one of distinguishing yourself in science and discoveries."[200] Himself the singular figure of destruction and creation,[201] Victor acts as the anchor to stabilize *Frankenstein* as a text, just as the arctic ice pack that immobilizes Walton's ship functions (just long enough) as the internal staging ground for the novel's unfolding tale. Shelley's ultimate imaginative act, therefore, is to leave the process of decay suspended *in the story* for the novel itself to be read *as story*. Whereas an absence of worms toward the end of the novel allows for the action of the novel to end, to terminate (as outlined earlier) without the possibility, as Victor presciently remarked of himself, to "begin life anew,"[202] this absence is also what, paradoxically, secures the novel itself as always already having been retold.[203]

Like the budding of one of Trembley's polyps, *Frankenstein* is a novel made up of a thrice-generated tale, from a single source, of "how dangerous is the acquirement of knowledge."[204] Often compared to Russian nesting dolls, the structure of the novel tracks the action through three autobiographical frames. First the reader is drawn backward through the events of Walton's, then Victor's, then the creature's lives, only to then move forward again to the point of Walton's encapsulating narrative. It is important to remember, therefore, that the outermost frame is of Walton's final letter to his sister Margaret Saville. We, the reader, gain the story of *Frankenstein* as a result of Walton's final refusal to live it.[205] As a testament to Walton's decision (however forced by a mutinous crew), this letter presents the reader with a kind of original out of which three contingent tales are reproduced. Yet the letter itself functions in turn as the selfsame reproduction of what would be the original tales that make up the final narrative. If the letter serves as both original and reproduction simultaneously, then *Frankenstein* displays "a process of literal recreation"[206] that can perform as a totality only as a result of its diplopic narrative.

But in a final complication, the novel closes not on Victor or Walton but on the creature, "lost in darkness and distance."[207] Reversing the decompositional effects of the worm work detailed in previous chapters, and at the start of this one, the concluding dissolution of the creature occludes, rather than stimulates, any further imaginative act. Never created, but always rather re-created, or (re)animated, the creature appropriately dies in a conflagration of the creative act. In doing so, however, he also recasts death as precisely that marker of renewal Victor himself had attempted to reconstruct, making the moment of annihilation also one of self-actualization. At the point of self-sacrifice, the creature manifests what Paul Cantor identifies as the Romantic ideal of autonomy: "total self-determination ultimately requires total self-creation."[208] The creature's intended self-immolation, juxtaposed to Victor's suspended and irresolute state, allows for the creature to relinquish his symbolic role of Victor's failed ambition. The apparent fusion of image and idea that the creature has come to represent finally breaks down,[209] confirming Victor alone to be the matter of invention.

# Conclusion

# "Wherefore All This Wormy Circumstance?"

"IT MAY BE THE CASE that science and poetry are incompatible, that the ascendancy of the former will mean the ultimate extinction of the latter." With this prescriptive evolution, Clark Emery concluded his 1941 article "Scientific Theory in Erasmus Darwin's 'The Botanic Garden'." Although this fatal ascendancy has proven largely unfounded in the seventy years since its expression, the sentiment of how exactly science and poetry relate to one another remains an intensely studied and contested question. While the academy today, for example, recognizes a formal division between the arts and the sciences, we, as individual scholars, should also acknowledge the cross-pollination and ultimate ambiguity of such constructed and frequently isolated and isolating fields so that causal mechanisms might be superseded by heuristic practices. So I have to wonder if, with all the recent and ongoing talk about trans-, inter-, or multidisciplinarity, with what are increasingly becoming known as *multi-X collaborations,* we aren't attempting to repair what Nichols has defined as the "postromantic phenomenon" of a "radical split between 'science' and 'art'" through an ironic return to a kind of "romantic ecology."[1]

As many conservationists, deep ecologists, posthumanists, and radical homemakers (to name a few) might agree, "man has lost / His desolating privilege, and stands / An equal amidst equals."[2] No longer can we set ourselves "apart from all other phenomena of the material world, to claim special status, and to exercise control through knowledge."[3] But this doesn't mean we don't try, adverse effects notwithstanding. Nor does this mean we should cease to investigate the implications of (re)discovering unity, exultant harmony even, in the face of fragmentation and under the portent of disintegration.

With Abraham Trembley's discovery of and experiments with the freshwater polyp in the 1740s, this virtually microscopic, regenerative organism fueled already smoldering contests of ontotaxonomic delineations. It not only disrupted eighteenth-century ideas on the supposed boundaries separating plant from animal, animate from inanimate, life from nonlife; it showcased a query into the principle of life consistent with naturalist studies from Aristotle to Linnaeus (and on to the present day). Fantastically speculative yet empirically sound texts such as *La Rêve de d'Alembert* and *Frankenstein* attest to the force with which the simple posing of such a query captured (and even scandalized) the materialist conceptions of Enlightenment thinkers forward. The focus on the minutiae of life tended to have what Dawson recognizes as "unsettling metaphysical implications . . . [such that] the superiority of man as the object in creation to which all other animals were subordinate was called into question."[4] It also presents further evidence of how the trends of what we have delineated as Enlightenment or Romantic were missed well before the era we now call "Romanticism"—and carry far beyond it—so that the taxonomic challenge equally posed by several types of vermiform call into view a larger set of disputable boundaries.

With what I defined as the diplopic paradox of man's approach to or approximation of his own vitalizing milieu, Erasmus Darwin constructed an holistic representation of the natural world by laying to view its interconnected parts. He adhered to an irony of individuation to capture nature as an epistemic totality. In consequence, he effectively circumlocuted the presentation of any actualized principle of life in favor of performing an infinite recession of origin through spontaneously generated means. In like fashion, the illuminated poems of William Blake elided any point of origin for life's unfolding in favor of representing the processes resulting *from* mortal existence. Such poems defined and displayed progress in the natural world via cyclic causality. With both *The Book of Thel* and "The Sick Rose" portraying a mutability in nature through the paradox of still life, the latter poem suspends animation between the seat of putrefaction and the hope of rebirth, while the former presents a natural process interrupted when the poem's mythic protagonist ironically denies her mortal existence by adopting vermicular behaviors. As a contributing factor to the displacement of clear taxonomic and aesthetic fixities, the changeling worm fructifies a romantic ecological rendering of man's natural vision to coincide with this vision's a priori loss of innocence.

In *Frankenstein*, Mary Shelley reimagines the processes of decay and generation to inform her text at the level of narrative and to execute the experiment of (re)animation represented within it. She reconfigures the supposed vermicelli experiment of "Dr. Darwin" into an avatar of man from which Victor is made to reassess his own place in a perceived hierarchy of beings. The diffused relationship of creator and created breaks down at the moment of its installation, revealing a shifting ground of definition that further emphasizes the taxonomic instability suggested by the worm work in the text. I am thinking here of Robert Richard's *The Romantic Conception of Life*, in which he thinks through Romanticism in terms of a paradox of the self—that of *natura naturans* (the creator) and *natura naturata* (the created) and the quest for unification: "Human beings had to face the fragmented and contending elements of life, yet as progressive creatures, they continue to strive toward the ideal of unity, perhaps never achieving it. Yet the goal of unity lay before them."[5] Read as another type of impossible ideal like that of completing the Catalogue of Nature, this "goal of unity" is demonstrably undermined by the factitious body of the creature. Such a body discloses natural vision as an artifice invented by Romantic narrative.

From Trembley's polyp to Shelley's creature, natural historical and literary landscapes of the eighteenth and early nineteenth centuries register a synthetic sensibility, filtered through the figure of the worm, that can accommodate apparently vile anomalies to make empirical and imaginative modes for representing the natural world also those that (re)invent it. The vermicular trappings found in the texts under scrutiny in this book help to raise questions of category stability and to suggest a new aesthetic imaginary that operates as an exemplary model of the inescapable processes of decay and generation.

## A New Romance

To promote this model's application to a-recasting of Romanticism, I close this study with a brief look at John Keats's *Isabella; or, the Pot of Basil* (1818/1820) and Charles Darwin's *The Formation of Vegetable Mould, through the Action of Worms, with Observations on Their Habits* (1881). Although asking directly, "Wherefore all this wormy circumstance?"[6] Keats's poem does not present actual worms. As a purely figurative device with which to identify the conditions of decay and dissolution that structure the poem (itself a recycled story "from Boccaccio," "Wherein is plainly proved, That Love cannot be rooted up"[7]), the poem's pivotal question marks not a protest against its grotesquery but an endorsement of worm work as *the* defining trait of a new kind of romance built on and out of the ruins of the old.

Rather than rely on any direct presentation of zoological material, *Isabella* posits its new aesthetic sensibility by assuming only a wormy affect.[8] The insistent figure of the vermiform as seen in the writings and illuminations of Blake, and on which both Trembley and Victor grounded their momentous experiments, disappears, but a sense or feeling of its at once decompositional and compositional work does not (like that constantly rehearsed in *The Temple of Nature*). In a poem whose central image is that of a beautiful girl (Isabella) reduced to loving the putrefying yet fertile head of her murdered lover (Lorenzo), "wormy circumstance" ironically calls attention to what Erasmus Darwin would define as the pleasure, or organic happiness, intrinsic to "animate creation."[9] Keats would define this as Love.

Exactly when Keats inserts what has become the hallmark query of my own project, Isabella is digging out the untimely, terrestrial tomb of Lorenzo. Murdered by Isabella's brothers, as a result of his being "the servant of their trade designs" and thus not "some high noble" to which they had planned to wed their sister, Lorenzo had been left to rot in the forest with only "a large flint-stone" to mark his crude grave.[10] By juxtaposing the perpetrators of the homicide to their victim, any venerable nobility in the poem takes on the sordid quality of worm food (the "form that *hungry* Death hath marr'd"[11]), and the rotten servant assumes a respectable character. "Wormy circumstance" in this way helps to structure a chiasmus of unfixed interpretive significance to mirror the poem's familiar shifts in tone and its notable variety of vegetated forms.

In tandem with the site/sight of Lorenzo's rancid body ("the horrid thing")—though unearthed and decapitated by Isabella ("With duller steel than the Perséan sword"), it presented "no formless monster's head, / But one, whose gentleness did well accord / With death, as life"[12]—is set a scene of plant life in varying stages of reproduction and generation. Not only do beech and chestnut trees "shed / Their leaves and prickly nuts" over Lorenzo's grave site, but a heather grows over it, existing as a kind of proxy for Lorenzo himself: "my heather-bloom."[13] Such serenely lush imagery corroborates the aura of consuming "gentleness" accompanying Lorenzo in death with the mild pastels of trees and bushes having come into flower. In fact, it is on the emergent heather plant, rather than on the corpse lying beneath it, that the spirit of Lorenzo asks Isabella to "shed one tear" of comfort.[14] Because the body of Lorenzo is (being) absorbed into the surrounding organic elements (so that any "accord" of "gentleness" alludes also to a kind of soft physical decay); because it is watered by the tears of Isabella (who has herself, in her bereavement, "By gradual decay from beauty fell"[15]); and because this body has grown to be the food of worms that Thel rejected and Victor manipulated, Lorenzo is repurposed from animal to plant without disrupting his position as lover. This vital repurposing presages in turn the ensuing placement of Lorenzo's head into "A garden-pot" of "Sweet basil,"[16] as if to contain and domesticate a moldering memory in (with) the face of its wild dispersion.

Like Thel, who was stripped of her passivity when confronted by the lowly worm, Isabella exchanges her demure manner for a bold commitment. She not only "dig[s] more fervently" to expose the corpse of her lover but she actively "cut[s] away" his likely worm-eaten head.[17] The matter of Lorenzo's instability, coupled with the constancy of love, thus urges the cultivating act with which Isabella mourns her loss:

And so she fed it with thin tears,
   Whence thick, and green, and beautiful it grew,
So that it smelt more balmy than its peers
   Of basil-tufts in Florence; for it drew
Nurture besides, and life, from human fears,
   From the fast mouldering head there shut from view:
So that the jewel, safely casketed,
Came forth, and in perfumed leafits spread.[18]

Just as decay consumes this portion of the poem, with its images betraying the effects of an organic wasting away, so, too, does an idea of growth and renewal infuse such putridity. The "sweet stench of rotting decay" doubles what Stacey McDowell highlights as the basil's own "balmy" sweetness; this in turn reflects what emerges as the "tension between 'modern rhyme' and 'old romance'" on which Keats grounds his poem.[19] Likewise, when Isabella first arrived at Lorenzo's grave, it was "Upon this murderous spot she seem'd to grow."[20] Her tears nourished the "casketed" head of Lorenzo—itself "vile with green and livid spot"—into the "thick, and green, and beautiful" basil plant bearing "perfumed leafits."[21] In doing so, pleasure and beauty appear to emerge out of what is most "vile" in nature. Such unpleasantness is exactly the substance on which the entangled registers of material processing and aesthetic expression can be read.

The cycle of decay and generation, as well as its associated aesthetic imaginary, hangs on the poem's profuse and diplopic treatment of the word *green,* for example, "loiter'd in a *green* churchyard"; "Whence thick, and *green,* and beautiful it grew"; "Why she sat drooping by the Basil *green*"; "The thing was vile with *green* and livid spot."[22] By alluding to both unsettling death and unyielding birth, an aged, disintegrating, perhaps blighted existence set to a young, immature, green life, *green* marks a shared and permeable barrier between the two lovers. Blindly crossing the divide between animal and plant, life and death, beauty and repulsion, Isabella's and Lorenzo's love proves as fecund as the thriving, though confined, basil plant—and as pitiable. All such "wormy circumstance" thus exposes a familiar scene of Love in its most loathsome yet sympathetic of presentations. It produces the vile countenance of romance—with its "leafits spread" from the "fast mouldering head . . . shut from view."

Active decomposition subverts aesthetic expectation in Keats's poem; it foregrounds not the beauty of romance per se but what I have been arguing is an aesthetic sensibility of decay underwritten by the worm work of the period. By posing the conditions of romance as a literal question ("Wherefore all this wormy circumstance?"), followed immediately by the leading question "Why linger at the yawning tomb so long?"[23] the poem calls attention to its aesthetic project to reimagine the "gentleness of old Romance," or "the simple plaining of a minstrel's song," with "that vision pale" of a vile yet thriving Romanticism.[24] Decay, the mutability of matter, therefore emerges in *Isabella* as an engendering trope for the piteous representation of Love's immutability.

The text of *Isabella,* as a narrative body at once doubled by the body of Lorenzo and doubling the tale of Boccaccio, relies on a culture of worms to disseminate, on one hand, what McDowell proposes is "an art that is two removes from the organic model: art imitating art as opposed to art imitating nature."[25] On the other hand, the worminess of Keats's poem reveals an essential diplopia of art *and* nature. With the beauty and delicacy of the natural world reconfigured to reveal a darker, moldering side of Love's secret(ed) domain, *Isabella* deploys worminess as a mechanism for recasting "old Romance," "the old tale" for which the poem might be read as a tributary lament, through its surfacing palimpsestic replacement: "O turn thee to the very tale, / And taste the music of that vision pale."[26] By proclaiming the "minstrel's song" to be an inadequate vehicle with which to characterize the type of Love—whether organic or aesthetic—that remains mutable in its immutability, able to transgress form to preserve its content, Keats's poem suggests the utility in exhibiting nature's most base processes to realize the radiant complexity of Romanticism's experiment in representation.

## "These Lowly Organized Creatures"

It should come as no surprise that when introducing her chapter on "analogy, metaphor, and narrative" in *Darwin's Plots,* Gillian Beer equates the worldview of Charles Darwin to that of John Keats: both rejected the idea that "one 'must begin with an Idea of the world, in order not to be prevailed over by the world's multifariousness.'"[27] To this end, Beer remarks that "Darwin's copious imagination constantly tried out and extended possibilities, drawing upon the richness of the perceptual world," until his theory emphasized "variation and change," accepted "the *shifting* energies of congruities," and used the "multifariousness of the world . . . as both material and idea."[28] Thus it is not so far a stretch to propose, as I believe Beer would agree, that Darwin approached *On the Origin of Species* in much the same way that Keats and many of his Romantic counterparts looked to "all of animated nature" like "organic Harps diversely fram'd"[29]: stimulated and stimulating in lasting variety.

Twenty-two years after Darwin published *Origin,* he wrote what has become known, in refreshing shorthand, as his "earthworm treatise," or *The Formation of Vegetable Mould, through the Action of Worms, with Observations on Their Habits.* It was to be Darwin's last and perhaps most undervalued work, just as *The Temple of Nature* was for his grandfather. That these two English naturalists looked, in their golden years (eighty years apart), to life's minutiae—be it a single filament, a kindred worm, or the beneficial action of many worms—as what we might call the *moved* movers of terrestrial existence, deserves some pause. Charles Darwin, as if in mature confirmation of what the elder Darwin and the poet Keats (as just two in a plethora of eighteenth- and nineteenth-century thinkers) introduced in their own fully developed ruminations, firmly plants the worm as an essential organism and fundamental symbol. It is demonstrative of a vital mutability emblematic of the relative association of all life and indicative of decomposition as cultivation and preservation.

Most often discussed for its contribution to farming and gardening, Charles Darwin's earthworm treatise is as timely today (if not entirely accurate) as it was unfortunately overlooked when it first appeared in 1881. Owing in large part to industrialization and the nineteenth century's agricultural focus on "the chemistry of soil water, i.e. [on] a single factor of a vast biological complex," Darwin's name was largely absent from any pertinent lectures of that period—neglected in favor of pushing "the virtues of artificial manures for increasing crops and of the efficacy of poison sprays for controlling plant diseases."[30] If this sounds like a preamble for Rachel Carson's veil-rending *Silent Spring*, it should. If this reads like a rally cry for modern organic farming initiatives, and, by extension, for today's Sisyphean environmental movement, you've got it. Darwin's earthworm treatise might well be read alongside such contemporary iconic texts as Thoreau's *Walden* and Aldo Leopold's *A Sand County Almanac*. It advocates for a kind of land ethic that treats what Aristotle called "the intestines of the earth" as some of the most influential organisms in/for the world.

Worms, according to Charles Darwin, "prepare the ground in an excellent manner for the growth of fibrous-rooted plants and for seedlings of all kinds. They periodically expose the mould to the air, and sift it so that no stones larger than the particles which they can swallow are left in it. They mingle the whole intimately together, like a gardener who prepares fine soil for his choicest plants."[31] Given the evident grace and utility of such organisms, is it finally so strange to think that such excellent preparation might extend metaphorically to the writings of those in which worms or worminess readily appear? That, for Darwin and others, worms are as crucial to studies in physiology, geology, botany, and agriculture as they are to myth, prophetic vision, and the creation of poetry and prose?[32] In all the works discussed in this book, worms indeed "prepare[d] the ground" from which my readings grew. In fact, such worm work has convinced me that any deconstructive or poststructuralist analysis might indeed be understood more fully as vermicular reading, a "sift[ing]" or breaking down of meaningful "particles" of thought only to be "mingle[d] . . . intimately together" to form a rich humus of ideas—at once unstable and stabilizing. No longer should we take for granted the action of worms, in life or in literature.

"It may be doubted," claims Darwin in the closing lines of his earthworm treatise, "whether there are many other animals which have played so important a part in the history of the world, as have these lowly organized creatures."[33] That Darwin values "these lowly organized creatures" is clear. The double entendre contained in the preceding description, however, also speaks to the intrigue and admiration with which he approached a study of what one critic denied as their "stupendous" contribution. Darwin embraces the worms for their astonishing character: of a simple physiology ("low[er] organiz[ation]") capable of executing complex, largely ignored, yet highly effective—essential—methodical work ("organized creatures"). But as he also recounts, this was not a collective view: "In the year 1869, Mr. Fish rejected my conclusion with respect to the part which worms have played in the formation of vegetable mould, merely on account of their assumed incapacity to do so much work. He remarks that 'considering their weakness and their size, the work they are represented to have accomplished is stupendous.'"[34] Although specifically targeted to what Darwin himself stubbornly put forward as the subject of his 1881 treatise, that is, "the share which worms have taken in the formation of the layer of vegetable mould, which covers the whole surface of the land in every moderately humid country," Mr. Fish's earlier rejection exposes the prejudice and biases against which Darwin and others of his era had to work—from the cases of geology and evolutionary theory forward.[35] It also underscores a seemingly knee-jerk response of incredulity, which is perhaps fed by the discomforting realization that man might be both indebted to and threatened by an organism that, as Blake observed, "shall remove the mountains."

Such a sober realization, coupled with the derision and scandal with which both Darwin's evolutionary theory and his sponsorship of the earthworm were met, led to the production of one of the more famous and recognizable caricatures from *Punch's Almanack*. In 1882 *Punch* released a cartoon titled "MAN IS BVT A WORM," shortly after publication of the earthworm treatise and just prior to Darwin's death in that same year. The cartoon displayed in spiraling fashion a kind of evolutionary transformation from common earthworm through primate and English dandy to arrive at a central caricature of Darwin looking unmistakably (and tiredly) like Father Time (see Figure 6.1). With "Time's Meter" clearly inscribed along the bottom of the ring helping to focus this image, and four visible clock faces inside the ring (three of which murkily register time in "units" from "[tho]usands of centuries" to "millions"), we are given to see in a single drawing the principle of evolution as Darwin himself expressed it: as the sum of "effects of a continually recurrent cause."[36] Thus are we confronted

FIGURE 6.1. *Man is but a worm. Punch's Almanack* for 1882. Reproduced with permission of Punch Ltd., http://www.punch.co.uk/.

with a segmented worm transforming into a primate, as the eye moves right and up around the outside of the ring, and a primate into a man, as the eye moves inward, to prove visually that "man is but a worm."

But we also cannot ignore the singular worm, at the bottom middle of the image, pointed in a direction opposite to that of its, shall we say, brother worms. This particular worm, with its tail end paralleling the tail of another worm, has its front end stuck through the middle of a rocky letter "A." Its body is thus set firmly in, as well as on, what looks to be a terrain of various rocks and gravels. It appears to be behaving as a worm should, "prepar[ing] the ground in excellent manner" by breaking down a "CHAOS" of matter into its more manageable and fertile bits. As a worm enters disorder, then, order emerges—an order readily reflected in the evolutionary performance that consumes the image (however satirically rendered).

The order that worms ultimately brought to the works of naturalists, philosophers, poets, and novelists who took up the vermiform as both an animal to be studied and a trope to be developed, filtered, as it was, through an abiding chaos of taxonomic and aesthetic implications, reveals the relationship between man and worm to be indeed "something far more deeply interfused" than mere evolutionary birthright. Just as we will become fodder for the worm, so should the worm be recognized as fodder: for us, worms are simply good to think with (Figure 6.2).

CHARLES ROBERT DARWIN, LL.D., F.R.S.

IN HIS *DESCENT OF MAN* HE BROUGHT HIS OWN SPECIES DOWN AS
LOW AS POSSIBLE—*I.E.*, TO " A HAIRY QUADRUPED FURNISHED
WITH A TAIL AND POINTED EARS, AND PROBABLY *ARBOREAL*
IN ITS HABITS "—WHICH IS A REASON FOR THE VERY GENERAL
INTEREST IN A " FAMILY TREE." HE HAS LATELY BEEN
TURNING HIS ATTENTION TO THE " POLITIC WORM."

FIGURE 6.2. *Charles Robert Darwin, L.L.D., F.R.S.* Punch's fancy portraits—No. 54, 1881. "In his *Descent of Man* he brought his own Species
down as low as possible—*i.e.,* to 'A Hairy Quadruped furnished with
a Tail and Pointed Ears, and probably *Arboreal* in its habits'—which is
a reason for the very general Interest in a 'Family Tree.' He has lately
been turning his attention to the 'Politic Worm.'" Reproduced with
permission of Punch Ltd., http://www.punch.co.uk/.

# Notes

## Introduction

1   "Human-like Brain Found in Worm," DiscoveryNews, http://news.
discovery.com/animals/worm-human-brain.html. For the original study
of which the former is a popular summary, see Tomer et al., "Profiling
by Image Registration."

2   "Human-like Brain Found in Worm."

3   See, e.g., book XIX, v. 30–40, in *The Iliad* and Aristotle, *On Generation
and Corruption, The History of Animals,* and *On the Generation of Animals,*
in *Basic Works*. For a discussion of worms and their effect on Western
ideas concerning the nature of life, beginning with the invention of the
modern microscope in the seventeenth century, see chapter 1 of this
book. For additional recent examples of how worm studies continue to
call into question the primacy of the human, particularly with regard
to new discoveries not only of worm species but of worm genera, see
Rouse et al., "*Osedax,*" and Osborn et al., "Deep-Sea Swimming Worms."

4   See, e.g., Bearzi and Stanford, *Beautiful Minds*; Dudzinksi and Frohoff,
*Dolphin Mysteries*; Wynne, *Do Animals Think?*

5   It cannot help but be mentioned that the worm's lowly—unassuming
yet base—characteristics found great acclaim in the fictional character
of "Lowly Worm," created by Richard Scarry. Recurring in a multitude
of Scarry's children's books, animated series, and video games since
1963, Lowly is an anthropomorphic earthworm dressed in a hat, tube
shirt, and trousers, and one shoe, and he drives an apple-shaped car.
In effect, he epitomizes the man–worm approximation through the
innocence of a child's imagination. And yet, though Lowly is certainly
an endearing character, able to efface any sense of aversion found in a
creature who bores through an otherwise tasty apple and excretes slimy

fluids, he cannot escape the insult of his namesake—however playful. Tom Bierbaum, of *Variety* magazine, says it best with this review of *The Busy World of Richard Scarry*: "Lowly Worm is the real star of the series, with his goofily deprecating name and natty ensemble." It also bears mention here that Lowly Worm, while perhaps the most profuse and lovable vermiform, is not alone. Jim Henson's 1986 film *Labyrinth*, for example, includes a cameo appearance by a tiny male Cockney worm, adorned with a red sweater, blue hairy tufts, and red eyes. One of several puppet creatures to gain a cult following in the film, this nameless worm appears as an amiable denizen of the labyrinth, inviting in the female protagonist, Sarah (played by Jennifer Connelly), for "a nice cup of tea." But he also serves to point out that Sarah "ain't lookin' right" as she tries to find her way through the labyrinth. "Things are not always what they seem in this place," he says. "You can't take anything for granted." The Cockney worm might be a precious character, but he nonetheless foreshadows all the trickery and illusions working to impede Sarah's quest. In Henson's film, therefore, the worm harbors a certain wisdom and vigilance against which the ignorance and impetuousness of the human appears amplified. Last, I thought I'd mention "Earthworm Jim" as just one more example in a long list of how the worm has wormed its way into popular culture. An earthworm that mutated into a "large and intelligent (at least by earthworm standards) superhero," and equipped with a robot suit, Earthworm Jim can be found fighting evil in a "run and gun platform video game" developed by Shiny Entertainment in 1994. Since then, the game Earthworm Jim has enjoyed successful and unsuccessful sequels, the eponymous character has made cameo appearances in subsequent video games, and there were once plans to make an animated film. I find it increasingly intriguing that this particular character proves a continued and attractive persona seventeen years after its creation, forcing man to play the role of a worm to save the galaxy!

6    This particular sense of the worm in *Paradise Lost* occurs in book IX, v. 1068. Prior to this, during the narration of the creation of the world by the archangel Gabriel to Adam, Milton introduces the worm in its multiplicitous significations: "At once came forth whatever creeps the ground, / Insect or Worme; . . . / These [i.e., the worms] as a line their long dimensions drew, / Streaking the ground with sinuous trace; not all Minims of Nature; // some of Serpent kinde / Wondrous in length and corpulence involv'd / Thir Snakie foulds, // and added wings" (book VII, v. 475–84). Through to the word "Nature" (v. 482), it is clear that

what is being spoken of is what we would now commonly refer to as a worm, with no admixture of a snake or reptile. And in these lines, the worm appears synonymous with "Insect" (v. 467). Then, from this point through to "foulds" (v. 484), the long-standing conflation of worm and serpent (any animal form with a long, sinuous body that creeps on the ground) pertains; furthermore, when this creature sprouts wings (v. 484), it has departed the realm of natural history and is approaching the realms of myth and moral allegory, where worm suggests Satan (e.g., book IX, v. 1068). See Milton, *Paradise Lost*, in Flannagan, *The Riverside Milton*. I owe a great debt and thanks to Dr. Ted Cotton, professor emeritus at Loyola University New Orleans for pointing out the surreptitious hand with which Milton moves through these varied forms of the worm.

7  Brown, *Insect Poetics*, 356.

8  Agamben, *The Open*, 26–27.

9  Ibid., 27.

10  I am playing here in part with Jacques Derrida's "The Autobiographical Animal," a ten-hour address given at the 1997 Cerisy conference, during which he presented a discursive catalog of the line separating the human from other animal species in both his and other significant thinkers' theoretical works. See Derrida, *The Animal That Therefore I Am*.

11  Cunningham and Jardine, *Romanticism and the Sciences*, xix.

12  Because Romanticism has been read as harboring disputed boundaries of time and structure, this identified genre of the literary displays transgressive properties similar to those I will demonstrate throughout this study as being found in the worm. See the essays collected in Rajan and Wright, *Romanticism, History, and the Possibilities of Genre*, on the permeable boundaries of Romanticism as a literary genre.

13  Stafford, *Body Criticism*, 21, 329, 341, 348.

14  Heringman, *Romantic Rocks, Aesthetic Geology*; Kelley, "Romantic Exemplarity." See also Kelley, *Clandestine Marriage*.

15  Kelley, "Romantic Exemplarity," 225.

16  Morton, *Ecological Thought*, 106.

17  Nichols, "Anxiety of Species," "Loves of Plants and Animals," and *Beyond Romantic Ecocriticism*.

18  McLean, "*The Monk* and the Matter of Reading," 111–31.

19  See Beer, *Darwin's Plots*; Perkins, *Romanticism and Animal Rights*; Ritvo, *Platypus and the Mermaid*.

20  "Since anomaly is by definition comparative, [the unusual animals']

violation of expectations reciprocally called into question both the zoological assumptions current before their advent and the systems in which
those assumptions were embedded." Moreover, such anomalies called
"systematic flexibility into question at a different level, undermining
the very categories that could not be stretched to accommodate them,
as well as the principles on which those categories were based, and
compromising the authority of the experts who endorsed and applied
them." Ritvo, *Platypus and the Mermaid,* 10–11.

21  Vartanian, "Trembley's Polyp," 260.

## 1. Transitional Tropes

1   In *The Ecological Thought,* Morton employs juxtaposition as a tool to
begin thinking the ecological thought: "[It] is about warmth and strangeness, infinity and proximity, tantalizing 'thereness' and head-popping,
wordless openness" (12). He effectively reproduces such juxtapositions
throughout the text to emphasize the "utterly mind-blowing idea" that
"the ecological thought permits no distance. . . . Thinking interdepen-
dence involves thinking difference. This means confronting the fact that
all beings are related to each other negatively and differentially, in an
open system without center or edge" (39). Morton's ecological project
therefore relies on a representative containment of its own openness
(i.e., the physical book) to perform its meaning. Ecology qua ecology is thus simply a matter of calibrated relationships set on an ever-
changing scale.

2   Bennett, *Vibrant Matter,* 94.

3   Ibid., pxiii.

4   See also Wolfe, *Zoontologies,* for a postmodern study of the animal as
the nonhuman Other.

5   Bennett, *Vibrant Matter,* 3.

6   Ibid., 94.

7   Ibid.

8   Darwin, *Formation of Vegetable Mould,* 311–12.

9   Ibid., 316.

10  Ibid., 177.

11  Bennett, *Vibrant Matter,* 2.

12  Ibid., 96.

13  Ibid., 108.

14  Morton, *Ecological Thought,* 94.

15  Ibid., 72; emphasis mine.

16  Ibid., 94.

17  Ibid., 18.

18  Ibid., 109, 96.

19  Ibid., 18.

20  Ibid., 109, 112.

21  Watts, *Divine and Moral Songs for Children,* Song 22.

22  Isaiah 51:8, KJV.

23  In a special issue of the journal *Genetics,* on *Arabidopsis thaliana* (a small, invasive, self-pollinating weed belonging to the mustard family, with small, white flowers), Watts's Song 22 was used as an epigraph to introduce a discussion on this "popular model system" for today's genetic research. "The flowering plant *Arabidopsis thaliana* has in the last decade joined the small group of popular model systems well suited to laboratory studies in classical, population, evolutionary, developmental, and molecular genetics. In addition to the fly and the worm (and yeast, the mouse, and others), we now have the weed." *Arabidopsis thaliana,* commonly called mouse-ear cress, was the first higher plant to have its complete genome sequence described. Meyerowitz et al., "Foreword to the Special Issue on Arabidopsis Genetics," *Genetics,* 471.

24  Edwards, *Basic Writings,* 57.

25  Psalm 22:6, KJV.

26  Burke, *Selected Works,* 142.

27  See chapter 3 of this book for my in-depth discussion of the polyp as a revolutionary vermiform.

28  Breynius, "Some Corrections and Amendments," 444.

29  Baster, "A Dissertation on the Worms," 277.

30  Ibid., 279.

31  My gratitude to Dr. Hillary Eklund, assistant professor of English literature at Loyola University New Orleans, for suggesting this particular extension of worm studies from natural historical import to historical impact.

32  Bonnet, "An Abstract of Some New Observations upon Insects," 479.

33  Ibid., 487.

34  Ibid., 479.

35  Ibid., 480.

36  La Mettrie, *Machine Man and Other Writings*; d'Holbach, *System of Nature.*

37  Bonnet, "An Abstract of Some New Observations upon Insects," 484.

38  Baker, "A Letter from Mr. Henry Baker," 576.

39  Ibid., 582.

40  Bigelow, "Regeneration," SM13.

41  The 2010 Nobel Prize in Physiology or Medicine, for example, was given to Dr. Robert G. Edwards for his development of in vitro fertilization. Likewise, twentieth-century science fiction works by such authors as Octavia Butler (the Xenogenesis Trilogy), Larry Niven and Jerry Pournelle *(The Mote in God's Eye),* and David Brin (the Uplift series) tread extensively on biological speculation and what it means to "save" human life. Special thanks to Kathryn Bell, whose senior thesis, completed under my direction in fall 2009 at Loyola University New Orleans and now part of a collection under review at Rodopi Press, suggested this trio of authors.

42  For a summary of the developments in microscopy throughout the late seventeenth and eighteenth centuries, see chapter 5, "Microsopic Seers," in Stafford, *Body Criticism.*

43  See, e.g., Jardine et al., *Cultures of Natural History,* for a collection of essays covering the culture of natural history. In particular, see Andrew Cunningham's essay "The Culture of Gardens." See also Spary, *Utopia's Garden,* for a complementary study of the Jardin du Roi in Paris.

44  A phenomenon in the Renaissance that proliferated in Europe throughout the sixteenth and seventeenth centuries, the cabinet of curiosities was in essence a personal collection of rare, unknown, and marvelous objects displayed for and by the wealthy and the well connected. Popular, visual, and encyclopedic in their approach, these cabinets, or *Wunderkammern,* included a diversity of specimens from both known and newly discovered worlds—from unicorn tails to monkey teeth, Indian canoes to phosphorescent minerals, exotic botanicals to pinned insects. In this act of collecting, categorizing, displaying, and recording, the idea of a Natural Order and what it meant to be human were thrown into question by philosophers, scientists, theologians, and poets alike. See, e.g., chapter 4 on "Exhibitionism" in Stafford, *Artful Science.*

45  See Beavis, *Insects and Other Invertebrates,* for an index of specific examples.

46  Farley, *Spontaneous Generation Controversy,* 8.

47  Redi, *Experiements on the Generation of Insects,* 18.

48  Ibid., 31.

49  Keeping in mind that the excerpt from Redi's experiment is Mab Bigelow's 1909 English translation from the original Italian, it bears noting here

the curious flourishes contained in the experiment's descriptive rhetoric. By employing a combination of alliteration, sibilance, and mute vowel sounds, like those found in "floating fragments of flesh," "swam and sported about," "fetid liquid," and "soft and slimy," Bigelow's translation appears as if worked out under the influence of Lewis's lyricism in *The Monk*. Read as such, it is as if Bigelow drew on the writing that was itself inspired by the original text she worked to translate. In other words, while Redi arguably inspired the imagery with which Lewis constructed his scene of putrefaction, Lewis arguably inspired the style and tone with which Bigelow then reconstructed the experiment that inspired Lewis. Bigelow's translation can therefore be read as one such final casting manufactured out of this cycle of impressions.

50  Lewis, *The Monk,* 273.

51  Job 7:5, KJV.

52  Farley, *Spontaneous Generation Controversy,* 15.

53  See Strick, "Darwinism and the Origin of Life," 1–42, for a discussion of Redi's role in the history of the spontaneous generation debates as that which helped to contribute a narrative of "dueling experiments" to these debates' methodology.

54  Farley, *Spontaneous Generation Controversy,* 12.

55  Ibid. Preformationism itself was internally divided between the ovists and the animalculists (or spermists). Swammerdam, for example, was an ovist who believed that life in miniature sprung from the female egg. Leeuwenhoek, with his discovery of spermatozoa, was by contrast a committed spermist, believing that the whole of the embryo was found in the male sperm.

56  Gasking, *Investigations into Generation,* 62–63.

57  Stafford, *Body Criticism,* 348.

58  Gasking, *Investigations into Generation,* 63.

59  See Linnaeus, *Systema Naturae,* and Lamarck, *Zoological Philosophy.*

60  Roger, *Buffon,* 71.

61  Cited in the *Oxford English Dictionary,* 2nd ed., vol. V (Oxford: Clarendon Press, 1989), 301. This statement appeared first in Bonnet's philosophical treatise *Contemplation of Nature.*

62  Atran, *Cognitive Foundations of Natural History,* 6.

63  Bynum et al., *Dictionary of the History of Science,* 411. For a full study of the metaphysical implication of taxonomic efforts, see Lovejoy, *Great Chain of Being.*

64  See Hooke, *Micrographia.*

65 Ritvo, *Platypus and the Mermaid,* 6.

66 Réaumur, *Mémoires pour servir à l'histoire des insectes,* 5:xliii.

67 Stewart, *On Longing,* 41.

68 Stafford, "Voyeur or Observer?," 100–3.

69 Stafford, *Body Criticism,* 330.

70 Ibid., 341.

71 Atran, *Cognitive Foundations of Natural History,* 3.

72 Linnaeus, *Systema Naturae,* 18.

73 Ibid., 19; emphasis mine.

74 Ibid.

75 Introduced in *Species Plantarum* (1753), this binomial system focused on a single visible structure (e.g., the number of stamens, or male parts to a flower, and the number of pistils, or female parts to the same) rather than attempting to account for the totalized morphology of a plant.

76 Linnaeus, *Systema Naturae,* 19.

77 Réaumur, *Mémoires pour servir à l'histoire des insectes,* 5:xlv.

78 Winsor, "Development of Linnaean Insect Classification," 64.

79 Corcos, "Fontenelle and the Problem of Generation," 364.

80 Diderot, *Rameau's Nephew and D'Alembert's Dream,* 57.

81 Paley, *Natural Theology,* 346.

82 Ibid., 12.

83 Ibid., 16.

84 Ibid., 366.

85 Roger, *Life Sciences in Eighteenth-Century French Thought,* 164.

86 Paley, *Natural Theology,* 370.

87 Ibid., 373.

88 Bennett, *Vibrant Matter,* 98.

## 2. "Unchanging but in Form"

1 King-Hele, *Collected Letters of Erasmus Darwin,* pxiv; Logan, *Poetry and Aesthetics of Erasmus Darwin,* 46.

2 King-Hele, *Erasmus Darwin: A Life of Unequalled Achievement,* ix.

3 "Taking available evidence into account," Cook and King-Hele reevaluate Darwin's death. They overturn the "view that Erasmus died from a 'heart attack,'" submitting instead the diagnosis of "infective illness." Cook and King-Hele, "Doctor Erasmus Darwin's Death," 264.

4 Jones, "Vogue of Natural History in England," 345.

5 Uglow, *Lunar Men,* xv.

6  Logan, *Poetry and Aesthetics of Erasmus Darwin,* 147.

7  See Fulford et al., *Literature, Science, and Exploration in the Romantic Era.*

8  Darwin, *Temple,* III:433–34. The edition from which my citations of the poem are drawn is Martin Priestman's 2006 annotated edition in digital copy (http://www.rc.umd.edu/editions/darwin_temple/). This edition also includes supplementary materials: "About this Edition," "Introduction," and Darwin's early draft of *Temple,* "Progress of Society." Thus my citations of the work appear as follows: when citing from Darwin's verse, I list canto and line number separated by a colon, as such: I:222. Darwin's notes will be designated the same, with the addition of an "n" following the line number: I:222n. Priestman's editorial notes will compound this format, with the addition of an "E" after the line of verse or note from which he draws his annotation: I:222E or I:222nE.

9  Darwin, *Temple,* I:137n.

10  Porter, "Scientific Analogy and Literary Taxonomy," 214.

11  Ibid., 215.

12  Darwin was invited by George III to be royal physician, but he turned down the offer.

13  For a brief discussion of Darwin's earliest poems, specifically "The Death of Prince Frederick" and "To Mr. Gurney," revisited as a result of Darwin's later fame, see Ritterbush, "Erasmus Darwin's Second Published Poem," 158–60.

14  Seward, *Memoirs of the Life of Doctor Darwin,* 4–5.

15  Ibid., 68.

16  Darwin, *Zoonomia,* XXIX.4.8. Anticipating transformism and the theory of inheritance of acquired characteristics, as presented in Jean-Baptiste Lamarck's 1809 *Philosophie Zoologique,* Darwin applied David Hartley's psychological theory of associationism from his 1749 *Observations on Man, His Frame, His Duty, and His Expectations* toward his own materialist ideas of evolution.

17  Seward, *Memoirs of the Life of Doctor Darwin,* 61.

18  Ibid., 68.

19  For innumerable examples of experiments and scientific performances that sought to unravel the mysteries of nature as well as human technologies, see King-Hele, *Collected Letters of Erasmus Darwin,* in which diagrams abound and an inflamed intellect excites many a correspondence. For an historian's view of the performance of science and its sociocultural contexts, see Morus, *Frankenstein's Children.*

20 For a succinct summary of some of Darwin's miscellaneous prose, see Hassler, *Erasmus Darwin,* 78. For a complete chronology of scholarly affiliations and inventions, see King-Hele, *Charles Darwin's "The Life of Erasmus Darwin,"* 135–40, appendix A.

21 Badger and Harrison, *Midland Naturalist,* 265.

22 Seward recounts that Darwin undertook "the translation of the Linnæan system of vegetation into English from Latin" with Sir Brook Boothby, with whom he "commenced a botanical society" just before leaving Lichfield. Seward, *Memoirs of the Life of Doctor Darwin,* 70. William Jackson has also been mentioned as "a useful aide" to Darwin in his translations, with special consideration given to the rhetorical-linguistic challenges Darwin faced in this and an additional translation of another one of Linnaeus's works, *Genera et Species Plantarum.* Uglow, *Lunar Men,* 379–83.

23 As the stated (read published) purpose of *The Loves of the Plants,* this phrase has come to define the aim of the whole of Darwin's poetic works.

24 From April 16, 1798, to May 7, 1798, a parodic critique of Darwin's first long poems, titled *Loves of the Triangles,* appeared in installments in the *Anti-Jacobin* periodical. In her biography, Seward lightly chastises Darwin for taking the ridicule to heart: "Instead of pretending, as he did, never to have heard of the Loves of the Triangles, when questioned on the subject, he should voluntarily have mentioned that satire every where, and praised its wit and ingenuity." She also graciously—given her accusation that Darwin published some of her lines as his own in his first long poem—attempts to reclaim a scandalized Darwin by claiming that "the verse of this ironical poem [*Loves of the Triangles*] is not only Darwinian, but it is beautifully Darwinian": she calls it a bastion of "brilliant satire" echoing the indefatigable original. Seward, *Memoirs of the Life of Doctor Darwin,* 150–51. For a summary of anti-Darwin writings, including the infamous *Loves of the Triangles*; the book-length refutation of *Zoonomia* by Thomas Brown also published in 1798; and even the account of a little girl's memory of the horror at the sight of Darwin's ample size, see Hassler, *Erasmus Darwin,* 96–97. For a full discussion of the Romantic poets' critical reception of Darwin, namely, Coleridge and Wordsworth, see King-Hele, *Erasmus Darwin and the Romantic Poets,* 62–147.

25 Coleridge, *Letters,* 305.

26 For an alphabetical listing of subjects to which Darwin's writings contributed, see King-Hele, *Erasmus Darwin,* 373n50.

27  Porter, *Enlightenment*, 23.

28  Page, "Darwin before Darwin," 168.

29  Published by Joseph Johnson, who also published such poets as Anna Seward, William Blake, and William Wordsworth, *The Temple of Nature* "appears as the title only once—on the title page, with *The Origin of Society* in smaller type as an alternative," whereas *The Origin of Society* "appears as the running head at the top of every even-numbered page, and in the subtitles; for example, page 1 reads, 'ORIGIN OF SOCIETY. CANTO I. PRODUCTION OF LIFE.'" King-Hele, *Erasmus Darwin*, 346. "Johnson was well known for his radical sympathies and was, as John Brewer expresses it, 'Willing to publish tracts that many others thought too hot to handle.'" Harris, *Erasmus Darwin's Enlightenment Epic*, 9; see also 19 for a brief analysis of the impact of Darwin's twice-titled work. King-Hele also mentions the unmistakable affinity of Darwin's original title with his grandson's 1859 *Origin of Species*. King-Hele, *Erasmus Darwin and the Romantic Poets*, 28. Furthermore, King-Hele notes that "one early notebook is confidently entitled 'The Progress of Society: a poem in five cantos,'" which told "a tale of continual progress from rude human beginnings to the golden 'Age of Philosophy.'" King-Hele, *Erasmus Darwin*, 354. Priestman, however, contends that this early version was "an unfinished historical poem" in its own right, "probably drafted in 1798–9," and later transformed into *The Temple of Nature*. Priestman, introduction to *Temple of Nature*, para. 1.

30  Priestman, introduction to *Temple of Nature*, para. 11.

31  Ibid., para. 5.

32  According to definition 5a. in the *Oxford English Dictionary*, "marriage, *n.*" signifies "an intimate union; a merging or blending of two things." Of further interest here, the dictionary cites directly from Darwin's *The Golden Age, A Poetical Epistle* (1794): "The Marriage Table its degrees extend, / And to our great, great Grandmother ascend." http://dictionary.oed.com/cgi/entry/00302422. For an expanded discussion of "the theme of marriage" in *The Temple of Nature*, see Hassler, *Erasmus Darwin*, 83–86.

33  Emery, "Scientific Theory in Erasmus Darwin's 'The Botanic Garden' (1789–91)," 325.

34  Primer, "Erasmus Darwin's *Temple of Nature*," 76.

35  King-Hele, *Erasmus Darwin*, 197.

36  See Botting and Williams, "Evolution of the Species Argument for Women's Rights."

37 Darwin's 1797 *A Plan for the Conduct of Female Education in Boarding Schools* touches on the education of women moving outside of the home and entering a multitude of disciplines in the arts and sciences. This suggests that Darwin's modernizing tendencies extended into—if not being a distinct defense for—the rights of women and a more balanced approach to the dynamic between male and female educational systems.

38 Richardson, "Erasmus Darwin and the Fungus School," 114.

39 Priestman, introduction to *Temple of Nature,* para. 1.

40 Porter, "Scientific Analogy and Literary Taxonomy," 213, 218.

41 Wordsworth, "Lines Written a Few Miles above Tintern Abbey," in *Poetical Works,* 262, ln93–102.

42 Sewall, *Orphic Voice*; Primer, "Erasmus Darwin's *Temple of Nature.*" See also King-Hele, *Erasmus Darwin,* 354.

43 Priestman, introduction to *Temple of Nature,* para. 8.

44 See http://www.rc.umd.edu/editions/darwin_temple/engravings.html for Priestman's editorial notes discussing the history and significance of these engravings to Darwin's work.

45 Logan, *Poetry and Aesthetics of Erasmus Darwin,* 120.

46 In fact, the verse of *Temple* has been said to "[fail] in its obsessive attempt to convey a striking succession of visual images." Primer, "Erasmus Darwin's *Temple of Nature,*" 76. Its very status of poetry has been attacked, though peculiarly still in appeal to its poetic form: "if there is science in the poem there is little poetry." Emery, "Scientific Theory in Erasmus Darwin's 'The Botanic Garden' (1789–91)," 325. As a result of its "deep exhilaration" for the varied studies of nature, it has earned more ridicule than sympathy. Logan, *Poetry and Aesthetic of Erasmus Darwin,* 147.

47 Logan, *Poetry and Aesthetics of Erasmus Darwin,* 120.

48 King-Hele, *Erasmus Darwin,* 353.

49 Coleridge, *Letters,* 135.

50 For a complete accounting for and contextualization of Charles Darwin's *Origin of Species,* see Browne, *Darwin's Origin of Species.* For a recent discussion of how creationism transforms biology, see Wood et al., *Understanding the Pattern of Life.*

51 King-Hele, *Erasmus Darwin,* 353.

52 By this, I am not suggesting that Darwin is purely Aristotelian; instead, he engages with Aristotelian physics and metaphysics together to display his own causative theory of nature. He goes beyond Aristotle, as Ross notes, "to understand *why* seeing and liveliness are so closely associated." Ross, "To Charm Thy Curious Eye," 385. For a succinct discussion of

Aristotle's natural science, see McKeon's introduction to *Basic Works of Aristotle*, xxii–xxvi.

53  See my discussion of Bennett's *Vibrant Matter* in chapter 1.

54  See also Canto I:137n for Darwin's explanation of the significance that the Eleusinian mysteries hold for his construction of the poem. Likewise, Priestman offers his own in-depth discussion of these mysteries' bearing on the structure and content of the poem in Canto I:137nE.

55  See Yolton, *Thinking Matter,* and Richardson, *British Romanticism and the Science of the Mind.*

56  Hassler, *Erasmus Darwin,* 13.

57  Ibid., 15.

58  Darwin, *Temple,* I:2.

59  Ibid., Additional Note VIII. The importation of such phrases, contends King-Hele, is used "to cover up the fact that his theory left the Creator without a role." King-Hele, *Erasmus Darwin and the Romantic Poets,* 142. Moreover, King-Hele states that "Darwin is careful to be tender with religious susceptibilities. He salutes the 'GREAT FIRST CAUSE' as maker of the living filament: he probably accepted this as consistent with deism. But he also has to make it clear that he is depriving God of his traditional role as officer-in-charge of changing species, and Darwin devises euphemistic phrases to say that evolution proceeds naturally, without divine intervention." The "vagueness in Darwin's summary that all creatures arise from 'one living filament,'" he continues, "is clarified in *The Temple of Nature*: 'all vegetables and animals now existing were originally derived from the smallest microscopic ones, formed by spontaneous vitality in primeval oceans' [Add. Note VII]." King-Hele, *Erasmus Darwin,* 300. Likewise, as Priestman attests, "it is wholly typical of Darwin to introduce an emphatic reference to God early on, but—as usual—the 'Creator' here need be no more than the deist 'First Cause,' under whose cover Darwin slips in the key evolutionary suggestion that organisms may literally have a single physical parent." Darwin, *Collected Writings,* xix.

60  King-Hele, *Erasmus Darwin,* 353.

61  Darwin, *Zoonomia,* vii.

62  King-Hele, *Erasmus Darwin,* 353.

63  Bynum et al., *Dictionary of the History of Science,* 248.

64  Ross, "To Charm Thy Curious Eye," 384.

65  Bynum et al., *Dictionary of the History of Science,* 248.

66  Hassler, *Erasmus Darwin,* 15.

67  Ross, "To Charm Thy Curious Eye," 388.

68  Ibid., 384.

69  Ibid., 381.

70  Teute, "Loves of the Plants," 328.

71  Hassler, *Erasmus Darwin*, 72, 65.

72  Page, "Darwin before Darwin," 164.

73  Darwin, *Temple*, preface.

74  Ibid.

75  Ibid.

76  Ibid., I:1, 3–4.

77  Ibid., I.

78  Ibid., I:27–28.

79  Ibid., I:29–30.

80  Ibid., I:32.

81  Ibid., II:1.

82  Ibid., I:446.

83  Darwin notes, "The thinking few in all ages have complained of the brevity of life, lamenting that mankind are not allowed time sufficient to cultivate science, or to improve their intellect. Hippocrates introduces his celebrated aphorisms with this idea; 'Life is short, science long, opportunities of knowledge rare, experiments fallacious, and reasoning difficult.'— A melancholy reflection to philosophers!" Darwin, *Temple*, II:1n.

84  Ross, "To Charm Thy Curious Eye," 388.

85  Darwin, *Temple*, II:19–20.

86  Ibid., II:4.

87  Ibid., I:227.

88  Ibid., Additional Note I.

89  Ibid., I:126n.

90  King-Hele, *Doctor of Revolution*, 267. King-Hele provides this succinct paraphrase of a lengthy, crucial section of *Temple*, III:409–34.

91  Nichols, "Loves of Plants and Animals," para. 4.

92  McKeon, *Basic Works of Aristotle*, xxiii.

93  Darwin, *Temple*, III:432.

94  King-Hele, *Doctor of Revolution*, 293.

95  Harris, *Erasmus Darwin's Enlightenment Epic*, 70, 69.

96  Primer, "Erasmus Darwin's *Temple of Nature*," 76.

97  Lovejoy, *Great Chain of Being*, 186, 190.

98  See my discussion from chapter 1 of how the modern theory of Morton's *Ecological Thought* can echo what I understand as the vermicular activities of eighteenth-century natural history study.

99   With his verse "as skillful as ever," states King-Hele, Darwin "calmly
     [presented what] was not to be scientifically established for a further
     hundred years, and then only after long argument." King-Hele, *Erasmus
     Darwin,* 346. In *Charles Darwin's "The Life of Erasmus Darwin,"* Krause
     reveals that "on the second page of the later editions of Darwin's 'Origin
     of Species' (sixth edition, p. xiv, note) we find the following brief obser-
     vation: 'It is curious how largely my grandfather, Dr. Erasmus Darwin,
     anticipated the views and erroneous grounds of opinion of Lamarck in
     his *Zoonomia* (vol. i., pp. 500–510), published in 1794.' Being quite
     aware of the reticence and modesty with which the author expresses
     himself, especially in speaking *pro domo,* I thought immediately that here
     we ought to read between the lines, and that this ancestor of his must
     certainly deserve considerable credit in connection with the history of
     the Darwinian theory" (148, appendix D).

100  Darwin, *Temple,* I:309–14.

101  Ibid., I:234. I use "natural philosophy" here, rather than the perhaps more
     accurate "biology," given that the latter term wasn't used in its modern
     sense until 1800 (by Karl Friedrich Burdach) and 1802 (by Gottfried
     Reinhold Treviranus). Also, with the eighteenth century's understanding
     of fossil theory, along with its invention of the geological survey map,
     the age of the earth went from being a mere one hundred thousand years
     old to over a million. This new age of the world was termed "geologic
     time," set between the considerably younger "historic time," in which
     humans reside, and the inconceivably older "astronomical time," con-
     noting the origin of the universe. See Lyell, *Principles of Geology,* and
     Rudwick, *Georges Cuvier, Fossil Bones, and Geological Catastrophes.* For a
     creative nonfictional account of the development of the geologic survey
     map, see Winchester, *Map That Changed the World.*

102  Darwin, *Temple,* I:232.

103  Ibid., I:229–30.

104  Ibid., I:224.

105  Ibid., I:224n.

106  Ibid., I:259.

107  Ibid., I:281.

108  Ibid., I:291.

109  Ibid., I:283–94.

110  This selfsame progression is later found in Wells's 1895 novel *The Time
     Machine,* in which the Time Traveller's vision of futurity ("in great strides
     of a thousand years or more") brings him through another of life's begin-
     nings. From recognizing "the green slime on the rocks," which "alone

testified that life was not extinct," he is finally confronted by "a monstrous crab-like creature," "a round thing, the size of a football perhaps, or it may be, bigger, tentacles trailed down from it; it seemed black against the weltering blood-red water, and it was hopping fitfully about" (146–48).

111 Darwin, *Temple,* I:295–96.

112 Ibid., I:297–98, I:297n.

113 Ibid., I:299.

114 Ibid., I:327.

115 Ibid., II:61–116.

116 Ibid., II:165–66.

117 Ibid., II:277–78, 262.

118 Ibid., IV:383–90.

119 Ibid., IV.383nE.

120 Ibid., II:250.

121 Ibid., II:307, 312.

122 Ibid., II:307–424.

123 Ibid., II:333, 347, 353, 357.

124 Ibid., II:361, 377–78.

125 Ibid., II:223n.

126 For more on this subject, particularly on the butterfly collections of the eighteenth century, see Russell, *An Obsession with Butterflies.* See also Todd, *Chrysalis,* an exquisite discussion of metamorphic obsession in the seventeenth century, focusing on the works of Maria Sibylla Merian.

127 Darwin, *Temple,* II:44.

128 Ibid., II:122n.

129 Ibid., I:176n.

130 Ibid., I:173nE.

131 Ibid., I:137–38.

132 Ibid., I:137n.

133 Ibid., I:137nE.

134 Priestman, introduction to *Temple of Nature,* para. 5. Gillian Beer claims a similar motivation for Charles Darwin's investigations into the natural world: "In the process of [Charles] Darwin's thought, one movement is constantly repeated: the impulse to substantiate metaphor and particularly to find a real place in the natural order for older mythological expressions." Beer, *Darwin's Plots,* 74.

135 Darwin, *Temple,* I:137n.

136 For a discussion of how the Portland Vase figured as an influential aestheticocultural object before, during, and after Darwin's era, see Keynes, "Portland Vase," 237–59.

137  Darwin, *Temple,* I:137n.

138  Ibid., Additional Note XV.

139  See King-Hele, *Letters of Erasmus Darwin,* 225. In a letter addressed to "My dear old friend [Richard Dixon]," dated October 25, 1792, Darwin writes that "the success of the French against a confederacy of kings gives me great pleasure, and I hope they will preserve their liberty, and spread the holy flame of freedom over Europe."

140  See Beer, *Darwin's Plots,* for a narratological study of Charles Darwin's *On the Origin of Species* that highlights Darwin's own creative and imaginative debts to his Romantic predecessors and Victorian counterparts.

141  Hamilton, *Metaromanticism,* 22.

142  Darwin, *Temple,* I:137nE.

143  Packham, "Science and Poetry of Animation," 202.

144  For more on this subject, see Saunders, *Picturing Plants*; Stafford, *Visual Analogy* and *Body Criticism*; and Kemp's illustrated catalog accompanying the Hayward Gallery's 2000 exhibition, *Spectacular Bodies.*

145  For purposes of clarity, I have maintained the italicized title of *The Temple of Nature* when discussing the poem as a literary work; when discussing the Temple of Nature as an actualized structure within this literary work, I leave it in roman text. However, I maintain capitalization, given its presentation as a sacred place.

146  I allude here to the space–place dynamic in de Certeau, *Practice of Everyday Life.*

147  Darwin, *Temple,* I:137nE.

148  Jordanova, *Languages of Nature,* 36.

149  Darwin, *Temple,* III:144.

150  Ibid., III:342.

151  Priestman, introduction to *Temple of Nature,* para. 5.

152  Darwin, *Temple,* I:65–66, 69–74.

153  Ibid., I:65nE.

154  Harris, *Erasmus Darwin's Enlightenment Epic,* 81.

155  Such a construction reverberates in Coleridge's "Kubla Khan," e.g., "I would build that dome in air, / That sunny dome! those caves of ice!" (ln46–47).

156  Darwin, *Temple,* I:227.

157  This is reflective of Foucault's idea of the *heterotopia,* but rather than being a "place without a place" that is "absolutely different from all the sites that [it] reflect[s] and speak[s] about," the Temple literally inscribes itself in the diplopia of figure and form. See Foucault, "Of Other Spaces," 27, 24.

158 In part, the frame for the space of the Temple could have been suggested by illustrations Darwin saw of a banyan tree, with what we now know as its positively gravitropic root system that allows lateral spread to coincide with vertical growth. William Hodges, for example, made several drawings of a banyan tree he saw while in Calcutta (1781), in service of the East India Company, and Warren Hastings, Governor of Bengal at this time, later received a painting of this composition. For one discussion of this circulation, see Stuebe, "William Hodges and Warran Hastings." For another, see de Almeida and Gilpin, *Indian Renaissance.* Thank you to Dr. Theresa M. Kelley, Marjorie and Lorin Tiefenthaler Professor of English Literature, University of Wisconsin–Madison, for bringing this possible botanical inspiration for Darwin's Temple to my attention.

159 Darwin, *Temple,* I:173–76.

160 Ibid., I:9–10.

161 Ibid., I:177–78.

162 One such object that fascinated Darwin was the Portland Vase: "Darwin believed the figures on the Vase represented a ritual of death and rebirth deriving from the Eleusinian mysteries." King-Hele, *Erasmus Darwin,* 243–45.

163 Ibid., 345.

164 Darwin, *Temple,* IV:516, 522–24.

165 Ibid., I:443–44. Percy Shelley's *Prometheus Unbound* (1820) inversely treats such consequences of voice, focused as it is on a recalling of the curse responsible for "this Earth / Made multitudinous with [Jupiter's] slaves" (I:4–5).

166 Primer, "Erasmus Darwin's *Temple of Nature,*" 76.

167 Darwin, *Temple,* III:401n.

168 Priestman, introduction to *Temple of Nature,* para. 4.

169 "*Romantic Circles* is a refereed scholarly website devoted to the study of Romantic-period literature and culture. It is published by the University of Maryland and supported, in part, by the Maryland Institute for Technology in the Humanities (MITH), and the English Departments of Loyola University of Chicago and the University of Maryland." General editors are Neil Fraistat, Steven E. Jones, and Carl Stahmer. http://www.rc.umd.edu/. *The Temple of Nature* is part of the Romantic Circles Electronic Editions, which "offers a searchable archive of texts of the Romantic era, enhanced by technology made possible in an online environment. Each edition is based on the highest scholarly standards

and is peer-reviewed." Edited by Tilar Mazzeo. http://www.rc.umd.edu/editions/.

170 Priestman, "About This Edition," in *Temple of Nature,* para. 3.

171 Ibid.

172 I am engaging here Deleuze and Guattari's concept of the rhizome from *A Thousand Plateaus.*

## 3. Not without Some Repugnancy

1 The citation is taken from Trembley's *Mémoires, pour servir à l'histoire d'un genre de polypes d'eau douce, à bras en forme de cornes (Memoirs Concerning the Natural History of a Type of Freshwater Polyp with Arms Shaped Like Horns)* (1744), which can be found as an English translation in Lenhoff and Lenhoff, *Hydra and the Birth of Experimental Biology, 1744.* I want to clarify here the structure of this treatise and my manner of citation of it, which I use throughout this chapter: the *Mémoires* themselves are divided into four "Memoirs," preceded by a general preface and an explanatory contents page. When citing this work, I maintain Trembley as the author so that the citations appear as such: Trembley, *Mémoires,* 1:27. The number to the left of the colon designates the memoir, and the number to the right of the colon is the page number on which the quoted or paraphrased material can be found. The particular citation for this note thus reads Trembley, *Mémoires,* 1:4–5.

2 Together, Typhaon and Echidna are known as the "Father and Mother of all monsters," creating not only the Hydra but the Nemean Lion, Cerberus, Ladon, the Chimera, and the Sphinx. While Echidna is described as being "half woman, half serpent," Typhaon is recounted as a "flaming monster with a hundred heads / Who rose up against all the Gods." Interestingly, both parents exhibit attributes most commonly equated with the Old English *wyrm,* making any notion of the vermicular always already burdened with the terror and fiendishness found in their offspring. Hamilton, *Mythology,* 69, 342.

3 In modern terminology, Trembley would have been working in the field of developmental biology. His observations and experiments on the polyp in particular have since earned him the nickname "Father of Experimental Zoology." Schiller, "Queries, Answers, and Unsolved Problems," 184.

4 Kuhn, *Structure of Scientific Revolutions,* xi.

5 Ritvo, *Platypus and the Mermaid,* 10.

6 Ibid., 11, and Kuhn, *Structure of Scientific Revolutions*, 64, 80, 84.

7 Youngquist, *Monstrosities*, xi.

8 Curran and Graille, "Faces of Eighteenth-Century Monstrosity," 3.

9 Vartanian, "Trembley's Polyp, La Mettrie, and Eighteenth-Century French Materialism," 262.

10 Ibid., 285–86.

11 Ritvo, *Platypus and the Mermaid*, xii.

12 Ibid., 260.

13 Ibid., 270.

14 Kuhn, *Structure of Scientific Revolutions*, 6.

15 Vartanian, "Trembley's Polyp, La Mettrie, and Eighteenth-Century French Materialism," 285.

16 Baker, *Abraham Trembley of Geneva*, vii.

17 Ibid.

18 In a review of Baker's biography shortly after its publication, Vartanian rightly comments that the "treatment of the crucial impact made by the polyp on the theory of generation in the eighteenth century is inadequate." Vartanian, "Book Review: *Abraham Trembley of Geneva*," 388.

19 Along with Trembley's own 1744 *Mémoires*, which had been published in Leiden, pirated copies appeared immediately in France, an abstract of the treatise was published in London in 1745, and a German translation was completed by 1775. See Baker, *Abraham Trembley of Geneva*, 42–43, for this publication history.

20 Dawson, *Nature's Enigma*, 185.

21 Ibid., appendices A–C, 189–252.

22 Ibid., 12.

23 Ibid., 83.

24 It bears mentioning here that Dawson's text is the last book-length, critical project to be completed on Trembley and the polyp. It is subsumed under the prescription of a "memoir," completed for the American Philosophical Society (vol. 174).

25 Ibid., 143.

26 Ibid., 186. Prior to this full-length study, Dawson published "The Problem of Soul in the 'Little Machines' of Réaumur and Charles Bonnet." This article serves as a kind of introduction to the ideas she developed further in *Nature's Enigma* but does not spend any significant time on Trembley himself.

27 Anderson, "Charles Bonnet's Taxonomy and Chain of Being," 46.

28 Ibid., 58.

29  Roe, "John Turberville Needham and the Generation of Living Organisms," 159.

30  Ibid., 182.

31  See Cooper, "Rediscovering the Immortal *Hydra*," and Sainson, "Le Régénérateur de la France."

32  For further details concerning the role of the Trembley family in Genevan history and the fate of Abraham Trembley's father, see Baker, *Abraham Trembley of Geneva*, 1–11.

33  Ibid., 16.

34  Gasking, *Investigations into Generation*, 122.

35  Winsor, "Development of Linnaean Insect Classification," 65.

36  Corcos, "Fontenelle and the Problem of Generation in the Eighteenth Century," 371.

37  Baker, *Abraham Trembley of Geneva*, 21.

38  Dawson, *Nature's Enigma*, 92.

39  Kuhn, *Structure of Scientific Revolutions*, 4.

40  For the complete letters of these two men, see the *Philosophical Transactions* 23 (1702–3): 1304–11, 1494–1501.

41  Trembley, *Mémoires*, 1:4.

42  Ibid.

43  Ibid.

44  Kuhn, *Structure of Scientific Revolutions*, 65.

45  Trembley, "Observations and Experiments upon the Freshwater Polypus," 42:iii.

46  Trembley, *Mémoires*, 1:1.

47  Trembley, "Observations and Experiments upon the Freshwater Polypus," 42:xi.

48  Ibid.

49  Trembley, *Mémoires*, 1:5.

50  As precursors to the glass aquaria (and the petri dish), Trembley's powder jars effectively displayed to him and to his students the flora and fauna he had collected. These jars also acted as rudimentary magnifying glasses, helping to reveal the presence of the freshwater polyp to the human eye.

51  Ibid., 1:6.

52  Ibid.

53  Ibid.

54  Ibid.

55  Lenhoff and Lenhoff, "Abraham Trembley and His Polyps," 4.

56  Trembley, *Mémoires*, 1:6.

57 Ibid.
58 Ibid., 1:7.
59 Ratcliff, *Quest for the Invisible,* 105.
60 Trembley, *Mémoires,* 1:7.
61 Ibid., 1:38.
62 Rouse et al., "*Osedax.*"
63 Grassle, "Hydrothermal Vent Animals."
64 See Deleuze, *The Fold,* 8–9, for the determination of raw matter vs. organic matter, "machinelike" vs. "mechanical," and the Leibnizian notion of plastic forces vs. compressive or elastic forces.
65 Dawson, *Nature's Enigma,* 184.
66 Ibid., 185.
67 Trembley, *Mémoires,* 1:7.
68 Ibid.
69 Dawson, *Nature's Enigma,* 117.
70 Trembley, *Mémoires,* 1:8.
71 Ibid., 1:9.
72 Ibid., 1:11.
73 Ibid., 3:117.
74 Ibid., 1:10.
75 Dawson, *Nature's Enigma,* 7.
76 Trembley, *Mémoires,* 1:11.
77 Quoted in Dawson, *Nature's Enigma,* 101.
78 Trembley, *Mémoires,* 3:125.
79 Ibid., 1:11.
80 Ibid.
81 See Baker, *Abraham Trembley of Geneva,* 33–36, for a detailed discussion of the naming of Trembley's polyp, its derivations, and its implications.
82 Trembley, *Mémoires,* preface, v.
83 See Roberts and Oosting, "Responses of Venus Fly Trap," for an historical account of the discovery of the Venus flytrap.
84 Trembley, *Mémoires,* 2:70. See chapter 4 for a discussion inclusive of Blake's interpretation of the intrinsic limitations wrought by the human faculties.
85 Ibid., 4:183.
86 Ibid., preface, vi.
87 Ratcliff, *Quest for the Invisible,* 105.
88 Trembley, *Mémoires,* 4:141.
89 Trembley, "Observations and Experiments upon the Freshwater Polypus," 42:viii.

90  Trembley, *Mémoires*, 4:151.

91  Ibid., 4:170–78. Trembley is credited with the first successful grafting of animal tissue, an operation he pursued in significant measure as a consequence of his ongoing comparison of the polyp to a plantlike nature—however subordinated to its animal classification. See Lenhoff, "Tissue Grafting in Animals," 1–10.

92  Trembley, *Mémoires*, 4:154–69.

93  Ibid., 3:129.

94  Trembley, "Observations and Experiments upon the Freshwater Polypus," 42:xi.

95  Trembley, *Mémoires*, 1:2.

96  Trembley, *Mémoires*, preface, v.

97  Ratcliff, *Quest for the Invisible*, 110.

98  Bonnet, "An Abstract of Some New Observations upon Insects," 42:458–88.

99  Anonymous, "Part of a Letter," 42:232, and Bonnet, "An Abstract of Some New Observations upon Insects," 42:468.

100  Stafford, *Body Criticism*, 349–50.

101  See Baker, *Abraham Trembley of Geneva*, 41–43, for a full account of this particular appropriation of Trembley's discovery.

102  Trembley, *Mémoires*, 1:3.

103  Collinson, *"Forget Not Mee & My Garden,"* 124.

104  Dawson, *Nature's Enigma*, 8.

105  Sarton, *A Guide to the History of Science*, 87–88.

106  Gronovius, "Extract of a Letter," 42:220. It will be remembered that Linnaeus created the *Zoophyta, Cryptogamia, Paradoxa,* or otherwise grab-bag categories with which to contain apparent natural anomalies.

107  Stafford, "Voyeur or Observer?," 96.

108  Gronovius, "Extract of a Letter," 42:218.

109  Anonymous, "Part of a Letter," 42:227.

110  Ibid., 42:229.

111  Ibid.

112  Kuhn, *Structure of Scientific Revolutions*, 52.

113  Ibid., 96.

114  Ibid., 191.

115  Anonymous, "Part of a Letter," 42:233–34.

116  Trembley, *Mémoires*, 4:185–86.

117  See Baker, *Abraham Trembley of Geneva*, 44–47, for a pragmatic summary of the polyp's role in the literary works listed previously.

118  Diderot, *Rameau's Nephew and D'Alembert's Dream*, 233.

119   Ibid., 137 (Tancock's introduction).

120   Ibid., 172.

121   Spangler, "Science, philosophie et littérature," 93.

122   Ibid., 89–90.

123   Diderot, *Rameau's Nephew and D'Alembert's Dream,* 171.

124   Ibid., 189; emphasis mine.

125   Vartanian, "Diderot and the Technology of Life," 21, 20.

126   Diderot, *Rameau's Nephew and D'Alembert's Dream,* 230.

127   Ibid., 200.

128   Naigeon, "Unitarians."

129   Vartanian, "Diderot and the Technology of Life," 21.

130   Diderot, *Rameau's Nephew and D'Alembert's Dream,* 181.

131   Curran, "Monsters and the Self in the *Rêve de d'Alembert,*" 48.

132   Diderot, *Rameau's Nephew and D'Alembert's Dream,* 222.

133   Spangler, "Science, philosophie et littérature," 94.

134   Diderot, *Rameau's Nephew and D'Alembert's Dream,* 182.

135   Ibid., 154.

## 4. "Art Thou but a Worm?"

1   While much of Blake's vermicular imagery also resonates with dragons, serpents, and the serpentine, which would also raise the starting sum of eighty-eight exponentially, I continue to focus specifically on the myriad invertebrate vermiforms.

2   Damon, *A Blake Dictionary,* 451.

3   Ibid., 451–52.

4   Gigante, "Blake's Living Form," 464.

5   Blake, *Letters,* 35.

6   Kawasaki, "Form and Worm in William Blake," 102.

7   Warner, *Blake and the Language of Art,* 33; Mitchell, *Blake's Composite Art,* 166.

8   See, e.g., Digby, *Symbol and Image in William Blake,* 8–10. (In particular, Digby draws on the prevalence of caterpillar–butterfly imagery throughout Blake's work.)

9   Gigante, *Life* and "Blake's Borders," 1. (Both this full text and essay primarily investigate Blake's *Jerusalem,* focusing on the images and imagery of the polyp as a regenerative motif.)

10   Although multiple print editions of the illuminated works were produced and colored by Blake, resulting in variations executed over a series of years, I am using the representative illuminations chosen by the

William Blake Trust and Princeton University Press in their Illuminated Books of William Blake series (David Bindman, general editor). For an intricate study of Blake's etching and printing procedures, including an accounting of their unavoidable variances and chronological confusion, see Viscomi, *Blake and the Idea of the Book,* and Eaves et al., *Illuminated Books of William Blake,* 3:71–74. While certainly deserving of continued study, neither the nuances of printed editions, which lack what Frye, as cited in Essick, *Visionary Hand,* 154, observes as any "fixed color symbolism in the designs: every copy is colored differently," nor the debates of an ur-text are emphasized in this study. Consequently, the Princeton series serves as the standard edition from which I examine Blake's work. For *The Book of Thel,* I am looking at copy J, from the first printing in green, at the Houghton Library, Harvard University, Cambridge, Massachusetts, and for "The Sick Rose," I am looking at the King's College copy, in London, England.

11  "I have said to corruption, Thou art my father: to the worm, Thou art my mother, and my sister." Job 17:14, KJV.

12  Remember that Darwin's ultimate aim in *The Temple of Nature* is to display the "origin of [*human*] society," but combined with Darwin's own botanical and zoological texts, this poem calls greater attention to the natural world than to the vital trajectory of one of its particular inhabitants.

13  Blake to Revd Dr Trusler, Englefield Green, Egham, Surrey, on August 23, 1799, in Blake, *Complete Poetry and Prose,* 702.

14  Blake, *All Religions Are One,* in *Complete Poetry and Prose,* plate 9 (Principle 6) and plate 6 (Principle 3d).

15  Blake, *There Is No Natural Religion* (c. 1794), in *Complete Poetry and Prose,* plate a5, II, and plate b3, I.

16  Ibid., plate b6, IV (circa 1795).

17  For a discussion of these and the other plates making up Blake's emblem book, see Mellor, *Blake's Human Form Divine,* 67–85. See also Digby, *Symbol and Image in William Blake,* 7–14, 50–52, for a specific discussion of the frontispiece image and the Worm–Mother image (the latter of which I go on to discuss in this paragraph).

18  See Blake, *For the Sexes: The Gates of Paradise,* plate 15.

19  Beer, *William Blake,* 27.

20  Essick, *Visionary Hand,* 517.

21  Blake, *Milton a Poem in 2 Books,* in *Complete Poetry and Prose,* plate 20, ln17–19.

22  Blake, *Jerusalem,* plate 56, ln33–37.

23 Blake, *For the Sexes: The Gates of Paradise,* Key 16, ln46–50; emphasis mine.

24 Beer, *William Blake,* 37.

25 For a full assessment of Blake's view of eighteenth-century rationalism and the philosophies of Bacon, Locke, and Newton, see Beer, *William Blake,* 29–40, and Peterfreund, *William Blake in a Newtonian World.* For an examination of Blake's antimaterialism, as read through a recuperation of materialism itself, see Adams, "The Blakean Aesthetic," in Essick, *Visionary Hand,* 173–200.

26 Blake, *For the Sexes: The Gates of Paradise,* prologue, ln1–2.

27 Blake, *For the Sexes: The Gates of Paradise,* copy D, *The William Blake Archive,* "Copy Information," http://www.blakearchive.org/.

28 Blake, *Marriage of Heaven and Hell,* in *Complete Poetry and Prose,* plate 15, ln17–19.

29 Ibid., plate 15, ln11–16.

30 Essick, *William Blake,* xxi.

31 Ibid., 3, 5.

32 I am careful here to name Blake an "etcher" rather than an "engraver," given what Essick defines as their categorical difference: "Very simply, engraving is any process by which incisions are made in a plate with a tool; in etching the incisions are made with acid." Essick, *William Blake,* 10. While Blake practiced general engraving (most often in his commercial work), as well as the more specific process of etching, his particular invention of relief etching is what concerns me most for my discussions in this chapter. See Essick, *William Blake,* 8–28, for a full account of the use of and debate over engraving and etching in the eighteenth century.

33 Essick, *Visionary Hand,* 493, and *William Blake,* xxi.

34 See King-Hele, *Erasmus Darwin and the Romantic Poets,* 35–41, for an introductory discussion of the intellectual, textual, and print parallels between Darwin and Blake. See also Erdman, *Illuminated Blake,* 33–34, 39, in which *The Book of Thel* is discussed specifically as a "curious counterpart" to *The Loves of Plants.*

35 Essick, *William Blake,* 16–18, 87–88.

36 Ibid., 255.

37 The idea for relief etching is attributed, by Blake himself, to his brother Robert. Having died in February 1787, Robert Blake soon afterward "stood before [William Blake] in one of his visionary imaginations, and so decidedly directed him in the way in which he ought to proceed [to publish his illustrated songs without their being subject to the expense

of the letter press], that he immediately followed his advice." Qtd. in Essick, *William Blake,* 85.

38 Ibid., 87.

39 Ibid., 115, 87.

40 Mitchell, *Blake's Composite Art,* 37.

41 See Essick, *William Blake,* 208–9, and Eaves et al., *Illuminated Books of William Blake,* 3:135–36.

42 Essick, *Visionary Hand,* 499.

43 Blake, *Book of Thel,* plate 3, ln2, 4.

44 Ibid., plate 3, ln1; emphasis mine.

45 Blake, *Book of Thel,* copy J, *The William Blake Archive,* editor's notes, http://www.blakearchive.org/.

46 Blake, *Book of Thel,* plate 3, ln5–6.

47 Damon, *A Blake Dictionary,* 174.

48 Blake, *Book of Thel,* plate 8, ln22, and plate 3, ln3.

49 Mitchell, *Blake's Composite Art,* 80.

50 Damon, *A Blake Dictionary,* 80.

51 Mitchell notes that "Thel" may be derived from the Greek word for "will" or "wish," for example. Mitchell, *Blake's Composite Art,* 101n. For further discussion of this and other source associations, including possible anagrams for "Thel," see Eaves et al., *Illuminated Books of William Blake,* 3:78–80.

52 Mellor, *Blake's Human Form Divine,* 21–28.

53 Beer, *William Blake,* 89.

54 Blake, *Book of Thel,* plate 3, ln2–3, 25; emphases mine.

55 Ibid., plate 6, ln2.

56 Ibid., plate 3, ln1.

57 Ibid., plate 3, ln8–11.

58 Ibid., plate 3, ln25, and plate 4, ln11–12.

59 Ibid., plate 4, ln4, 5, 10, and plate 5, ln2.

60 Ibid., plate 5, ln2, 4.

61 Ibid., plate 5, ln17, 12, 8.

62 Ibid., plate 3, ln16–17, and plate 5, ln5.

63 Ibid., plate 5, ln22–23.

64 Ibid., plate 5, ln25–27.

65 "For I walk through the vales of Har, and smell the sweetest flowers; / But I feed not the little flowers: I hear the warbling birds, / But I feed not the warbling birds. they fly and seek their food;" Blake, *Book of Thel,* plate 5, ln18–20.

66 Fuller, *Blake's Heroic Argument,* 35.

67 Blake, *Book of Thel,* plate 5, ln29.

68 Ibid., plate 5, ln27–28.

69 Nichols, "Anxiety of Species," 134.

70 Blake, *Book of Thel,* plate 6, ln2, 5.

71 Ibid., plate 7, ln7, and plate 6, ln3.

72 Eaves et al., *Illuminated Books of William Blake,* 3:84.

73 "Blake's imagination constantly saw natural objects in terms of their interconnectedness rather than their discrete separateness. His caterpillars and butterflies have human faces. His human figures often sprout roots and branches. His bird's tails and wings echo flower stalks and vines, while his mythic figures often connect the human form with the botanic or the bestial. In Blake's imaginative universe, to be in 'Nature' is to be always fallen, but that does not prevent him from suggesting a powerful connectedness that unites all living things." Nichols, "Anxiety of Species," 133.

74 Mellor, *Blake's Human Form Divine,* 147. See also Mitchell, *Blake's Composite Art,* 101–3, and Warner, *Blake and the Language of Art,* 105.

75 Blake, *Book of Thel,* plate 6, ln5.

76 Eaves et al., *Illuminated Books of William Blake,* 3:84.

77 Blake, *Book of Thel,* plate 6, ln1.

78 Ibid., plate 6, ln2, 5.

79 Ibid., plate 7, ln17, and plate 8, ln3.

80 Erdman, *Illuminated Blake,* 39, and Mitchell, *Blake's Composite Art,* 101.

81 Frye, in Essick, *Visionary Hand,* 155.

82 Mitchell, *Blake's Composite Art,* 102.

83 Blake, "Annotations to *Lavater's Aphorisms on Man,*" in *Complete Poetry and Prose,* 589.

84 Blake, *Book of Thel,* plate 7, ln9–11.

85 Ibid., plate 8, ln1, 2–4, 9.

86 Mellor, *Blake's Human Form Divine,* 28. Mellor goes on to speculate for Thel an experience of "ecstasy" and "sexual union with a lover," as a result of the contested final plate that Blake would have added in 1789 had he not postponed its addition until circa 1791. See also Erdman, *Blake Newsletter 2,* 24, and Mitchell, *Blake's Composite Art,* 78–106, for a related discussion of the etching dates for *The Book of Thel.*

87 Blake, *Book of Thel,* plate 8, ln9–10.

88 Mitchell, *Blake's Composite Art,* 91.

89 Blake, *Marriage of Heaven and Hell,* in *Complete Poetry and Prose,* plate 25, chorus.

90  Blake, *Book of Thel,* plate 8, ln11–20.

91  Ibid., plate 8, ln21–23.

92  See Beer, *William Blake,* 186, and Mellor, *Blake's Human Form Divine,* 34–35, for two examples of the opposing interpretations of Thel's "shriek" and ensuing flight "back . . . into the vales of / Har."

93  Fuller, *Blake's Heroic Argument,* 35.

94  This is not to ignore the idea that Thel herself is set up *to arrive at* this seat of decay from the poem's opening description but rather to emphasize the discursiveness with which *The Book of Thel* approaches its endgame against the immediacy projected by "The Sick Rose."

95  Blake, "The Sick Rose," in *Songs of Experience,* plate 39, ln1.

96  Ibid., plate 39, ln2.

97  Lincoln, *Illuminated Books of William Blake,* 2:183.

98  See Raine, "Blake's Debt to Antiquity," for the probable sources of Blake's symbolic poetry, esp. with regard to those poems in *Songs of Experience.* See also Fuller, *Blake's Heroic Argument,* 23, in which he remarks that "where no specific interpretation of the central symbol is assigned within the poem, Blake was working at least partly with a traditional language of symbols in which the tradition acts as a guide to interpretation."

99  Blake, "The Sick Rose," plate 39, ln7, 5–6.

100  With the "invisible worm" as a phallic image, the poem easily draws on sexual generative processes through their more destructive physical, psychological, and cultural effects. See Gillham, *Blake's Contrary States,* 148–90, for an in-depth discussion of how "The Sick Rose" draws on the experience of the reader to elicit its negative sexual theme. Mellor sides with Gillham here, noting that this poem "propagate[s] the notion that sexual pleasure is evil." Mellor, *Blake's Human Form Divine,* 55. In contrast, Wilkie consistently reads *Thel* as a lesson in sexual delight, one that gives to Thel a "noble enough role, the epitome of a higher form of usefulness." Wilkie, *Blake's Thel and Oothoon,* 63.

101  Mitchell, *Blake's Composite Art,* 78; Fuller, *Blake's Heroic Argument,* 33.

102  Blake, "The Sick Rose," plate 39, ln8.

103  Fuller, *Blake's Heroic Argument,* 34.

104  Blake, "The Sick Rose," plate 39, ln3–6.

105  See chapter 3 of this book for my examination of Bonnet's discovery of parthenogenesis in aphids and Trembley's discovery of regeneration in the freshwater polyp.

106  See chapters 1 and 3 of this book for a full discussion of these debates.

107  This discussion responds, in part, to Mitchell's query about "in what

precise sense Blake's poems 'need' their illustrations." Mitchell, *Blake's Composite Art*, 3.

108   This kinship is especially visible in copy R of "The Sick Rose."

109   The inchworm is a likely referent given that after metamorphosis, this worm becomes a geometer moth (with the moth, again, being the most likely referent for a "worm" in nocturnal flight). It is most readily visible in copy AA of "The Sick Rose," in which the inchworm is tinted blue.

110   The mirrored effect between this miniaturized figure and the globular blossom of the Rose is most readily seen in copy V of "The Sick Rose," wherein Blake has colored both forms with the same pink (rose) tint.

111   Such second rose stems appear also in copies V, Y, and Z of "The Sick Rose," but none of these share the completeness of the stem I discuss here in the King's College copy.

112   For a summary interpretation of the designs represented on the title page–frontispiece of *The Book of Thel,* see Eaves et al., *Illuminated Books of William Blake,* 3:81–82.

113   Ibid., 82.

114   Mellor, *Blake's Human Form Divine,* 19.

115   Blake, *Visions of the Daughters of Albion,* in *Complete Poetry and Prose,* plate 8, ln39–41.

116   Ibid., plate 6, ln10–11.

117   Ibid., plate 6, ln15–17.

118   Blake, *[First] Book of Urizen,* in *Complete Poetry and Prose,* plate 17, ln19–23.

119   Ibid., plate 17, ln35–36.

120   Blake, *Jerusalem,* plate 12, ln1–4.

121   Ibid., plate 17, ln43–46.

122   Ibid., plate 80, ln1–4.

123   Ibid., plate 55, ln36–37.

124   Beer, *William Blake,* 186.

125   Blake, *Visions of the Daughters of Albion,* plate 9, ln2.

126   For a summary description of this title page, see Blake, *Jerusalem,* copy E, *The William Blake Archive,* "Copy Information," http://www.blakearchive.org/. See also Keynes, *The Note-book of William Blake,* for another facsimile image of copy E, in which Blake's added gold leaf over the lettering is readily apparent.

127   Blake, *Jerusalem,* plate 67, ln35, and plate 55, ln36.

128   Blake, "On Virgil," in *Complete Poetry and Prose,* 270, and *Visions of the Daughters of Albion,* plate 8, ln40.

## 5. A Diet of Worms

1  "The Big Picture," *Boston Globe,* April 15, 2010, http://www.boston. com/bigpicture/2010/04/icelands_disruptive_volcano.html.

2  "Mount Tambora," Wikipedia, http://en.wikipedia.org/wiki/Mount_ Tambora (accessed April 8, 2011).

3  Phillips, "*Frankenstein* and Mary Shelley's 'Wet Ungenial Summer,'" 59.

4  "Year without a Summer," Wikipedia, http://en.wikipedia.org/wiki/ Year_without_a_summer (accessed April 8, 2011).

5  Shelley, *Frankenstein: The Original 1818 Text,* 354.

6  Ecocritical interpretations of *Frankenstein* make this intriguing connection between climactic disturbance and Romantic creativity. For in-depth discussions of weather as an influential element both within the text and for the existence of the text itself, see Phillips, "*Frankenstein* and Mary Shelley's 'Wet Ungenial Summer,'" and Clubbe, "The Tempest-toss'd Summer of 1816."

7  Shelley, *Frankenstein: The Original 1818 Text,* 353.

8  Because "the [creature], an explicit image of his genitor's hidden secrets, appears as Victor's alter ego . . . generations of readers have mistaken the name of the father [Frankenstein] for that of the 'son.'" Huet, *Monstrous Imagination,* 138. To avoid this confusion, I follow the critical tradition of referring to Victor Frankenstein by his first name, rather than his last, throughout this chapter.

9  Shelley, *Frankenstein: The Original 1818 Text,* 358.

10  Ibid.

11  Ibid.

12  Ibid., 231.

13  Ibid., 62.

14  As Walton relates, "Sometimes I endeavoured to gain from Frankenstein the particulars of his creature's formation; but on this point he was impenetrable." Shelley, *Frankenstein: The Original 1818 Text,* 231.

15  Shelley, *Frankenstein* (1982), xxvii. Editor Rieger's infamous declaration appears as part of his introduction to the first modern scholarly edition of the 1818 *Frankenstein.*

16  See Vasbinder, *Scientific Attitudes in Mary Shelley's Frankenstein.*

17  This essay, often reproduced, can be found in Mellor, *Mary Shelley.*

18  While Mellor's essay explores both the 1818 and 1831 texts of *Frankenstein,* my own study in this chapter focuses only on the original 1818 text

owing to its more stringent treatment of science without the pressure of theism from which the 1831 edition suffers.

19  Mellor, "A Feminist Critique of Science," in *Mary Shelley,* 90.

20  Shelley, *Frankenstein* (1993), xv–xvi.

21  As Shelley states in her 1831 introduction, "I certainly did not owe the suggestion of one incident, nor scarcely of one train of feeling, to my husband, and yet but for his incitement, it would never have taken the form in which it was presented to the world. For this declaration I must except the preface. As far as I can recollect, it was entirely written by him." Shelley, *Frankenstein: The Original 1818 Text,* 358.

22  For a study that draws out Shelley's individual identity through the act of writing *Frankenstein,* see Sharp, "If It Be a Monster Birth."

23  See Shelley, *Journals of Mary Shelley.* This text includes an appendix with an alphabetical list (by author) of Shelley's reading history. She is cited as reading Buffon, *Histoire naturelle générale et particulière* (1749–67), on June 16, 18, and 26, 1817, and July 3, 9, and 10, 1817, which included summaries of the natural historical investigations I discussed at length in chapters 1 and 3. She also read Smellie, *Philosophy of Natural History* (1790, 1799), on October 25, 1814.

24  Shelley, *Frankenstein: The Original 1818 Text,* 81.

25  Gigante, "Facing the Ugly," 567.

26  Ibid., 565, 567.

27  Ibid., 569.

28  McLane, *Romanticism and the Human Sciences,* 86.

29  Ibid., 95, 108.

30  Ibid., 86.

31  Darwin, *Temple,* III:401n.

32  Shelley, *Frankenstein: The Original 1818 Text,* 356.

33  Ibid., 357.

34  Ibid.

35  Shelley, *Frankenstein: The Original 1818 Text,* 47. Small notes in *Mary Shelley's Frankenstein,* 43, that "in a technical sense [the novel] belonged in the same category of Romantic fiction as the works of Radcliffe or the American Charles Brockden Brown, in which a 'natural' explanation for apparently supernatural happenings was always provided. . . . Indeed in this narrow sense it was not a 'ghost story' at all, but a forerunner of those tales of the marvelous but possible which we now call science fiction." "Being not of impossible occurrence," then, echoes the manner of extrapolation with which Diderot constructed the thought experiments

in *La Rêve de d'Alembert* and suggests the speculative or extrapolative fiction label that many have attached to *Frankenstein*. See also Aldiss, *Billion Year Spree.*

36 Shelley, *Frankenstein: The Original 1818 Text,* 357.

37 Vasbinder, "A Possible Source of the Term 'Vermicelli,'" 116–17.

38 King-Hele, *Erasmus Darwin and the Romantic Poets,* 53.

39 Seligo, "Monsters of Botany," 78–80.

40 Qtd. in Nichols, "Erasmus Darwin and the Frankenstein 'Mistake.'" See also Darwin, *Temple,* Additional Note 1:III, IV.

41 Shelley, *Frankenstein: The Original 1818 Text,* 357.

42 Ibid.

43 Ibid., 356.

44 Ibid., 79.

45 Ibid., 357.

46 Ibid., 84.

47 See Davy, *Elements of Chemical Philosophy* (1812) and *A Discourse, Introductory to a Course of Lectures on Chemistry* (1802); and Galvani, *De Viribus Electricitatis in Motui Musculari* [Commentary on the Effects of Electricity on Muscular Motion] (1791). Mellor and Butler, as already mentioned, provide significant contextualization of Shelley's novel within eighteenth- and early-nineteenth-century electricity debates, using Percy Shelley's education as one dominant source of his wife's scientific knowledge.

48 Shelley, *Frankenstein: The Original 1818 Text,* 79.

49 Ibid., 77.

50 Ibid., 357.

51 Caldwell, *Literature and Medicine in Nineteenth-Century Britain,* 25.

52 Shelley, *Frankenstein: The Original 1818 Text,* 358.

53 Ibid., 79.

54 Rauch, "Monstrous Body of Knowledge," 238.

55 Shelley, *Frankenstein: The Original 1818 Text,* 61.

56 Ibid., 63.

57 Ibid., 64.

58 Ibid., 67, 66.

59 Ibid., 66.

60 Ibid., 67, 69.

61 Ibid., 69.

62 Ibid., 69–70. Anticipating the mid-nineteenth century's fascination with the performance of electrical experimentation, during which "shocks and

sparks were well calculated to impress a paying audience," Victor's father presents experimentation as a matter of display to excite his children into application. Morus, *Frankenstein's Children*, 7.

63 Rauch, "Monstrous Body of Knowledge," 234–35.

64 Shelley, *Frankenstein: The Original 1818 Text*, 75.

65 Ibid., 69.

66 Ibid.

67 Ibid., 79.

68 Ibid., 356.

69 Ibid.

70 Ibid., 76–77.

71 Vasbinder, *Scientific Attitudes in Mary Shelley's Frankenstein*, 73.

72 Shelley, *Frankenstein: The Original 1818 Text*, 80.

73 Ibid., 77.

74 Ibid., 78.

75 Ibid., 79.

76 Vasbinder, *Scientific Attitudes in Mary Shelley's Frankenstein*, 76.

77 "The word 'science' had yet to restrict its range to what we now denominate the physical and social sciences; yet Shelley carefully differentiates among the bodies of knowledge available to and cultivated by the various figures in the novel." McLane, *Romanticism and the Human Sciences*, 95.

78 Shelley, *Frankenstein: The Original 1818 Text*, 77.

79 Ibid., 79.

80 Caldwell, *Literature and Medicine in Nineteenth-Century Britain*, 5.

81 Shelley, *Frankenstein: The Original 1818 Text*, 81.

82 Ibid., 79.

83 Ibid.

84 Ibid.

85 Vasbinder, *Scientific Attitudes in Mary Shelley's Frankenstein*, 39.

86 Shelley, *Frankenstein: The Original 1818 Text*, 79.

87 Vasbinder, *Scientific Attitudes in Mary Shelley's Frankenstein*, 67. Although Vasbinder recognizes Victor as being "patterned after the extreme materialists of the eighteenth century," it proves another interesting oversight that what Vasbinder understands to be "the minute aspects of nature" actually neglect the role of the worm. Instead, he states that Victor "views the human body in decay as *merely* food for the worm" (75; emphasis mine). Such diminutive rhetoric might imply that the worm is no more influential for the creature's existence than the "body in decay" is needed for the creature's construction.

88 Shelley, *Frankenstein: The Original 1818 Text*, 79–80.

89  See the introduction to Botting, *Frankenstein,* for a discussion of the gothic as an aesthetic monster of eighteenth-century ideals of beauty and proportion.

90  Shelley, *Frankenstein: The Original 1818 Text,* 80; emphasis mine.

91  Ibid., 356.

92  Ibid., 62; emphasis mine.

93  Ibid., 356.

94  "Galvanism," cites Morus, "was intimately linked to the processes of life. It arose directly, if serendipitously, from Galvani's interest in the relationship between muscular action and electrical agency." Morus, *Frankenstein's Children,* 126. He goes on to state that "electricity seemed in many ways to simulate the properties of vitality. The galvanic fluid could be used to bring back at least the semblance of life to the dead" (152). See also Caldwell, *Literature and Medicine in Nineteenth-Century Britain,* for a discussion of Andrew Abernethy and the role of electricity as a possible analogy for life. Caldwell, citing Butler's 1993 introduction to the 1818 edition of *Frankenstein,* also lays claim to the fact that Percy Shelley attended Abernethy's anatomy lectures at St. Bartholomew's Hospital, which could have contributed to electricity's use as a "life fluid" in Shelley's novel. See also Mellor, *Mary Shelley,* 102–4, for another discussion of the source of the "spark of being." Mellor discusses this "spark of being," as electricity, in terms of the interrelations of Humphrey Davy, Percy Shelley, and Erasmus Darwin.

95  The electrical experiments that Victor performed with his father, like those with the kite string or the "small electrical machine," mark the only actualized experiments mentioned in the text. Moreover, when Victor claims that he "collected the instruments of life around me, that I might infuse a spark of being into the lifeless thing that lay at my feet," he noticeably sidesteps any direct articulation of galvanic mechanisms. Shelley, *Frankenstein: The Original 1818 Text,* 84. Accordingly, Rauch observes in "Monstrous Body of Knowledge," 239, that there is not one recounted attempt by Victor "to actually restore life." As a result, there is an "unmistakable subtext . . . that [Victor] deliberately chose to pursue creation over restoration" (239).

96  Vasbinder, *Scientific Attitudes in Mary Shelley's Frankenstein,* 75.

97  McLane suggests that the "natural" materials with which Victor constructs the creature are "extremely heterogeneous" (being human and beast), which, in turn, leaves the creature "physiologically indeterminate." McLane, *Romanticism and Human Sciences,* 87.

98  Shelley, *Frankenstein: The Original 1818 Text,* 82.

99   Ibid., 81.

100  Ibid.

101  Hustis, "Responsible Creativity," 849.

102  Shelley, *Frankenstein: The Original 1818 Text,* 85.

103  Ibid., 84.

104  Rauch, "Monstrous Body of Knowledge," 236.

105  Shelley, *Frankenstein: The Original 1818 Text,* 82.

106  Ibid., 84.

107  Ibid., 85, 82.

108  Ibid., 84.

109  Ibid., 82.

110  Ibid., 61.

111  Ibid., 79.

112  Ibid.

113  Huet, *Monstrous Imagination,* 132.

114  Shelley, *Frankenstein: The Original 1818 Text,* 50.

115  Ibid., 76.

116  Ibid., 168, 190.

117  Ibid., 81.

118  Ibid., 82; emphasis mine.

119  Ibid., 147.

120  Ibid., 125.

121  de Man, *Blindness and Insight,* 28.

122  Shelley, *Frankenstein: The Original 1818 Text,* 130.

123  Ibid., 81.

124  Ibid., 85.

125  Ibid.

126  Ibid., 82.

127  Ibid., 154.

128  Ibid., 85.

129  Ibid.

130  For groundbreaking feminist criticism of *Frankenstein,* see Homans, *Bearing the Word*; Poovey, *Proper Lady and the Woman Writer*; Gilbert and Gubar, *Madwoman in the Attic*; Moers, *Literary Women.*

131  Shelley, *Frankenstein: The Original 1818 Text,* 85.

132  Gigante, "Facing the Ugly," 582.

133  Randel, "Political Geography of Horror," 475.

134  For a recent article considering *Frankenstein* and the narrative consequences of Victor's repression of death, love, nature, and spirit, see Adams, "Making Daemons of Death and Love."

135  Shelley, *Frankenstein: The Original 1818 Text,* 103.

136  Ibid., 85.

137  Ibid., 86.

138  Ibid., 85.

139  Gigante, "Facing the Ugly," 568.

140  McLane, *Romanticism and the Human Sciences,* 87.

141  Gigante, "Facing the Ugly," 566.

142  Shelley, *Frankenstein: The Original 1818 Text,* 98.

143  Rauch, "Monstrous Body of Knowledge," 238.

144  Shelley, *Frankenstein: The Original 1818 Text,* 99.

145  McLane identifies the creature as just such a "rupture, a 'most astonish-
     ing thing' not unlike the French Revolution according to Burke." She
     discusses how the creature's position as a descriptive and hence categorical
     "problem" affects our understanding and definition of human being.
     In what I discuss earlier, I read this rupture in its most literal impact,
     with the creature acting directly to remove an anthropological barrier
     in an attempt to gain definition while simultaneously securing himself
     as his own "monstrous critique." McLane, *Romanticism and the Human
     Sciences,* 86–91.

146  Shelley, *Frankenstein: The Original 1818 Text,* 80, 103.

147  Ibid., 86.

148  Ibid., 89, 88.

149  Ibid., 88.

150  Ibid., 89.

151  Ibid., 89, 97.

152  Ibid., 97; emphasis mine.

153  Ibid., 103.

154  Ibid., 102.

155  Ibid., 103.

156  Ibid., 104.

157  As Miller discusses at length in "Being and Becoming of *Frankenstein,*"
     68, "the use of the noun 'object'" in reference to the creature implies
     "a consistent link between life and nonlife." Thus, when Victor sees his
     creature as an object, illuminated by a flash of lightning, it is of significant
     consequence that he must later reflect, or consider, the nature of this
     appearance. That he cannot maintain a constant belief in the creature's
     animated existence is what, in part, makes his surprise (and horror) at
     the creature's vengeful acts valid yet nonetheless misappropriated.

158  Shelley, *Frankenstein: The Original 1818 Text,* 125.

159  "Remember," pronounced the creature to Victor, "thou hast made me

more powerful than thyself; my height is superior to thine; my joints more supple." Ibid., 126.

160 Ibid., 92, 108.

161 Ibid., 115.

162 Ibid. This recalls one of the lamentations of Los in Blake's *Jerusalem*, regarding "Negations" (as opposed to "Contraries"): "And he shall be a *never dying Worm*, mutually tormented by / Those that thou tormentest, a Hell & Despair for ever & ever." Blake, *Jerusalem*, 17:44–47; emphasis mine.

163 Ibid., 115, 79.

164 Ibid., 79.

165 Ibid., 108.

166 Ibid., 115.

167 Freeman, "*Frankenstein* with Kant," 27, presents an in-depth discussion of the word *monster* and the effect its various derivational uses has on the text of *Frankenstein*.

168 Ibid.

169 McLane, *Romanticism and the Human Sciences*, 100.

170 Shelley, *Frankenstein: The Original 1818 Text*, 127–28.

171 Gigante, "Facing the Ugly," 576.

172 I.e., the creature's narrative forms the center of the novel, with Victor's narrative encapsulating his creature's, and then Walton's narrative (in the letters to his sister) encapsulating both Victor's and the creature's. However, the frame is permeated toward the end of the novel, when Victor dies on Walton's ship and Walton is then confronted by the creature directly. See my discussion in this chapter's final section for further development of the implication of this narrative framing.

173 Shelley, *Frankenstein: The Original 1818 Text*, 145.

174 Caldwell, *Literature and Medicine in Nineteenth-Century Britain*, 41. This is further emphasized by Cantor, who states that "[the creature's] repeated argument is that any ugliness in his soul is purely the result of the ugliness of his body; he is in no way responsible for his self because his self is the product of someone else's creativity; he was not given the freedom to create his self once he was placed in a warped body." Cantor, *Creature and Creator*, 128.

175 Shelley, *Frankenstein: The Original 1818 Text*, 171.

176 Ibid., 168.

177 Ibid., 144, 145.

178 Ibid., 144–45.

179  McLane, *Romanticism and the Human Sciences,* 91.

180  Ibid., 96.

181  Shelley, *Frankenstein: The Original 1818 Text,* 126.

182  Ibid., 156.

183  Ibid., 169.

184  Ibid., 74.

185  Ibid., 241.

186  Namely, the creature's strangulation of Elizabeth on her and Victor's wedding night. Of course, such vengeance is protracted; it includes next the death of Victor's father, Alphonse, then Victor himself, and finally, the creature.

187  Ibid., 200. "[Victor's] response [to Clerval's death] is to fall into one of his characteristic illnesses that return him to the helplessness of infancy and to the care of his father and family. In other words, the passivity of this hero is to be explained not only by the ideals of prudence and domestic harmony and natural affection, or by the ideal of civilized community, but by the irrational need to escape the consequences of adulthood, to retreat to the innocence and helplessness of the womb where the heroic expression of selfhood is denied and replaced by the comfort of dependence and the absorption of the love of others. Narratively, it is a retreat from the shaping energies of imagination." Levine, *Realistic Imagination,* 34.

188  Shelley, *Frankenstein: The Original 1818 Text,* 200.

189  Ibid., 205, 201.

190  Ibid., 201.

191  Ibid., 182.

192  Ibid., 201.

193  Ibid., 49.

194  Ibid., 146, 243.

195  Ibid., 243.

196  Huet, *Monstrous Imagination,* 144.

197  Shelley, *Frankenstein: The Original 1818 Text,* 237.

198  Ibid., 190.

199  As Mellor notes, Mary "analyze[d] and criticize[d] the more dangerous implications of the scientific method and its practical results. Implicitly, she contrasted what she considered to be 'good' science—the detailed and reverent description of the workings of nature—to what she considered 'bad' science, the hubristic manipulation of the elemental forces of nature to serve man's private ends." Mellor, *Mary Shelley,* 89.

200  Shelley, *Frankenstein: The Original 1818 Text,* 239.

201  "It is fairly obvious," claims Huet, "that by animating not just a corpse but a corpse that would bring death wherever he went," Victor is the true progenitor of death. Huet, *Monstrous Imagination,* 141.

202  Shelley, *Frankenstein: The Original 1818 Text,* 61.

203  A similar arrangement appears in Percy Shelley's *Alastor,* in which the Narrator (who is himself a reteller of tales) claims that the body of the wanderer Poet—whose "pallid lips" and "eyes / That image sleep in death" clearly betray the consummation of the Poet's death—is nevertheless "safe from the worm's outrage." Shelley, *Shelley's Poetry and Prose,* 110:ln699–702. In a poem that grounds itself in a kind of narrative decay—meaning where the death of the Poet *inside* the text translates to a fear of the dissolution of poetry *outside the text in the world*—the invocation of worms within the final twenty lines of the poem identifies a preservation (rather than a decomposition) of the Poet's body and thus of the text. Such inviolate remains of the Poet, like those of the scientist in *Frankenstein,* secure the site of literary creation and construction in the poem.

204  Shelley, *Frankenstein: The Original 1818 Text,* 81.

205  Levine and Knoepflmacher, *Endurance of* Frankenstein, 25.

206  Sharma, *Frankenstein,* 204.

207  Shelley, *Frankenstein: The Original 1818 Text,* 244.

208  Cantor, *Creature and Creator,* 24.

209  "In a successful fusion of image and idea, Mary [*sic*] had endowed the embodiment of [Victor's] ambition with a speaking voice that pleads most urgently for the presence of the very thing [Victor's] (and Walton's) dream of glory has rejected—genuine human relationship." Walling, *Mary Shelley,* 39. Although this view is certainly upheld by what we come to learn from the creature's developing intellect (not to mention from his overt acts of destruction), the close of the novel makes an important, if ironic, switch from Victor's failure of ambition to the creature's success.

## Conclusion

1  Nichols, "Anxiety of Species," 130.

2  Shelley, "Daemon of the World," in *Complete Poetical Works,* 10.

3  Beer, "Problems of Description in the Language of Discovery," in Levine, *One Culture,* 40.

4  Dawson, *Nature's Enigma,* 17.

5  Richards, *Romantic Conception of Life,* 203.

6  Keats, "Isabella," in *Complete Poems,* 49:385.

7  Qtd. in McDowell, "Grotesque Organicism," 23. See also McDowell's essay for a thorough discussion of how Keats's poem plays with the tension "between the natural and the artificial style of poetry" and so might be read as an adaptation of Boccaccio "prompted not so much through inspiration as at the instigation of William Hazlitt. Lecturing 'On Dryden and Pope,' Hazlitt had suggested that such a work could hardly 'fail to succeed'" (23).

8  Although I refer here to a kind of elision of any definitive zoological concern in Keats's poem, McDowell mounts a convincing argument for how Keats called on his practical knowledge of gardening and herbal lore to construct his organic metaphor. See McDowell, "Grotesque Organicism," 23, 25–26.

9  See Nichols, "Loves of Plants and Animals," para. 4, in which he discusses a kind of Darwinian organicism that not only "[extends] through the whole of the terrestrial biosphere" but reveals that "all emotional responses—pleasure, pain, happiness, and sadness—are thus based solely on the motion of material parts of each life form."

10  Keats, *Isabella,* 21:165, 168; 38:299.

11  Ibid., 45:35; emphasis mine.

12  Ibid., 48:381; 50:393–96.

13  Ibid., 38:300–3.

14  Ibid., 38:304.

15  Ibid., 32:255–56.

16  Ibid., 52:414, 416.

17  Ibid., 46:368; 50:394.

18  Ibid., 54:425–32.

19  McDowell, "Grotesque Organicism," 25, 23.

20  Keats, *Isabella,* 46:365.

21  Ibid., 60:475.

22  Ibid., 45:353; LIV:426; 58:458; 60:475; emphasis mine.

23  Ibid., 49:386.

24  Ibid., 49:387–88, 392.

25  McDowell, "Grotesque Organicism," 23–24.

26  Keats, *Isabella,* 49:389, 391–92.

27  Beer, *Darwin's Plots,* 73.

28  Ibid.

29  Coleridge, "Eolian Harp," in *Poetical Works,* ln45–46.

30 See Howard's introduction to Darwin, *Formation of Vegetable Mould* (1976), 10.

31 Darwin, *Formation of Vegetable Mould* (1881), 314.

32 I am borrowing here from the way Beer describes the importance of metamorphosis to Darwin's evolutionary project. See Beer, *Darwin's Plots*, 104–5.

33 Darwin, *Formation of Vegetable Mould* (1881), 316.

34 Ibid., vi.

35 Ibid., i, vi.

36 Ibid., vi.

# Bibliography

Adams, Will W. "Making Daemons of Death and Love: *Frankenstein,* Existentialism, Psychoanalysis." *Journal of Humanistic Psychology* 41, no. 4 (2001): 57–89.

Agamben, Giorgio. *The Open: Man and Animal.* Translated by Kevin Attell. Palo Alto, Calif.: Stanford University Press, 2004.

Aldiss, Brian. *The Billion Year Spree: The True History of Science Fiction.* New York: Doubleday, 1973.

Anderson, Lorin. "Charles Bonnet's Taxonomy and Chain of Being." *Journal of the History of Ideas* 37, no. 1 (1976): 45–58.

Anonymous. "An Abstract of What Is Contained in the Preface to the Sixth Volume of Mons. Reaumur's History of Insects, Relating to the Abovementioned Observations, and Delivered in to the Royal Society, Immediately after the Foregoing Paper." *Philosophical Transactions of the Royal Society of London* 42 (1742–43): xii–xvii. Available from http://www.jstor.org/.

———. "Part of a Letter from———of Cambridge, to a Friend of the Royal Society Occasioned by What Has Lately Been Reported Concerning the Insect Mentioned in Page 218 of This Transaction." *Philosophical Transactions of the Royal Society of London* 42 (1742–43): 227–34. Available from http://www.jstor.org/.

———. "Some Account of the Insect Called the Fresh-Water Polypus, Before-Mentioned in These Transactions, as the Same Was Delivered at a Meeting of the Royal Society, by the President, on Thursday, March 24." *Philosophical Transactions of the Royal Society of London* 42 (1742–43): 422–36. Available from http://www.jstor.org/.

———. "Two Letters from a Gentleman in the County, Relating to Mr. Leewenhoek's Letter in Transaction, No. 283." *Philosophical Transactions of the Royal Society of London* 23 (1702–3): 1494–1501. Available from http://www.jstor.org/.

Aristotle. *The Basic Works of Aristotle.* Edited by Richard McKeon. New York: Random House, 1941.

Atran, Scott. *Cognitive Foundations of Natural History: Towards an Anthropology of Science.* New York: Cambridge University Press, 1990.

Badger, E. W., and W. J. Harrison, eds. *The Midland Naturalist: The Journal of the Associated Natural History, Philosophical, and Archaeological Societies and Field Clubs of the Midland Counties.* 2 vols. London: Hardwicke and D. Bogue, 1878–79.

Baker, Henry. "A Letter from Mr. Henry Baker F.R.S. to the President, Concerning the Grubbs Destroying the Grass in Norfolk." *Philosophical Transactions of the Royal Society of London* 44 (1746–47): 576–82. Available from http://www.jstor.org/.

———. "Some Observations on a Polype Dried." *Philosophical Transactions of the Royal Society of London* 42 (1742–43): 616–19. Available from http://www.jstor.org/.

Baker, John R. *Abraham Trembley of Geneva: Scientist and Philosopher.* London: Edward Arnold, 1952.

Bann, Stephen, ed. *Frankenstein, Creation and Monstrosity.* London: Reaktion Books, 1994.

Baster, Job. "A Dissertation on the Worms Which Destroy the Piles on the Coasts of Holland and Zealand, by Job Baster, M.D. F.R.S. Communicated by the President of the Royal Society. Translated from the Latin by T.S. M.D. F.R.S." *Philosophical Transactions of the Royal Society of London* 41 (1739–41): 276–88. Available from http://www.jstor.org/.

Bearzi, Maddalena, and Craig B. Stanford. *Beautiful Minds: The Parallel Lives of Great Apes and Dolphins.* Cambridge, Mass.: Harvard University Press, 2008.

Beavis, Ian C. *Insects and Other Invertebrates in Classical Antiquity.* Oxford: Alden Press, 1988.

Beer, Gillian. *Darwin's Plots: Evolutionary Narrative in Darwin, George Eliot, and Nineteenth-Century Fiction.* Cambridge: Cambridge University Press, 1983.

Beer, John. *William Blake: A Literary Life.* New York: Palgrave Macmillan, 2005.

Bennett, Jane. *Vibrant Matter: A Political Ecology of Things.* Durham, N.C.: Duke University Press, 2010.

Bierbaum, Tom. "The Busy World of Richard Scarry." *Variety,* March 7, 1994. Available from http://www.variety.com/review/.

Bigelow, M. A. "Regeneration." *New York Times,* March 30, 1902, SM13+.

Blake, William. *The Book of Thel.* Copy J, title page, plate 6-7. The William

Blake Archive, April 27, 2008. Available from http://www.blakearchive.org/.

———. *The Complete Poetry and Prose.* Revised edition. Edited by David V. Erdman. New York: Anchor Books, 1988.

———. *For the Sexes: The Gates of Paradise.* Copy D, frontispiece. The William Blake Archive, April 27 2008. Available from http://www.blakearchive.org/.

———. *For the Sexes: The Gates of Paradise.* Copy D, plate 16. The William Blake Archive, April 27, 2008. Available from http://www.blakearchive.org/.

———. *Jerusalem.* Copy E, title page. The William Blake Archive, April 27, 2008. Available from http://www.blakearchive.org/.

———. *The Letters of William Blake.* Edited by Geoffrey Keynes. New York: Macmillan, 1956.

Bonnet, Charles. "An Abstract of Some New Observations upon Insects: By M. Charles Bonnet of Geneva. Communicated in a Letter to Sir Hans Sloane, Bart. Late President of the Royal Society, &c. Translated from the French by P.H.Z. Esq; F.R.S." *Philosophical Transactions of the Royal Society of London* 42 (1742–43): 458–88. Available from http://www.jstor.org/.

———. *The Contemplation of Nature (1764–1765).* Translated from the French of C. Bonnet. London: T. Longman, T. Becket, and P. A. da Hondt, 1766. http://www.galenet.galegroup.com/servlet/ECCO.

Botting, E. H., and M. Williams, M. "The Evolution of the Species Argument for Women's Rights." Paper presented at the 67th annual meeting of the Midwest Political Science Association, Chicago, Ill., December 27, 2010.

Botting, Fred. *Frankenstein: Contemporary Critical Essays.* New York: Palgrave, 1995.

Bour, Isabelle. "Sensibility as Epistemology in *Caleb Williams, Waverley,* and *Frankenstein.*" *Studies in English Literature* 45, no. 4 (2005): 813–27.

Breynius, J. P. "Some Corrections and Amendments by J. P. Breynius, M.D. F.R.S. concerning the Generation of the Insect Called by Him Coccus Radicum, in His Natural History Thereof, Printed in the Year 1731, an Account of Which Is Given in These Philosophical Transactions, No. 421, Translated from the Latin by Mr. Zollman, F.R.S." *Philosophical Transactions of the Royal Society of London* 37 (1731–32): 444–47. Available from http://www.jstor.org/.

Brown, Eric C., ed. *Insect Poetics.* Minneapolis: University of Minnesota Press, 2006.

Browne, Janet. *Darwin's Origin of Species.* New York: Grove Press, 2008.

Buffon, George Louis Leclerc, comte de. *Histoire naturelle générale et particuliére: avec la description du Cabinet du Roi.* Paris: De l'Imprimerie royale, 1758–69.

Burke, Edmund. *A Philosophical Enquiry into the Origin of Our Ideas of the*

*Sublime and Beautiful.* Edited by Adam Phillips. Oxford: Oxford University Press, 1998.

———. *Selected Works of Edmund Burke.* Vol. 1. Edited by E. J. Payne. Indianapolis, Ind.: Liberty Fund, 1999.

Bynum, W. F., E. J. Browne, and Roy Porter, eds. *Dictionary of the History of Science.* Princeton, N.J.: Princeton University Press, 1981.

Caldwell, Janis McLarren. *Literature and Medicine in Nineteenth-Century Britain: From Mary Shelley to George Eliot.* Cambridge: Cambridge University Press, 2004.

Cantor, Paul A. *Creature and Creator: Myth-making and English Romanticism.* Cambridge: Cambridge University Press, 1984.

Clubbe, John. "The Tempest-toss'd Summer of 1816: Mary Shelley's *Frankenstein.*" *Byron Journal* 19 (1991): 26–40.

Coleridge, Samuel Taylor. "Kubla Khan; Or, a Vision in a Dream. A Fragment." [1797–98/1816]. In *Norton Anthology of English Literature: The Romantic Period, Volume D.* 8th ed. Edited by Stephen Greenblatt. New York: W. W. Norton, 2006.

———. *Letters of Samuel Taylor Coleridge.* Boston: Houghton, Mifflin, 1895.

———. *Poetical Works.* Edited by E. H. Coleridge. Oxford: Oxford University Press, 1969.

Collinson, Peter. *"Forget Not Mee & My Garden . . .": Selected Letters 1725–1768.* Edited by Alan W. Armstrong. Philadelphia: American Philosophical Society, 2002.

Cook, Gordan C., and Desmond King-Hele. "Doctor Erasmus Darwin's Death in 1802." *Notes and Records of the Royal Society of London* 52, no. 2 (1998): 261–65.

Cooper, Melinda. "Rediscovering the Immortal *Hydra*: Stem Cells and the Question of Epigenesis." *Configurations* 11 (2003): 1–26.

Corcos, Alain F. "Fontenelle and the Problem of Generation in the Eighteenth Century." *Journal of the History of Biology* 4, no. 1 (1971): 363–72.

Cunningham, Andrew, and Nicholas Jardine, eds. *Romanticism and the Sciences.* Cambridge: Cambridge University Press, 1990.

Curran, Andrew. "Monsters and the Self in the *Rêve de d'Alembert.*" *Eighteenth-Century Life* 21, no. 2 (1997): 48–69.

Curran, Andrew, and Patrick Graille. "The Faces of Eighteenth-Century Monstrosity." *Eighteenth-Century Life* 21, no. 2 (1997): 1–15.

Curran, Stuart, and Joseph Anthony Witterich Jr., eds. *Blake's Sublime Allegory.* Madison: University of Wisconsin Press, 1973.

Damon, S. Foster. *A Blake Dictionary: The Ideas and Symbols of William Blake.* New York: E. P. Dutton, 1971.

Darwin, Charles. *The Formation of Vegetable Mould, through the Action of Worms, with Observations on Their Habits.* London: John Murray, 1881.

———. *The Formation of Vegetable Mould, through the Action of Worms, with Observations on Their Habits.* Facsimile ed. With a foreword by James P. Martin and an introduction by Sir Albert Howard. Ontario, Calif.: Bookworm, 1976.

Darwin, Erasmus. *The Collected Writings of Erasmus Darwin.* 9 vols. Selected and introduced by Martin Priestman. Bristol, U.K.: Thoemmes Continuum, 2004.

———. *The Letters of Erasmus Darwin.* Edited by Desmond King-Hele. Cambridge: Cambridge University Press, 1981.

———. *Phytologia; or, the Philosophy of Agriculture and Gardening.* London: J. Johnson, 1800.

———. *A Plan for the Conduct of Female Education: In Boarding School, Private Families, and Public Seminaries.* Derby, U.K.: privately printed, 1797.

———. *The Temple of Nature: or, the Origin of Society.* London: privately printed, 1803.

———. *The Temple of Nature; or the Origin of Society.* Annotated ed. Edited by Martin Priestman. 2006. http://www.rc.umd.edu/editions/darwin_temple/.

———. *Zoonomia; or, the Laws of Organic Life.* London: J. Johnson, 1794.

Davy, Humphrey, Sir. *A discourse, introductory to a course of lectures on chemistry; delivered in the theatre of the Royal Institute on the 21st of January, 1802.* London: J. Johnson and messrs. Cadell and Davies, 1802.

———. *Elements of Chemical Philosophy.* London: privately printed, 1812.

Dawson, Virginia P. *Nature's Enigma: The Problem of the Polyp in the Letters of Bonnet, Trembley, and Réaumur.* Philadelphia: American Philosophical Society, 1987.

———. "The Problem of Soul in the 'Little Machines' of Réaumur and Charles Bonnet." *Eighteenth-Century Studies* 18, no. 4 (1985): 503–22.

de Almeida, Hermione, and George H. Gilpin. *Indian Renaissance: British Romantic Art and the Prospect of India.* Aldershot, U.K.: Ashgate Press, 2005.

de Certeau, Michel. *The Practice of Everyday Life.* Berkeley: University of California Press, 1988.

Deleuze, Gilles. *The Fold.* New York: Continuum, 2006.

Deleuze, Gilles, and Félix Guattari. *A Thousand Plateaus.* Translated by Brian Massumi. London: Continuum, 2004.

de Man, Paul. *Blindness and Insight: Essays in the Rhetoric of Contemporary Criticism.* Minneapolis: University of Minnesota Press, 1983.

Derrida, Jacques. *The Animal That Therefore I Am.* Translated by David Wills. New York: Fordham University Press, 2008.

D'Holbach, Paul Henri Thiry, baron, and Denis Diderot. *The System of Nature: or, Laws of the Moral and Physical World.* Translated by H. D. Robinson. New York: B. Franklin, 1970.

Diderot, Denis. *Rameau's Nephew and D'Alembert's Dream.* Translated by Leonard Tancock. London: Penguin Books, 1966.

———. *Thoughts on the Interpretation of Nature and Other Philosophical Works.* Translated by Lorna Sandler. Manchester, U.K.: Clinamen Press, 1999.

Digby, George Wingfield. *Symbol and Image in William Blake.* Oxford: Clarendon Press, 1957.

Dudzinksi, Kathleen M., and Toni Frohoff. *Dolphin Mysteries: Unlocking the Secrets of Communication.* New Haven, Conn.: Yale University Press, 2010.

Eales, Nellie B. "A Satire on the Royal Society, Dated 1743, Attributed to Henry Fielding." *Notes and Records of the Royal Society of London* 23, no. 1 (1968): 65–67.

Earthworm Jim. Doug TenNapel, creator. Devid Perry, designer. Tokyo: Sega Corporation, 1994.

Eaves, Morris. *William Blake's Theory of Art.* Princeton Essays on the Arts 13. Princeton, N.J.: Princeton University Press, 1982.

Eaves, Morris, Robert N. Essick, and Joseph Viscomi, eds. *The Illuminated Books of William Blake.* Vol. 3, *The Early Illuminated Books.* Princeton, N.J.: Princeton University Press, 1998.

Edwards, Jonathan. *Basic Writings.* Edited by Ola Elizabeth Winslow. New York: New American Library, 1978.

Emery, Clark. "Scientific Theory in Erasmus Darwin's 'The Botanic Garden' (1789–91)." *Isis* 33, no. 3 (1941): 315–25.

Erdman, David V. *Blake: Prophet against Empire.* Princeton, N.J.: Princeton University Press, 1954.

———. *A Concordance to the Writings of William Blake.* Ithaca, N.Y.: Cornell University Press, 1967.

———, ed. *Blake Newsletter* 2, nos. 1–2 (1968).

———. *The Illuminated Blake: William Blake's Complete Illuminated Works with a Plate-by-Plate Commentary.* New York: Dover, 1992.

Essick, Robert N., ed. *The Visionary Hand: Essays for the Study of William Blake's Art and Aesthetics.* Los Angeles, Calif.: Hennessey and Ingalls, 1973.

———. *William Blake: Printmaker.* Princeton, N.J.: Princeton University Press, 1980.

Farley, John. *The Spontaneous Generation Controversy from Descartes to Oparin.* Baltimore: Johns Hopkins University Press, 1974.

Farre, Arthur. "Observations on the Minute Structure of Some of the Higher Forms of Polypi, with Views of a More Natural Arrangement of the Class." *Philosophical Transactions of the Royal Society of London* 127 (1837): 387–427. Available from http://www.jstor.org/.

Fisch, Audrey A., Anne K. Mellor, and Esther H. Schor, eds. *The Other Mary Shelley: Beyond* Frankenstein. Oxford: Oxford University Press, 1993.

Foucault, Michel. "Of Other Spaces." Translated by Jay Miskowiec. *Diacritics* 16, no. 1 (1986): 22–27.

———. *The Order of Things: An Archaeology of the Human Sciences.* New York: Vintage Books, 1970.

Fox, Christopher, Roy Porter, and Robert Wokler, eds. *Inventing Human Science: Eighteenth-Century Domains.* Berkeley: University of California Press, 1995.

Freeman, Barbara. "*Frankenstein* with Kant: A Theory of Monstrosity, or the Monstrosity of Theory." *SubStance* 16, no. 1 (1987): 21–31.

Frye, Northrop. *Fearful Symmetry: A Study of William Blake.* Princeton, N.J.: Princeton University Press, 1969.

Fulford, Tim, Debbie Lee, and Peter J. Kitson. *Literature, Science, and Exploration in the Romantic Era: Bodies of Knowledge.* Cambridge: Cambridge University Press, 2007.

Fuller, David. *Blake's Heroic Argument.* London: Croom Helm, 1988.

Gallant, Christine. *Blake and the Assimilation of Chaos.* Princeton, N.J.: Princeton University Press, 1978.

Galvani, Luigi. *De Viribus Electricitatis in Motui Musculari* [Commentary on the Effects of Electricity on Muscular Motion]. 1791. Translated by Robert Montraville Green. Cambridge, Mass.: E. Licht, 1953.

Gasking, Elizabeth B. *Investigations into Generation, 1651–1828.* Baltimore: Johns Hopkins University Press, 1967.

Gaull, Marilyn. "Joseph Johnson's World: Ancestral Voices, Invisible Worms, and Roaming Tigers." *Wordsworth Circle* 33, no. 3 (2002): 92–93.

Gigante, Denise. "Blake's Borders." Paper presented at the International Conference on Romanticism, Laredo, Tex., 2005.

———. "Blake's Living Form." *Nineteenth-Century Literature* 63, no. 4 (2009): 461–85.

———. "Facing the Ugly: The Case of *Frankenstein.*" *English Literary History* 67 (2000): 565–87.

———. *Life: Organic Form and Romanticism.* New Haven, Conn.: Yale University Press, 2009.

Gilbert, Sandra M., and Susan Gubar, eds. *The Madwoman in the Attic: The*

*Woman Writer and the Nineteenth-Century Literary Imagination.* 2nd ed. New Haven, Conn.: Yale University Press, 2000.

Gillham, D. G. *Blake's Contrary States: The Songs of Innocence and of Experience as Dramatic Poems.* Cambridge: Cambridge University Press, 1966.

Grassle, Frederick J. "Hydrothermal Vent Animals: Distribution and Biology." *Science* 229, no. 4715 (1985): 713–17.

Gronovius, J. F. "Extract of a Letter from J. F. Gronovius, M.D. at Leyden, November 1742 to Peter Collinson, F.R.S. Concerning a Water Insect, Which, Being Cut into Several Pieces, Becomes So Many Perfect Animals." *Philosophical Transactions of the Royal Society of London* 42 (1742–43): 218–20. Available from http://www.jstor.org/.

Grylls, Glynn R. *Mary Shelley: A Biography.* New York: Haskell House, 1969.

Guyer, Sara. "Testimony and Trope in *Frankenstein.*" *Studies in Romanticism* 45, no. 1 (2006): 77–115.

Hamilton, Edith. *Mythology: Timeless Tales of Gods and Heroes.* New York: Warner Books, 1969.

Hamilton, Paul. *Metaromanticism: Aesthetics, Literature, Theory.* Chicago: University of Chicago Press, 2003.

Harris, Stuart. *Erasmus Darwin's Enlightenment Epic: A Study of the Evidence for Sequential Design in "The Botanic Garden" [1791] and "The Temple of Nature" [1803].* Sheffield, U.K.: S. Harris.

Hartley, David. *Observations on Man, His Frame, His Duty, and His Expectations; in Two Parts.* London: privately printed by Samuel Richardson, 1749.

Hassler, Donald M. *Erasmus Darwin.* New York: Twayne, 1973.

Henson, Jim, director. *Labyrinth.* DVD. San Francisco: Henson Associates and Lucas Film, 1986.

Heringman, Noah. *Romantic Rocks, Aesthetic Geology.* Ithaca, N.Y.: Cornell University Press, 2004.

Hollingsworth, Christopher. *Poetics of the Hive: The Insect Metaphor in Literature.* Iowa City: University of Iowa Press, 2001.

Holmes, Richard. *The Age of Wonder: How the Romantic Generation Discovered the Beauty and Terror of Science.* New York: Pantheon, 2009.

Homans, Margaret. *Bearing the Word: Language and Female Experience in Nineteenth-Century Women's Writing.* Chicago: University of Chicago Press, 1986.

Homer. *The Iliad.* Translated by Robert Fagles. New York: Penguin Classics, 1998.

Hooke, Robert. *Micrographia: or, Some Physiological Descriptions of Minute Bodies Made by Magnifying Glasses. With Observations and Inquiries Thereon.* London: J. Martyn and J. Allestry, 1665.

Huet, Marie Hélène. *Monstrous Imagination*. Cambridge, Mass.: Harvard University Press, 1993.

Hustis, Harriet. "Responsible Creativity and the 'Modernity' of Mary Shelley's Prometheus." *Studies in English Literature* 43, no. 4 (2003): 845–58.

Jardine, N., J. A. Secord, and E. C. Spary, eds. *Cultures of Natural History.* Cambridge: Cambridge University Press, 1996.

Jones, W. P. "The Vogue of Natural History in England." *Annals of Science* 2, no. 3 (1937): 345–52.

Jordanova, Ludmilla J., ed. *Languages of Nature: Critical Essays on Science and Literature*. New Brunswick, N.J.: Rutgers University Press, 1986.

Kawasaki, Noriko. "Form and Worm in William Blake." In *Centre and Circumference: Essays in English Romanticism*. Tokyo: Kirihara Shoten, 1995.

Keats, John. *Complete Poems*. Edited by Jack Stillinger. Cambridge, Mass.: Belknap Press, 1982.

Kelley, Theresa M. *Clandestine Marriage: Botany and Romantic Culture*. Baltimore: Johns Hopkins University Press, 2012.

———. "Romantic Exemplarity: Botany and 'Material' Culture." In *Romantic Science: The Literary Forms of Natural History,* edited by Noah Heringman. Albany: State University of New York Press, 2003.

Kemp, Martin. *Spectacular Bodies: The Art and Science of the Human Body from Leonardo da Vinci to Now*. Berkeley: University of California Press, 2000. Published in conjunction with the exhibition "Spectacular Bodies" shown at the Hayward Gallery, 2000.

Keynes, Geoffrey, ed. *The Note-book of William Blake* [The Rossetti Manuscript]. London: Nonesuch Press, 1935.

Keynes, Milo. "The Portland Vase: Sir William Hamilton, Josiah Wedgwood, and the Darwins." *Notes and Records of the Royal Society of London* 52, no. 2 (1998): 237–59.

King-Hele, Desmond, ed. *Charles Darwin's "The Life of Erasmus Darwin."* Cambridge: Cambridge University Press, 2002.

———, ed. *The Collected Letters of Erasmus Darwin*. Cambridge: Cambridge University Press, 2007.

———. *Doctor of Revolution: The Life and Genius of Erasmus Darwin*. London: Faber and Faber, 1977.

———. *Erasmus Darwin and the Romantic Poets*. New York: St. Martin's Press, 1986.

———. *Erasmus Darwin: A Life of Unequalled Achievement*. London: Giles de la Mare, 1999.

Koyré, Alexandre. *From the Closed World to the Infinite Universe*. Baltimore: Johns Hopkins University Press, 1957.

Kuhn, Thomas S. *The Structure of Scientific Revolutions.* 3rd ed. Chicago: University of Chicago Press, 1996.

Lamarck, J. B. *Zoological Philosophy: An Exposition with Regard to the Natural History of Animals.* [1809]. English translation. Chicago: University of Chicago Press, 1984.

La Mettrie, Julian Offray de. *Machine Man and Other Writings.* Translated by Ann Thompson. Cambridge: Cambridge University Press, 1996.

Lashmet, David. "Unfurling the Worm: Insecto-theology in William Blake's *Thel.*" Panel discussion at Hypertexts and Textual Studies, Emory University, Atlanta, Ga., 1996. http://prometheus.cc.emory.edu/panels/1A/D .Lashmet.html.

Latour, Bruno. *Science in Action: How to Follow Scientists and Engineers through Society.* Cambridge, Mass.: Harvard University Press, 1987.

Lenhoff, Howard M. "My Link with the Trembleys—Abraham (1710–1784), Maurice (1874–1942), and Jean-Gustave (1903–1977)." In *Developmental Biology of Coelenterates,* edited by P. Tardent and R. Tardent. Amsterdam: Elsevier, 1986.

Lenhoff, Howard M., and Sylvia G. Lenhoff. "Abraham Trembley and the Discovery of Regeneration." In *History of Regeneration Research,* edited by C. Dinsmore. Cambridge: Cambridge University Press, 1991.

———. "Abraham Trembley and His Polyps, 1744: The Unique Biology of Hydra and Trembley's Correspondence with Martin Folkes." *Eighteenth-Century Thought* 1 (2003): 1–25.

———. "Challenge to the Specialist: Abraham Trembley's Approach to Research on the Organism—1744 and Today." *American Zoologist* 29 (1989): 1105–17.

———. "How the Animal Nature of Marine Cnidarians Was Recognized and the Nematocyst Discovered." In *Biology of Nematocysts,* edited by D. A. Hessinger and H. M. Lenoff. San Diego, Calif.: Academic Press, 1988.

———. "Tissue Grafting in Animals: Its Discovery in 1742 by Abraham Trembley as He Experimented with Hydra." *Biological Bulletin* 177 (1984): 1–10.

———. "Trembley's Polyps and the Dawn of Experimental Biology." *Scientific American* 258 (1988): 108–13.

Lenhoff, Sylvia G. "Abraham Trembley." In *Encyclopaedia of the Enlightenment,* edited by Alan Charles Kors. Oxford: Oxford University Press, 2002.

Leonard, David Charles. "Erasmus Darwin and William Blake." *Eighteenth-Century Life* 4 (1978): 79–81.

Levine, George. *One Culture: Essays in Science and Literature.* Madison: University of Wisconsin Press, 1987.

———, ed. *The Realistic Imagination: English Fiction from Frankenstein to Lady Chatterley.* Chicago: University of Chicago Press, 1981.

Levine, George, and U. C. Knoepflmacher, eds. *The Endurance of* Frankenstein: *Essays on Mary Shelley's Novel.* Berkeley: University of California Press, 1979.

Lewis, Matthew Gregory. *The Monk: A Romance.* Edited by D. L. MacDonald and Kathleen Scherf. Peterborough, Ont.: Broadview Literary Texts, 2003.

Lincoln, Andrew. *The Illuminated Books of William Blake.* Vol. 2, *Songs of Innocence and of Experience.* Princeton, N.J.: Princeton University Press, 1994.

Logan, James Venable. *The Poetry and Aesthetics of Erasmus Darwin.* New York: Octagon Books, 1972.

Lovejoy, A. O. *The Great Chain of Being: A Study of the History of an Idea.* Cambridge, Mass.: Harvard University Press, 1964.

Lyell, Charles. *Principles of Geology.* Edited by James Secord. New York: Penguin Books, 1997.

Manson, Michael, and Robert Scott Stewart. "Heroes and Hideousness: Frankenstein and Failed Unity." *SubStance* 22, nos. 2–3 (1993): 228–42.

Marshal, David. *The Surprising Effects of Sympathy: Marivaux, Diderot, Rousseau, and Mary Shelley.* Chicago: University of Chicago Press, 1988.

McDowell, Stacey. "Grotesque Organicism in Keats's *Isabella; or, the Pot of Basil.*" *Keats–Shelley Review* 24 (2010): 22–28.

McKeon, Richard, ed. *The Basic Works of Aristotle.* New York: Random House, 1941.

McLane, Maureen N. *Romanticism and the Human Sciences.* Cambridge: Cambridge University Press, 2000.

McLean, Clara D. "*The Monk* and the Matter of Reading." In *Women, Revolution, and the Novels of the 1790s.* East Lansing: Michigan State University Press, 1999.

Mee, Jon. "The 'Insidious Poison of Secret Influence': A New Historical Context for Blake's 'The Sick Rose.'" *Eighteenth-Century Life* 22, no. 1 (1998): 111–22.

Mellor, Anne K. *Blake's Human Form Divine.* Berkeley: University of California Press, 1974.

———. *Mary Shelley: Her Life, Her Fiction, Her Monsters.* New York: Routledge, 1989.

Meyerowitz, Elliot, Daphne Preuss, and Venkatesan Sundaresan. "Foreword to the Special Issue on Arabidopsis Genetics." *Genetics* 149 (1998): 471.

Miller, Rand. "The Being and Becoming of *Frankenstein.*" *SubStance* 18, no. 3 (1989): 60–74.

Milton, John. *The Riverside Milton.* Edited by Roy Flannagan. Florence, Ky.: Wadsworth, 1998.

Mitchell, W. J. T. *Blake's Composite Art: A Study of the Illuminated Poetry.* Princeton, N.J.: Princeton University Press, 1978.

Moers, Ellen. *Literary Women.* New York: Doubleday, 1976.

Morton, Timothy. *The Ecological Thought.* Cambridge, Mass.: Harvard University Press, 2010.

Morus, Iwan Rhys. *Frankenstein's Children: Electricity, Exhibition, and Experiment in Early-Nineteenth-Century London.* Princeton, N.J.: Princeton University Press, 1998.

Naigeon, Jacques-André. "Unitarians." In *The Encyclopedia of Diderot and d'Alembert Collaborative Translation Project.* Translated by Dena Goodman and Susan Emanuel. Ann Arbor: Scholarly Publishing Office of the University of Michigan Library, 2010. http://hdl.handle.net/2027/spo .did2222.0001.224. Originally published as "Unitaires," *Encyclopédie ou Dictionnaire raisonné des sciences, des arts et des métiers* 17 (1765): 387–401.

Needham, Turberville. "A Summary of Some Late Observations upon the Generation, Composition, and Decomposition of Animal and Vegetable Substances." *Philosophical Transactions of the Royal Society of London* 45 (1748): 615–66. Available from http://www.jstor.org/.

Nichols, Ashton. "The Anxiety of Species: Toward a Romantic Natural History." *Wordsworth Circle* 28, no. 3 (1997): 130–36.

———. *Beyond Romantic Ecocriticism: Toward Urbanatural Roosting.* New York: Palgrave Macmillan, 2011.

———. "Erasmus Darwin and the Frankenstein 'Mistake.'" http://users .dickinson.edu/~nicholsa/Romnat/frankmis.htm.

———. "The Loves of Plants and Animals: Romantic Science and the Pleasures of Nature." In *Romanticism and Ecology,* edited by Orrin Wang. http:// www.rc.umd.edu/praxis/ecology/nichols/nichols.html.

Nitchie, Elizabeth. *Mary Shelley: The Author of* Frankenstein. New Brunswick, N.J.: Rutgers University Press, 1953.

Oerlemans, Onno. *Romanticism and the Materiality of Nature.* Toronto, Ont.: University of Toronto Press, 2002.

Osborn, Herbert. *A Brief History of Entomology; Including Time of Demosthenes and Aristotle to Modern Times with over Five Hundred Portraits.* Columbus, Ohio: Spahr and Glenn, 1952.

Osborn, Karen J., Steven H. D. Haddock, Fredrik Pleijel, Laurence P. Madin, and Greg W. Rouse. "Deep-Sea Swimming Worms with Luminescent 'Bombs.'" *Science* 325, no. 5943 (2009): 964.

Packham, Catherine. "The Science and Poetry of Animation: Personification, Analogy, and Erasmus Darwin's *Loves of the Plants.*" *Romanticism* 10, no. 2 (2004): 191–208.

Page, Michael. "The Darwin before Darwin: Erasmus Darwin, Visionary

Science, and Romantic Poetry." *Papers on Language and Literature* 41, no. 2 (2005): 146–69.

Paley, Morton D. *The Illuminated Books of William Blake.* Vol. 1, *Jerusalem: The Emanation of the Giant Albion.* Princeton, N.J.: Princeton University Press, 1997.

Paley, William. *Natural Theology: or, Evidences of the Existence and Attributes of the Deity, Collected from the Appearances of Nature.* London: Wilks and Taylor, 1802. Republished in facsimile edition by Gregg International, 1970.

Passano, L. M., and C. B. McCullough. "The Light Response and the Rhythmic Potentials of Hydra." *Proceedings of the National Academy of Sciences of the United States of America* 48, no. 8 (1962): 1376–82.

Perkins, David. *Romanticism and Animal Rights.* Cambridge: Cambridge University Press, 2003.

Peterfreund, Stuart. "Dissent and Ontological Space in Romantic Science and Literature." *Wordsworth Circle* 36, no. 2 (2005): 59–65.

———. *William Blake in a Newtonian World: Essays on Literature as Art and Science.* Norman: University of Oklahoma Press, 1998.

Phillips, Bill. "*Frankenstein* and Mary Shelley's 'Wet Ungenial Summer.'" *Atlantis* 28, no. 2 (2006): 59–68.

Poovey, Mary. *The Proper Lady and the Woman Writer: Ideology as Style in the Works of Mary Wollstonecraft, Mary Shelley and Jane Austen.* Chicago: University of Chicago Press, 1984.

Porter, Dahlia. "Scientific Analogy and Literary Taxonomy in Darwin's *Loves of the Plants.*" *European Romantic Review* 18, no. 2 (2007): 213–21.

Porter, Roy. *The Enlightenment.* 2nd ed. New York: Palgrave, 2001.

Primer, Irwin. "Erasmus Darwin's Temple of Nature: Progress, Evolution, and the Eleusinian Mysteries." *Journal of the History of Ideas* 25, no. 1 (1964): 58–86.

Raine, Kathleen. "Blake's Debt to Antiquity." *Sewanee Review* LXXI, no. 3 (1963): 352–450.

Rajan, Tilottama, and Julia M. Wright, eds. *Romanticism, History, and the Possibilities of Genre: Re-forming Literature 1789–1837.* Cambridge: Cambridge University Press, 1998.

Randel, Fred V. "The Political Geography of Horror in Mary Shelley's *Frankenstein.*" *English Literary History* 70 (2003): 465–91.

Ratcliff, Marc. *The Quest for the Invisible: Microscopy in the Enlightenment.* Surrey, U.K.: Ashgate, 2009.

Rauch, Alan. "The Monstrous Body of Knowledge in Mary Shelley's *Frankenstein.*" *Studies in Romanticism* 34 (1995): 227–53.

Réaumur, René-Antoine Ferchault de. *Letters on Entomology: Intended for the Amusement and Instruction of Young Persons, and to Facilitate Their Acquiring a Knowledge of the Natural History of Insects.* English translation. London: George B. Whittaker, 1825.

———. *Mémoires pour servir à l'histoire des insectes.* 6 vols. Amsterdam: P. Mortier, 1737–48.

Redi, Francesco. *Experiements on the Generation of Insects.* 1688. Translated by Mab Bigelow. Chicago: Open Court, 1909.

Richards, Robert. *The Romantic Conception of Life: Science and Philosophy in the Age of Goethe.* Chicago: University of Chicago Press, 2004.

Richardson, Alan. *British Romanticism and the Science of the Mind.* Cambridge: Cambridge University Press.

———. "Erasmus Darwin and the Fungus School." *Wordsworth Circle* 33, no. 3 (2002): 113–14.

Ritterbush, Philip C. "Erasmus Darwin's Second Published Poem." *Review of English Studies* 13, no. 50 (1962): 158–60.

Ritvo, Harriet. *The Platypus and the Mermaid and Other Figments of the Classifying Imagination.* Cambridge, Mass.: Harvard University Press, 1997.

Roberts, Patricia R., and H. J. Oosting. "Responses of Venus Fly Trap *(Dionaea muscipula)* to Factors Involved in Its Endemism." *Ecological Monographs* 28, no. 2 (1958): 193–218.

Roe, Shirley A. "John Turberville Needham and the Generation of Living Organisms." *Isis* 74, no. 2 (1983): 158–84.

———. *Matter, Life, and Generation: 18th Century Embryology and the Haller–Wolff Debate.* Cambridge: Cambridge University Press, 1981.

Roger, Jacques. *Buffon: A Life in Natural History.* Translated by Sarah Lucille Bonnefoi. Ithaca, N.Y.: Cornell University Press, 1997.

———. *The Life Sciences in Eighteenth-Century French Thought.* Translated by Robert Ellrich. Palo Alto, Calif.: Stanford University Press, 1997.

Rosenfield, Leonora Cohen. *From Beast-Machine to Man-Machine.* New York: Oxford University Press, 1941.

Ross, Robert. "'To Charm Thy Curious Eye': Erasmus Darwin's Poetry at the Vestibule of Knowledge." *Journal of the History of Ideas* 32, no. 3 (1971): 379–94.

Rouse, G. W., S. K. Goffredi, and R. C. Vrijenhoek. "*Osedax*: Bone-Eating Marine Worms with Dwarf Males." *Science* 305, no. 5684 (2004): 668–71.

Rudwick, Martin J. S. *Georges Cuvier, Fossil Bones, and Geological Catastrophes.* Chicago: University of Chicago Press, 1997.

Russell, Sharman Apt. *An Obsession with Butterflies: Our Long Love Affair with a Singular Insect.* Cambridge: Perseus Books, 2003.

Sainson, Katia. "'Le Régénérateur de la France': Literary Accounts of Napoleonic Regeneration 1799–1805." *Nineteenth-Century French Studies* 30, no. 12 (2001): 9–25.

Sanderson, Richard K. "Glutting the Maw of Death: Suicide and Procreation in *Frankenstein*." *South Central Review* 9, no. 2 (1992): 49–64.

Sarton, George. *A Guide to the History of Science: A First Guide for the Study of the History of Science, with Introductory Essays on Science and Tradition.* Waltham, Mass.: Chronica Botanica, 1952.

Saunders, Gil. *Picturing Plants: An Analytical History of Botanical Illustration.* Berkeley: University of California Press, 1995.

Schiller, Joseph. "Queries, Answers, and Unsolved Problems in Eighteenth-Century Biology." *History of Science* 12 (1974): 184–99.

Schofield, Robert E. "The Industrial Orientation of Science in the Lunar Society of Birmingham." *Isis* 48, no. 4 (1957): 408–15.

———. *Mechanism and Materialism: British Natural Philosophy in an Age of Reason.* Princeton, N.J.: Princeton University Press, 1970.

Schor, Esther, ed. *The Cambridge Companion to Mary Shelley.* Cambridge: Cambridge University Press, 2003.

Seligo, Carlos. "The Monsters of Botany and Mary Shelley's *Frankenstein*." In *Science Fiction, Critical Frontiers.* Edited by Karen Sayer and John Moore. New York: St. Martin's Press, 2000.

Sewall, Elizabeth. *Orphic Voice: Poetry and Natural History.* New Haven, Conn.: Yale University Press, 1960.

Seward, Anna. *Memoirs of the Life of Doctor Darwin.* Philadelphia: Classic Press, 1804.

Sharma, Anjana, ed. *Frankenstein: Interrogating Gender, Culture, and Identity.* Delhi: Macmillan India, 2004.

Sharp, Michele Turner. "If It Be a Monster Birth: Reading and Literary Property in Mary Shelley's *Frankenstein*." *South Atlantic Review* 66, no. 4 (2001): 70–93.

Shelley, Mary. *Frankenstein.* Edited by J. Paul Hunter. New York: W. W. Norton, 1996.

———. *Frankenstein.* Edited by Johanna M. Smith. New York: St. Martin's Press, 2000.

———. *Frankenstein; or the Modern Prometheus.* 1818. Edited by James Rieger. Chicago: University of Chicago Press, 1982.

———. *Frankenstein; or the Modern Prometheus.* 1818. Edited by Marilyn Butler. Oxford: Oxford University Press, 1993.

———. *Frankenstein; or the Modern Prometheus.* 1831. Edited by Maurice Hindle. New York: Penguin Books, 1985.

————. *Frankenstein: The Original 1818 Text.* 2nd ed. Edited by D. L. Macdonald and Kathleen Scherf. Peterborough, Ont.: Broadview Press, 1999.

————. *The Journals of Mary Shelley.* Edited by Paula R. Feldman and Diana Scott-Kilvert. Baltimore: Johns Hopkins University Press, 1995.

Shelley, Mary, and Percy Bysshe Shelley. *History of a Six Weeks' Tour.* 1817. Facsimile. Otley, U.K.: Woodstock Books, 2002.

Shelley, Percy Bysshe. *The Complete Poetical Works.* Edited by T. Hutchinson. Oxford: Oxford University Press, 1934.

————. *Shelley's Poetry and Prose.* 2nd ed. Edited by Donald H. Reiman and Neil Fraistat. New York: W. W. Norton, 2002.

Small, Christopher. *Mary Shelley's Frankenstein: Tracing the Myth.* Pittsburgh, Pa.: University of Pittsburgh Press, 1973.

Smellie, William. *The Philosophy of Natural History.* Philadelphia: privately printed for Robert Campbell, Bookseller, north-east corner of Second and Chestnut Street, 1791.

Smith, Christopher Upham Murray, and Robert Arnott, eds. *The Genius of Erasmus Darwin.* Surrey, U.K.: Ashgate, 2005.

Snow, C. P. *The Two Cultures.* Cambridge: Cambridge University Press, 1993.

Spangler, May. "Science, philosophie et littérature: le polype de Diderot." *Reserches sur Diderot et sur l'Encyclopédie* 23 (1997): 89–107.

Spary, E. C. *Utopia's Garden: French Natural History from Old Regime to Revolution.* Chicago: University of Chicago Press, 2000.

Stafford, Barbara Maria. *Artful Science: Enlightenment Entertainment and the Eclipse of Visual Education.* Cambridge, Mass.: MIT Press, 1994.

————. *Body Criticism: Imaging the Unseen in Enlightenment Art and Medicine.* Cambridge, Mass.: MIT Press, 1991.

————. *Visual Analogy: Consciousness as the Art of Connecting.* Cambridge, Mass.: MIT Press, 2001.

————. "Voyeur or Observer? Enlightenment Thoughts on the Dilemmas of Display." *Configurations* 1, no. 1 (1993): 95–128.

Stewart, Susan. *On Longing: Narratives in the Miniature, the Gigantic, the Souvenir, the Collection.* Durham, N.C.: Duke University Press, 1993.

Strick, James. "Darwinism and the Origin of Life: the Role of H. C. Bastian in British Spontaneous Generation Debates, 1868–1873." *Journal of the History of Biology* 32 (1999): 1–42.

Stuebe, Isabel. "William Hodges and Warran Hastings: A Study in Eighteenth-Century Patronage." *Burlington Magazine* 115, no. 847 (1973): 657–66.

Terrell, Mary. "Speculation and Experiment in Enlightenment Life Sciences." In *A Cultural History of Heredity I: 17th and 18th Centuries.* Berlin: Max Planck Institute for the History of Science, 2002.

Teute, Fredrika J. "The Loves of the Plants; or, the Cross-Fertilization of Science and Desire at the End of the Eighteenth Century." *Huntington Library Quarterly* 63, no. 3 (2000): 319–45.

Todd, Kim. *Chrysalis: Maria Sibylla Merian and the Secrets of Metamorphosis.* Orlando, Fla.: Harcourt, 2007.

Tomer, Raju, Alexandru S. Denes, Kristin Tessmar-Raible, and Detlev Arendt. "Profiling by Image Registration Reveals Common Origin of Annelid Mushroom Bodies and Vertebrate Pallium." *Cell* 142, no. 5 (2010): 800–9.

Trembley, Abraham. *Hydra and the Birth of Experimental Biology, 1744: Abraham Trembley's Memoirs Concerning the Natural History of a Type of Freshwater Polyp with Arms Shaped Like Horns.* Edited by Sylvia G. Lenhoff and Howard M. Lenhoff. Pacific Grove, Calif.: Boxwood Press, 1986.

———. "Observations and Experiments upon the Freshwater Polypus, by Monsieur Trembley, at the Hague." *Philosophical Transactions of the Royal Society of London* 42 (1742–43): iii–xi. Available from http://www.jstor.org/.

Uglow, Jenny. *The Lunar Men: Five Friends Whose Curiosity Changed the World.* New York: Farrar, Straus, and Giroux, 2002.

van Leeuwenhoek, Antony. "Part of a Letter from Mr. Antony van Leeuwenhoek, F.R.S. Concerning Green Weeds Growing in Water, and Some Animalcula Found about Them." *Philosophical Transactions of the Royal Society of London* 23 (1702–3): 1304–11. Available from http://www.jstor.org/.

Vartanian, Aram. "Book Review: *Abraham Trembley of Geneva: Scientist and Philosopher*, John R. Baker." *Isis* 44, no. 4 (1953): 387–98.

———. "Diderot and the Technology of Life." *Studies in Eighteenth-Century Culture* 15 (1986): 11–31.

———. "Necessity or Freedom? The Politics of an Eighteenth-Century Metaphysical Debate." *Studies in Eighteenth-Century Culture* 7 (1978): 153–74.

———. "Trembley's Polyp, La Mettrie, and 18th-Century French Materialism." *Journal of the History of Ideas* 11, no. 3 (1950): 259–86.

Vasbinder, Samuel Holmes. "A Possible Source of the Term 'Vermicelli' in Mary Shelley's *Frankenstein*." *Wordsworth Circle* 12 (1981): 116–17.

———. *Scientific Attitudes in Mary Shelley's Frankenstein.* Ann Arbor, Mich.: UMI Research Press, 1984.

Veeder, William. *Mary Shelley and Frankenstein: The Fate of Androgyny.* Chicago: University of Chicago Press, 1986.

Viscomi, Joseph. *Blake and the Idea of the Book.* Princeton, N.J.: Princeton University Press, 1993.

von Linné, Carl [Linnaeus, Carolus]. *Systema Naturae.* 1735. English translation. Nieuwkoop, Netherlands: B. de Graaf, 1964.

Walling, William A. *Mary Shelley.* New York: Twayne, 1972.

Warner, Janet A. *Blake and the Language of Art.* Kingston, Ont.: McGill-Queen's University Press, 1984.

Watts, Isaac. *Divine and Moral Songs for Children.* London: Sampson Low, Son, Marston, 1866.

Wells, H. G. *The Time Machine: An Invention.* Edited by Nicholas Ruddick. Peterborough, Ont.: Broadview Literary Texts, 2001.

Wilkie, Brian. *Blake's Thel and Oothoon.* Edmonton: University of Alberta Press, 1990.

Winchester, Simon. *The Map That Changed the World: William Smith and the Birth of Modern Geology.* New York: Perennial, 2002.

Winsor, Mary P. "The Development of Linnaean Insect Classification." *Taxon* 25, no. 1 (1976): 57–67.

Wohl, Robert. "Buffon and His Project for a New Science." *Isis* 51, no. 2 (1960): 186–99.

Wolfe, Carey. *What Is Posthumanism?* Minneapolis: University of Minnesota Press, 2010.

———. *Zoontologies: The Question of the Animal.* Minneapolis: University of Minnesota Press, 2003.

Wood, Todd Charles, Kurt P. Wise, and Megan J. Murray. *Understanding the Pattern of Life: Origins and Organization of Species.* Nashville, Tenn.: Broadman and Holman, 2003.

Wordsworth, William. *The Poetical Works of William Wordsworth.* Edited by E. de Selincourt. Oxford: Clarendon Press, 1965.

Worrall, David. *The Illuminated Books of William Blake.* Vol. 6, *The Urizen Books.* Princeton, N.J.: Princeton University Press, 1998.

———. "William Blake and Erasmus Darwin's *Botanic Garden.*" *Bulletin of the New York Public Library* 78 (1974–75): 397–417.

Wynne, Clive D. L. *Do Animals Think?* Princeton, N.J.: Princeton University Press, 2006.

Yolton, John W. *Thinking Matter: Materialism in Eighteenth-Century Britain.* Minneapolis: University of Minnesota Press.

Youngquist, Paul. *Monstrosities: Bodies and British Romanticism.* Minneapolis: University of Minnesota Press, 2003.

# Index

Abernethy, Andrew, 237n94

*Abraham Trembley of Geneva: Scientist and Philosopher* (Baker), 76

"Abstract of Some New Observations upon Insects, An" (Bonnet), 10

Academie des Sciences, 8, 82, 103

*Adventures of Peregrine Pickle, in which are included, memoirs of a lady of quality* (Smollett), 106–107

*Aeneid* (Virgil), 59

aesthetic, xv, xvi, xx, xxii, 29, 61, 181, 191; of decay, xxiv, 167–76; material and, 182

Agamben, Giorgio, on *Homo sapiens,* xix

agency, xvii, 1, 2, 3, 181

Agrippa, Cornelius, 151, 160, 161, 162–63

Akenside, Mark, 31

*Alastor* (Shelley), 242n203

Albinus, 80, 103

Albion, Worm and, 148

Allamand, 80, 103

*Alvinella pompejana,* 91

American Philosophical Society, 222n24

Anderson, Lorin, 78

*Anemone pulsatilla,* 143

animality, 33, 36

animation, 157, 166, 175, 182, 192, 196

"Annotations to Lavater's *Aphorisms on Man*" (Blake), 134

anomalies, xxiii, 18, 20, 101, 105, 106; biological, 176; classification and, 176; natural, 225n106

anthropomorphism, 19, 21, 74, 85, 125, 155

*Anti-Jacobin,* 39, 212n24

aphids, 81, 82; parthenogenesis and, 79, 82

apple worms, xvii

*Arabidopsis thaliana,* 207n23

Aristotle, xiv, xviii, 40, 190, 214n52; classification by, 18; natural science of, 215n52; physical explanation of, 49; on worms, 197

Armstrong, John, 31

art, science and, 189

"Artificial Spring of Water, An" (Darwin), 31

"Ascent of Vapor" (Darwin), 31

Associated Natural History, Philosophical, and

263

**Janelle A. Schwartz** is visiting assistant professor of comparative literature at Hamilton College. She is the coeditor of *Curious Collectors, Collected Curiosities: An Interdisciplinary Study.*